The Treason Trial of Aaron Burr
Law, Politics, and the Character Wars of the New Nation

The Burr treason trial, one of the greatest criminal trials in American history, was significant for several reasons. The legal proceedings lasted seven months and featured some of the nation's best lawyers. It also pitted President Thomas Jefferson (who declared Burr guilty without the benefit of a trial and who masterminded the prosecution), Chief Justice John Marshall (who sat as a trial judge in the federal circuit court in Richmond), and former Vice President Aaron Burr (who was accused of planning to separate the western states from the Union) against each other. At issue, in addition to the life of Aaron Burr, were the rights of criminal defendants, the constitutional definition of treason, and the meaning of separation of powers in the Constitution. Capturing the sheer drama of the long trial, R. Kent Newmyer's book sheds new light on the chaotic process by which lawyers, judges, and politicians fashioned law for the new nation.

R. Kent Newmyer received his PhD in history from the University of Nebraska in 1959. From 1960 to 1997, he taught American history at the University of Connecticut. Since 1997, he has been Professor of Law and History at the University of Connecticut School of Law. He has taught a wide range of graduate and undergraduate courses in American history, specializing in the political, constitutional, and legal history of the early national period. He received two awards for teaching and in 1988 was named Distinguished Alumni Professor for excellence in teaching and scholarship, the highest faculty honor bestowed by the university. As an author, Newmyer is best known for *Supreme Court Justice Joseph Story: Statesman of the Old Republic* (1985) and, most recently, *John Marshall and the Heroic Age of the Supreme Court* (2001). A second edition of his short volume on the Supreme Court under Marshall and Taney was published in 2006. Newmyer's books have been reviewed in various history journals and law reviews, as well as in the *New York Times*, the *Washington Post*, and the *New Republic*. Newmyer has appeared on C-Span's *Booknotes*, and most recently was a commentator in a National Public Television documentary on the U.S. Supreme Court, produced by Channel 13 in New York City.

CAMBRIDGE STUDIES ON THE AMERICAN CONSTITUTION

Series Editors

Maeva Marcus, The George Washington University
Melvin I. Urofsky, Virginia Commonwealth University
Mark Tushnet, Georgetown University Law Center
Keith Whittington, Princeton University

Cambridge Studies on the American Constitution publishes books that examine the American Constitution and offers a range of interpretations and approaches, from traditional topics of constitutional history and theory, case studies, and judicial biographies, to more modern and often controversial issues dealing with gender and race. While many estimable series have incorporated constitutional studies, none has done so exclusively. This series seeks to illuminate the implications – governmental, political, social, and economic – of the relationship between the American Constitution and the country it governs through a wide array of perspectives.

Titles in the Series

Mark A. Graber, *Dred Scott and the Problem of Constitutional Evil*
Christian G. Fritz, *American Sovereigns: The People and America's Constitutional Tradition Before the Civil War*
Pamela Brandwein, *Rethinking the Judicial Settlement of Reconstruction*

The Treason Trial of Aaron Burr

Law, Politics, and the Character Wars of the New Nation

R. KENT NEWMYER
University of Connecticut

CAMBRIDGE
UNIVERSITY PRESS

CAMBRIDGE UNIVERSITY PRESS
Cambridge, New York, Melbourne, Madrid, Cape Town,
Singapore, São Paulo, Delhi, Mexico City

Cambridge University Press
32 Avenue of the Americas, New York, NY 10013-2473, USA

www.cambridge.org
Information on this title: www.cambridge.org/9781107606616

© R. Kent Newmyer 2012

First published 2012
Reprinted 2013

A catalog record for this publication is available from the British Library.

Library of Congress Cataloging in Publication Data

Newmyer, R. Kent.
  The treason trial of Aaron Burr : law, politics, and the character wars
of the new nation / R. Kent Newmyer.
     p. cm. – (Cambridge studies on the American Constitution)
  Includes bibliographical references and index.
  ISBN 978-1-107-02218-8 (hardback) – ISBN 978-1-107-60661-6 (pbk.)
  1. Burr, Aaron, 1756–1836 – Trials, litigation, etc. 2. Trials (Treason) –
United States. 3. Burr Conspiracy, 1805–1807. 4. United States – Politics
and government – 1783–1809. I. Title
  KF223.B8N49 2012
  345.73´0231–dc23   2011051724

ISBN 978-1-107-02218-8 Hardback
ISBN 978-1-107-60661-6 Paperback

To my wife Rosanne Pelletier
To my brother Dan Newmyer
and his wife Paula Poppe Newmyer

"A trial in a Court of Justice is a trial of many things besides the prisoners at the bar."

William Maxwell Evarts, closing address to the jury in the case of the Savannah Privateers, 1861

Contents

Acknowledgments

I am immensely grateful to Lewis Bateman, Senior Editor for Political Science and History at Cambridge University Press, who has had faith in my work over the years; as always, it has been a pleasure and a privilege to work with him. I also very much appreciate the contributions of Anne Lovering Rounds and Shaun Vigil, Senior Editorial Assistants; Shari Chappell, Production Editing Manager; Mark Fox, Production Controller; and Laura Lawrie, Production and Copy Editor. I am grateful also to the two outside anonymous readers who critiqued the manuscript for the Press; their informed and insightful suggestions greatly improved the book. The suggestions of Maeva Marcus and Mark Tushnet, Series Editors of Cambridge Studies on the American Constitution were also helpful. Thanks also to Bill Keegan for preparing the map and helping me with the other illustrations in the book. Mary Ellen Curtin, of Red Owl Web Design, skillfully prepared the index.

My colleagues at the University of Connecticut School of Law, where I have been teaching for the last dozen years, have helped me more than they could know. To share ideas with so many fine lawyers has been a uniquely valuable experience for a historian trying to fathom the creative labors of the lawyers and judges who shaped the legal culture of the new nation.

I owe a special debt of gratitude to professors Hugh Macgill and Phillip Blumberg, both former deans of the Law School. The idea of doing a book on the Burr trial originated in an animated discussion with Hugh about David Robertson's stenographic report of the trial. Hugh was not only present at the book's creation, but he has also advised and encouraged me at each stage of its development. Dean Phillip Blumberg, who has inspired me in so many ways, generously took time from his own scholarly endeavors to help me with mine. Both Hugh and Phillip have given me valuable critical readings of the entire manuscript. Professor Tim Everett also read a portion of the manuscript and helped me puzzle my way through some of the mysteries of courtroom advocacy that I encountered in the trial record.

My former student at the Law School, Kelly Barrett, gave me helpful comments on an early draft of the manuscript and assisted me in tracking Marshall's opinions in the Burr case as they entered the stream of constitutional discourse. Monique Griffin, Sandi Browne, Rosa Colon, and Linda Kirk kindly assisted me during the various stages of preparing the manuscript.

I am deeply indebted to the late Professor Kathryn Preyer. "Kitty" did not write about the Burr trial, but her approach to the study of early national legal culture has done much to shape my own. I would like to think that she would have found something of value in my book; I know for sure it would have been better had she given it one of her famous critiques.

Kitty's friend and mine, John Gordan III, has generously shared with me his impressive knowledge of law and trial procedure, knowledge he honed as a federal attorney in the Southern District of New York and from 1994 to 2010 as Partner in Morgan, Lewis, & Bockius in New York City. In the midst of his demanding duties he has found time to read the reports of the trial and to give me a critical reading of my entire manuscript, some parts of it more than once. His critique has informed my thinking on key issues and has also saved me from some embarrassing errors. The errors that remain are my own and not John's, nor those of any of the other friends who have helped me.

My esteemed colleague, Emeritus Professor of History Edmund Wehrle, deserves special mention. I spared Ed from reading the book in manuscript, which he kindly offered to do; instead he listened to me vent for several years running about the joys and frustrations of my research. Dee Gosline, Graduate Secretary of the UConn History Department has come to my rescue on more occasions than I care to mention; so have my computer guru friends at the University, Geoffrey Meigs and Tim Ruggieri. Amanda Rosenberg generously volunteered her time to introduce me to the world of digitalized newspaper research.

The secondary scholarship on the Burr trial is extensive, and while I have consulted various accounts to support and/or clarify my argument, I have made no attempt to resolve the disputes among the numerous historians and biographers. Rather I have been guided as much as possible by the original documents – the reports of the trial and other court records, the newspapers, and the published and unpublished writings of the various participants. Accordingly, I owe a special debt to the editor-scholars and librarians who have made such research possible. My footnotes, I hope, pay suitable tribute to all of them, but two deserve special mention. Mary-Jo Kline's scholarly two-volume edition of *Political Correspondence and Public Papers of Aaron Burr* has been indispensable to me; especially important has been her critical reassessment of the famous cipher letter that played such an important role in both Jefferson's original decision to charge Burr with treason and also in the subsequent litigation.

Charles Hobson, past editor of the *Papers of John Marshall* and current editor of the St. George Tucker Law Papers at the College of William and Mary has as always been an invaluable source of information and advice to me, as well as to dozens of other scholars. Hobson's account of the Burr trial with accompanying documents, prepared for the Federal Judicial Center as part of the project "Federal Trials and Great Debates in United States History," is a model of exacting scholarship. Equally valuable has been his concise summary of Marshall's multiple opinions in the trial (in his edited Volume 7 of the *Papers of John Marshall*). I have used the original reports of David Robertson and also those of Thomas Carpenter when citing Marshall's opinions, but the full text of those opinions with useful introductory notes appears in Hobson's Volume 7, as does Marshall's correspondence relevant to the Richmond proceedings.

Librarians and archivists, past and present, have made my work possible. So it pleases me greatly to acknowledge the dedicated professionals at the American Antiquarian Society, especially Elizabeth Watts Pope, for helping me access the Society's incomparable collection of early American newspapers. Robert F. Karachuck, Associate Editor of the Adams Papers at the Massachusetts Historical Society, went out of his way to expedite my research in the Adams Family Papers. I am grateful to the archivists and librarians at the State Library of Virginia and the Virginia Historical Society for making my research trips to Richmond profitable and pleasant. E. Lee Shepard, Vice President for Collections at the VHS, has been most helpful and encouraging.

And so over many years have been the librarians and staff at the Homer Babbidge Library at the University of Connecticut, where I have been privileged to do much of my research and writing. Special thanks to Steve Batt, library liaison to the Federal Depository Program, and to curator of collections Melissa Watterworth Batt and the staff at the University's Thomas Dodd Research Center.

Finally, and above all, I want to express my love and gratitude to my wife Rosanne Pelletier, who advised and encouraged me in countless ways. Her aesthetic sense of language and skilled copyediting have made the book better on almost every page.

I'm delighted to dedicate the book to Rosie and also to my brother Dan and his wife Paula, who have been my best friends for longer than any of us care to remember.

Introduction

A leading constitutional historian called the Burr treason trial "the greatest criminal trial in American history and one of the notable trials in the annals of the law."[1] Edward Corwin did not explain why the trial was great and notable but several reasons come to mind. For one thing it involved a three-way legal, ideological, and personal contest among three prominent statesmen of the early republic. The clash between President Thomas Jefferson and his former vice president Aaron Burr set the case in motion, gave it a highly personalized and emotional cast, and defined many of the legal issues that emerged during the trial. President Jefferson's extensive and unprecedented involvement in the trial proceedings, in turn, brought him into conflict with his old enemy Chief Justice John Marshall, who was sitting as a trial judge in the federal circuit court in Richmond, Virginia. Given the three-way battle that raged in Marshall's courtroom, it is not surprising that historians have found the trial irresistible – and this is not to mention the mysterious intentions of Burr himself which the trial never fully revealed.

In addition to the leading figures involved, the legal and constitutional issues in the trial – the definition of treason, the constitutional rights of criminal defendants, and the meaning of separation of powers in the Constitution – have attracted the attention of constitutional and legal historians. Major biographers of Burr, Jefferson, and Marshall have also felt obliged to address the role their subjects played in the trial. As for Burr, it is tempting to make the study of the trial a study, if not of Burr himself, then of the "Burr conspiracy"; two pioneering scholars who

[1] Edward S. Corwin, *John Marshall and the Constitution* (New Haven, 1919), 86.

chose this approach are Walter F. McCaleb (a revised edition of whose 1903 book appeared in 1936, followed by a further revision in 1966), and Thomas P. Abernathys (*The Burr Conspiracy*, 1954). Two outstanding biographies of Burr, by Milton Lomask (1982) and Nancy Isenberg (2007), also discuss the trial at some length. Jefferson's response to Burr's conspiracy and his involvement in the Richmond proceedings are treated at length in Volume 5 of Dumas Malone's biography of Jefferson (1962). Leonard Levy's *Jefferson and Civil Liberties* (1963) focuses critically on Jefferson's role in the events leading up to, and including, the trial.

Constitutional historians, especially those interested in Chief Justice John Marshall, have weighed in on the trial and on Marshall's role in it. Edward Corwin's short study of Marshall's jurisprudence (1919) argued that Marshall's performance in the trial was a blemish on his record, while Albert Beveridge's extensive discussion of the trial in his four-volume Marshall biography, which also appeared in 1919, was highly praiseful. Robert Faulkner's superb essay in the September 1966 issue of *The Journal of American History* is a successful critique of Corwin. Recent biographies of Marshall – those of Jean Edward Smith (1996) and R. Kent Newmyer (2001), for example – have, like Faulkner, viewed Marshall's performance in a favorable light. Further evidence of the continuing fascination with the trial are two recent book-length studies by Buckner F. Melton Jr., a historian and professor of law at the University of North Carolina, and Peter Charles Hoffer, Distinguished Research Professor of History at the University of Georgia. Hoffer's thorough bibliography of works about the trial (in his *The Treason Trials of Aaron Burr*, 2008) attests to this ongoing scholarly fascination with the trial.

While I have been greatly aided by the many fine scholars who have studied the trial, I have not presumed to sort out and resolve the interpretive differences among them. Rather, in order to get a fresh view, I have concentrated on contemporary accounts by trial participants and by the firsthand observers of those directly involved. My particular focus has been on the remarkable trial record itself as reported in two stenographic transcriptions of the proceedings, one by David Robertson (two volumes, 1808), the other by Thomas Carpenter (three volumes, 1808).

A word of clarification is in order concerning my use of Robertson and Carpenter. Both men were experienced stenographic reporters, and both appear to have been in competition to get their reports of the trial before the public. Robertson seems to be the favorite among historians of the trial, perhaps because it was his account that appeared in serial form in the Richmond *Enquirer*, the paper that in turn was cited by other newspapers around the country. Carpenter was an equally competent reporter, however, and more to the point, he is the only source for the legal proceedings after the main treason trial ended. (Robertson stopped reporting on September 9, 1807; Carpenter's Volume Three, which covers the final stage of the proceedings, contains some of the most revealing material of the long trial.) Accordingly, for the principal treason trial I cite Robertson, while for the misdemeanor trial and the commitment hearings after the main trial, I have used Carpenter. Marshall's numerous opinions during the trial have been published in Volume Seven of the *Papers of John Marshall*, edited with scholarly head-notes by Charles F. Hobson.

To understand the principal treason trial of Burr in Richmond – the focus of the present book – I have found it necessary to discuss the other legal proceedings growing out of the conspiracy. The most relevant of these was the habeas corpus litigation involving Burr's associates, Erick Bollman and Samuel Swartwout in early 1807 in the federal circuit court for the Distinct of Columbia, and then on appeal to the Supreme Court, where Chief Justice Marshall wrote the majority opinion. Marshall's definition of treason in *Ex parte Bollman* and *Ex parte Swartwout* turned out to be a central point of dispute in the Richmond trial. As we shall see, Marshall as the trial judge in Richmond was forced to clarify what he said as Chief Justice in his Bollman and Swartwout opinion.

At roughly the same time that the Bollman and Swartwout case was taking shape, Burr himself faced two federal grand juries regarding his activities in the West: the first in Kentucky, in early November 1806, and the second in the Mississippi Territory, in early February 1807. While Burr was not indicted in either proceeding, this experience, I argue, shaped his defense strategy in the principal treason trial. To avoid confusion, readers should note that I have included a brief discussion of Burr's encounters with the two western grand juries in Chapter 3, the chapter that deals mainly with the grand jury phase of the principal trial in Richmond.

Readers should also keep in mind that there were three distinct phases in the Richmond proceedings. Burr was initially indicted for two crimes: treason and high misdemeanor. The government tried the treason charge first and after Burr was acquitted on that charge on September 1, 1807, he was tried on the misdemeanor charge, and again acquitted on September 15. The third phase of the Richmond trial, reported only by Thomas Carpenter as mentioned above, came when Jefferson instructed the prosecution in Richmond to charge Burr for misdemeanor and treason again – this time for actions that occurred subsequent to those that formed the basis of the original indictment. Marshall's ruling to commit Burr for trial in Ohio in late October 1807 ended the trial.

In approaching the Burr treason trials I have followed the path laid out by the late Professor Kathryn "Kitty" Preyer. What Kitty aimed to do in her remarkable life of scholarship and teaching was to capture the lawmakers of the new nation in the act of making law. Lawmaking in the Burr trial fits Kitty's scenario – which is to say it involved a collision between the inherited law of monarchical England concerning treason with the perceived needs of the new republic, as those needs were filtered through the ideological convictions, character traits, and personal quirks of the lawmakers and the political framework created by the new Constitution. Not surprisingly, given the complex factors involved, the law-making process was tedious, convoluted, and full of ironic twists and turns. The legal doctrines that emerged from the trial may have been less than perfect, but they were, I argue, remarkably suited to the aspirations of the new nation.

The challenge has been to capture the dynamics of the trial. Keeping all the plates in the air at the same time meant tracking the complex interaction of old law and new circumstances, while at the same time assessing the impact of political ideology and character on this process. In referring to "old law" I mean English treason law as it developed during the four centuries following the great treason statute of 25 Edward III, passed in 1351. Conflicting interpretations of treason during this long period meant that lawyers in the Burr trial could cherry-pick English case law to suit their own purposes. The lawyers, and of course Marshall, too, also had to weigh the intent of those who framed the treason provisions in the Constitution and the judicial rulings from the 1790s as to what the Framers intended.

Just as important as the legal arguments in my account, however, are the reasons that the parties involved in the proceedings chose to act as they did. Certainly legal reasoning has to be taken seriously in ascribing motivation, but hardly less determinative were the personality and character, and indeed temperament, of those involved. Concerning the matter of character, the reader should note that there are no separate chapters dealing with Jefferson, Marshall, and Burr. My approach has been to let their intertangled actions regarding the trial speak to the matter of their character and personality. What is revealed, I hasten to say, does not constitute a full portrait of these multifaceted and complex men; much less does it constitute an assessment of their places in history. That said, the Burr trial – because of its length, the intense public scrutiny, and the fact that trial procedure, especially when employed by gifted lawyers such as those in Richmond – brought to light the values, personalities, and character of the leading players. Not surprisingly, contemporaries such as John Adams came to see Jefferson, Marshall, and Burr as iconic figures in the cultural battles over republican truth.

A special word is merited regarding the way in which the contest between Jefferson and Marshall in Richmond bears on the lifelong constitutional battle between the two men – a struggle that pitted President Jefferson's states rights ideology against Chief Justice Marshall's constitutional nationalism. The important point to keep in mind is that the confrontation between the president and the chief justice in the Burr trial was not overtly about states rights and nationalism. Rather, the underlying constitutional issue concerned a struggle between two competing branches of the national government. In this contest, Marshall's performance as a trial judge was critical because it spoke to the credibility of the federal judiciary as an independent branch of the federal government – this at a time when judicial authority and independence had yet to be established, at both the state and national levels.

What makes the Burr trial unique in this struggle for judicial independence, and uniquely revealing for purposes of understanding Marshall, is the fact that the Chief Justice of the Supreme Court was sitting as a trial judge on circuit. Circuit court duties were a distinctive and vastly important feature of the federal court system from the outset and indeed for much of the nineteenth century. Supreme Court justices on circuit sat with the federal district court judges in their respective circuits, which in Marshall's case included Virginia and North Carolina. While federal district court judges sometimes had a real impact on circuit court decisions, such was not the case with district judge Cyrus Griffin, who sat with Marshall in the Burr trial. In fact, rarely in the extensive transcriptions of the proceedings do we see Griffin's name, and never in regard to any item of interest or importance. Jefferson was probably correct to think of him as a "cypher."

As the de facto sole trial judge, Marshall faced a daunting number of questions about law and about trial procedure that had not yet been settled. He did at one point attempt to consult his colleagues on the Supreme Court about the constitutional issues involved, but there is no evidence that they responded. As it turned out Marshall's main assistance came from the lawyers who argued before him.

The lawyers figure prominently in my account because, as Marshall himself took pains to recognize, they figured prominently in the law-making process. Doing justice to the lawyers is not easy, however, since – like Marshall himself – they rarely bothered to explain what they were about. It is nevertheless possible to determine what it was they said that Marshall considered useful. And although neither side left a blueprint of their battle plan, I indicate how their litigation strategies can be inferred from a close reading of their arguments. Additionally, by giving the lawyers their due, I hope to capture some of the excitement and confusion generated by the "Melo-drama" as witnessed by those who watched the trial firsthand.

A final point about the lawyers concerns my suggestion that their arguments and litigation strategies constitute a transitional moment in the emergence of a distinctly American adversarial tradition. For example, the unrestrained attack of Burr's lawyers on the government – and on the president personally – was certainly unprecedented. Also, the lawyers themselves, along with Marshall, embody a mixture of the old and the new in their approach to lawyering. To speak confidently about a transitional moment, however, historians need to know a lot more about the way American lawyers argued than we presently do; my heuristic remarks are meant to prompt others to study this important subject in depth. My guess is that when a full history of courtroom advocacy in America finally appears, the Burr treason trial will occupy a prominent place.

Finally, a brief comment must be made concerning the legal and constitutional principles that resulted from the trial: the meaning of treason ("levying war") in Article III of the Constitution; the rule of law in general and the concept of due process, especially as it applied to the rights of criminal defendants; and finally the separation of powers between the federal judiciary and the executive branch. These legal and constitutional principles, as I try to make clear, were not Marshall's creations alone, and neither were they settled conclusively for all time. I do insist that Marshall's decisions, coupled with his example of judicial independence, left an enduring legacy. How that legacy figures in our own time is an important subject I touch on only briefly, in the hope that readers will ponder the issue and come to their own conclusions.

Chronology of the Conspiracy
and Associated Trial Proceedings

1805

*March 2, 1805: Burr's Farewell Address to the U.S. Senate

*April–October 1805: Burr travels down the Ohio and Mississippi Rivers to New Orleans and back, visiting leading politicians along the way in order to gauge popular attachment to the Union and popular support for a military operation against Spanish territory.

*Late November 1805: Burr meets privately with Jefferson. No record of their conversation, but Jefferson knew of Burr's western trip and the rumors surrounding it. Jefferson apparently does not warn Burr about his activities in the West.

1806

*Late March 1806: Burr meets again with Jefferson, seemingly in a futile effort to extract a political appointment. Again no warning to Burr.

*Winter–Spring 1806: Burr's plans take shape for a military expedition against Spanish possessions, presumably in case of a war with Spain. Burr moves to acquire land on the Washita River to be settled by his men as a contingency plan in case there is no war.

*Summer 1806: Burr contacts friends in the East to raise money for his expedition, which now seems likely because of apparent Spanish military movements against American territory in the Southwest.

*July 22–29, 1806: Jonathan Dayton drafts the cipher letter, which is delivered to Wilkinson in Natchitoches in Louisiana by Samuel Swartwout on October 8, 1806. The purpose of the letter, which depicts

Burr's army as poised to move downriver, is to keep Wilkinson involved in the conspiracy; the letter had the opposite effect.

*Fall 1806: Jefferson receives more letters from various quarters warning of Burr's conspiracy.

*October 22, 1806: First of three Cabinet meetings discussing the reliability of Wilkinson's letters to Jefferson warning him of Burr's activities.

*November 4, 1806: Federalist district attorney Joseph Hamilton Daveiss, independently of President Jefferson, instigates grand jury proceedings against Burr in Kentucky, charging him with high misdemeanor for preparing a military action against Spanish territory in violation of the Neutrality Act of 1794. The grand jury refuses to indict.

*November 25, 1806: Wilkinson takes military control of New Orleans, nominally in order to resist Burr's invading "army," but in reality to silence those who knew of Wilkinson's own involvement in the conspiracy.

*December 1–5, 1806: Daveiss tries for another grand jury indictment in Kentucky and fails again.

*December 10, 1806: Harman Blennerhassett and a small band of Burr's men rendezvous on Blennerhassett's island in the Ohio River, only to make a hasty retreat downriver to avoid arrest.

1807

*January 18, 1807: Jefferson receives Wilkinson's decoded (and altered) copy of the cipher letter, written by Jonathan Dayton and purporting to describe Burr's military movements. In decoding the letter, Wilkinson altered its content in order to implicate Burr in treason and to cover his own involvement in the conspiracy.

*January 22, 1807: Largely on the basis of Wilkinson's cipher letter, President Jefferson addresses Congress declaring Burr guilty of treason.

*January 30, 1807: Federal circuit court for the District of Columbia rules by a vote of 2 to 1 to confine Burr's friends Bollman and Swartwout on the charge of treason.

*February 4, 1807: Burr faces another grand jury on the charge of treason, this time in the Mississippi Territory. The grand jury refuses to indict, but thanks to Jefferson's proclamation of January 22, 1807, Burr is now a wanted man.

February 13, 1807: Back in Washington, the U.S. Supreme Court in *Ex parte Bollman* and *Ex parte Swartwout* overrules the federal circuit court decision, freeing the two men on writs of habeas corpus. Marshall writes the majority opinion, in which he defines the meaning of treason in Article III of the Constitution.

*February 19, 1807: Burr is arrested in the village of Wakefield in the Mississippi Territory and sent under military guard to Richmond, Virginia to await trial in Marshall's federal circuit court.

*March 30, 1807: Burr is charged with treason and high misdemeanor before a special session of Marshall's circuit court.

*April 1, 1807: Marshall finds sufficient evidence to hold Burr on the misdemeanor charge but not the treason charge. Burr is bailed at $10,000.

*May 22, 1807: Grand jury sworn for Burr's treason trial; Marshall delivers the charge.

*June 13, 1807: Marshall issues subpoena *duces tecum* to President Jefferson, ordering him to produce certain documents requested by Burr's lawyers to be used in preparing his defense.

*June 24, 1807: Grand jury indicts Burr for treason and high misdemeanor.

*August 3, 1807: Principal treason trial against Burr begins.

*August 17, 1807: Trial jury sworn and treason charge read; prosecution opens the case against Burr.

*August 31, 1807: Marshall hands down the major decision of the trial, ruling in favor of Burr's motion of August 20 to exclude all further testimony by the government's witnesses not relating specifically to the events of December 10, 1806 on Blennerhassett's island, the matter charged in the formal indictment. Marshall clarifies his definition of treason in his opinion for the Supreme Court in *Ex parte Bollman*.

*September 1, 1807: The jury returns an unusually worded verdict, declaring Burr "not proved to be guilty under this indictment by any evidence submitted to us."

*September 9, 1807: Burr's trial on the misdemeanor charge begins.

*September 15, 1807: Marshall's ruling on evidence leads the jury to acquit Burr on the misdemeanor charge.

*September 18, 1807: At Jefferson's urging, federal attorney George Hay asks Marshall, now sitting as a committing magistrate, to hold Burr for trial for treasonable activities committed outside Virginia.

*October 20, 1807: Marshall rules that there is sufficient evidence to bring Burr to trial in Ohio on the misdemeanor charge or on the charge of treason should the grand jury in Ohio so determine. Burr is never brought to trial in Ohio.

Prologue

A Mind-Jostling Trial

"There never was such a trial from the beginning of the world to this day!"

George Hay[1]

"The far famed trial of Aaron Burr...has jostled the public mind from one end of the Union to the other..."

Richard Bates, September 20, 1807[2]

Americans in 1807, proud of their hard-won status as a nation among nations, were prone to exaggerate their own importance. Thus could George Hay, President Jefferson's chief prosecutor in the Burr treason trial, make his extravagant claim. The world at large, of course, took no notice of what was transpiring in Chief Justice Marshall's circuit court in Richmond. Such was decidedly not the case, however, with the several thousand people who swarmed into town to catch the action. Nor was it true of the tens of thousands across the country who followed the sensationalist coverage of the trial in the partisan newspapers of the day. What Americans saw and read about – what "jostled the public mind" – was in fact one of the most dramatic trials in American history, one that pitted the president against the chief justice of the United States, that saw some of America's finest lawyers locked in seven months of legal

---

[1] Hay is quoted in Richard B. Morris, *Fair Trial: Fourteen Who Stood Accused from Anne Hutchinson to Alger Hiss* (Rev. ed., New York, Evanston, and London, 1967), 121.
[2] Richard Bates to Frederick Bates, Sept. 20, 1807, Edward Bates Manuscript Collection, Va. Hist. Soc.

and personal combat, and featured a defendant whose fall from grace remains an enduring mystery.

Aaron Burr was one of the most promising young statesmen of the Revolutionary generation. As the grandson of Jonathan Edwards and the son of the president of Princeton, Burr was marked for distinction. He was also a military hero, a gifted lawyer, and a charismatic politician who delivered New York's electoral vote to Jefferson in 1800. Two events ended Burr's meteoric rise. One was his refusal to withdraw from the disputed presidential contest in 1800, in which he was tied for electoral votes with Jefferson. The House of Representatives settled the dispute after thirty-six ballots, making Jefferson president and Burr vice president. Burr served effectively in that position for four years, but Jefferson never forgave him for his hubris. The second blow to Burr's political aspirations was his duel with Hamilton, whose death ended Burr's prospects for advancement in the Federalist Party. Like so many Americans who were down and out in the East, Burr went west to recover his fortune and his honor. It was his suspicious comings and goings there in 1805 and 1806 that caused Jefferson to charge him with treason, which in turn brought him into Marshall's circuit court for trial.

Burr's presence alone was enough to make the Richmond trial a national event, but the president of the United States was also involved. Well before the proceedings opened in Richmond, it was clear that Jefferson was out to destroy his vice president – first by driving him from the party, and then in January 1807, by publicly declaring him to be guilty of treason (this without benefit of grand jury indictment or jury trial). The president also took personal charge of the prosecution in Richmond in order to secure Burr's conviction. Jefferson's role in the trial guaranteed yet another showdown with Marshall, who after *Marbury v. Madison* (1803) was on the president's list of enemies. Adding yet more drama and importance to the trial was the appearance of a remarkable array of talented lawyers competing for adversarial honors and fighting for truth and justice as they saw it.

Marshall's circuit court, which generally dealt with run-of-the-mill economic issues of Virginians, suddenly became the focal point of national political controversy and unprecedented press coverage in newspapers across the nation. If one includes arraignment and bail hearings and the grand jury selection, the proceedings lasted from April through October. If one also counts the trial of Burr's confederates before the federal Circuit Court for the District of Columbia (*U.S. v. Bollman et al.*) and the Supreme Court of the United States in early

1807 (*Ex parte Bollman and Ex parte Swartwout*) the legal proceedings lasted the better part of a year.

The stenographic report of the trial, running to well over one thousand pages, poses a number of intriguing issues. One concerns the vastly important (and generally underestimated) role of lawyers in the lawmaking process. Not all of the lawyers in the trial were memorable, of course, but the best had a striking command of law, rhetoric, and adversarial skill. The trial record also reveals the dynamic relationship among counsel, judge and jury during what appears to be a unique moment in courtroom advocacy.

Observing Chief Justice Marshall as trial judge is also revealing. On circuit in Richmond – in contrast to his role on the Supreme Court in Washington – he spoke and acted for himself alone. As presiding judge he was responsible for keeping nine highly competitive, partisan lawyers in line. Some fifteen on-the-spot rulings in the course of the trial put his legal knowledge and legal agility on display for the entire nation to criticize. His judicial duties varied widely: Sometimes he sat as a simple magistrate whose job was to settle arraignment and bail. He also oversaw both the grand and trial jury process, which in turn involved ruling on trial procedure and evidence, often without the guidance of precedent. While seeing to it that Aaron Burr got a fair trial, he necessarily had to determine the meaning of the constitutional provisions concerning treason – ironically by clarifying his own opinion for a divided Supreme Court in the case involving Burr's associates Erick Bollman and Samuel Swartwout, who were also charged with treason. Complicating matters further for Marshall was the tidal wave of public opinion, first against Burr and then against himself, generated by the partisan press with the active encouragement of the president.

More than drama, Jefferson's unprecedented role added constitutional significance to the trial. It was the president who decided to charge Burr with treason – mainly on the word of one James Wilkinson, who was widely recognized, even by Jefferson himself, as a questionable character. Having usurped the role of both the grand jury and the trial jury by publicly pronouncing Burr guilty, Jefferson also intervened in the Richmond proceedings. In doing so he drew fire from Burr's lawyers, which further intensified the partisan tone of the proceedings and inevitably drew Marshall into the political and ideological squabbles surrounding the trial. Whether his well-known antipathy toward the president and his party distorted Marshall's sense of fairness, as his enemies claimed, is a question begging for an answer.

Complicating matters for Marshall was the mystery of Aaron Burr himself. The former vice president was not only the catalyst for the case but also was the charismatic lawyer who masterminded his own defense. Whether the trial revealed or instead obscured the truth of his actual innocence or guilt remains an open issue. What the trial did do was to stir up a number of puzzling questions. How was it, for example, that Burr, who had so many advantages and so much promise, could fall so low? This particular question is a subject for Burr's biographers rather than for a book concerning his treason trial. Still, when considering the evidence against him presented at his trial, it is impossible not to wonder whether a soldier who had fought courageously to create the American nation would then undertake to destroy it, as Jefferson claimed. And, had Burr not been out to sever the Union, why (astute lawyer that he was) would he behave so as to make himself vulnerable to the charge? Why the secret association via cipher letters with Wilkinson, who was the chief witness against him at the trial? And how was it that Burr acting as private citizen thought he could drive Spain from Mexico and brashly attempt to enlist the British minister in such an enterprise while at the same time dealing with Spanish officials by playing on their hostility to Great Britain?[3] Such a plan, as John Adams observed, was so far-fetched that it would have had to be hatched by an "Idiot or a Lunatick," neither of which Burr was.

Jefferson's actions also defy easy explanation. As president and commander-in-chief, he was of course responsible for the security of the nation; he was also in charge of American foreign policy. In both capacities, Jefferson was rightly concerned about persistent rumors that Burr was raising money and men to attack New Orleans (an American territory) as a first step in a military expedition to free Mexico from Spanish colonial domination. Even though Burr had not yet committed himself to a course of action, Jefferson had reason to fear he was the leader of a criminal conspiracy – either to commit treason by attacking New

[3] The full extent and audacity of Burr's elaborate scheme to extort money from Spain and Great Britain is explained in Henry Adams, *History of the United States of America during the Administrations of Thomas Jefferson*. The Library of America Edition (New York, 1985), vol. 2, especially chs. 10 and 11, 754–87. Adams was the first to make extensive use of Spanish Archives, but, according to John Randolph, it was suspected as early as January 1807 that Burr was extorting money for his plan from both Spain and Great Britain. John Randolph to James Monroe, Jan. 2, 1807, Monroe Papers, LC, as quoted in William Cabell Bruce, *John Randolph of Roanoke, 1773–1833* (2 vols., New York, 1970), 1: 299.

Orleans, or to violate of the Neutrality Act of 1794 by attacking Spanish authorities in Mexico.

So why did the president not stop the conspiracy (whatever its objective) before it matured, which he could have done simply by putting the chief conspirator on warning? And why was it that Jefferson, once he decided to act, took the law into his own hands in order to secure Burr's conviction – especially since doing so invoked a concept of federal executive power that he and his party repudiated? And rather than prosecuting Burr for treasonably levying war against the United States (for which there was little solid evidence), why not prosecute him only for mounting a military campaign against Spanish Mexico in violation of the Neutrality Act – a high misdemeanor for which there was more evidence and a much less stringent standard of proof? Why as sitting president would he undertake to micromanage the prosecution in Richmond down to the manipulation of witnesses? And why as master strategist for the prosecution would he rely on the much-hated English doctrine of constructive treason – especially when that doctrine ran directly counter to his republican values and his distaste for English legal precedents?

The trial itself is also replete with puzzles, one of which was Marshall's decision to let it continue until both he and the lawyers were totally exhausted. Also, did public opinion have as much impact on the proceedings as lawyers on both sides claimed it did? And what does it say about the nature of the legal profession in 1807 that lawyers on both sides could hold forth so brilliantly? And why, in search of American law, did they spend so much time, in the words of one of them, traversing "a wilderness of investigation in England"?

Furthermore, there are questions about Marshall's conduct of the trial, questions asked by contemporaries and historians alike. How, for example, did the mutual hatred between the president and the chief justice play out during the trial; and in what way did this animosity affect the trial's final outcome? And what about "the Rhadamanthine calm" Henry Adams attributed to Marshall?[4] Was he really all that calm; or perhaps, as his critics insinuated, was Marshall's calm simply a cover to disguise a sinister determination to free Burr at any cost in order to embarrass the president? But if Marshall's aim was to free Burr, why, after Burr had been acquitted of all charges in Richmond, did Marshall commit him to yet another trial in Ohio?

---

[4] Adams, *History*, 915.

And indeed, what impact did the encounter between the chief justice and the president have on the yet to be defined principle of separation of powers in the Constitution? And what was settled – and left unsettled – regarding the constitutional meaning of treason that Marshall and the lawyers fashioned for the new nation?

Indeed it is the newness of the nation and the resulting fluidity of ideas, institutions, and national boundaries, that helps us understand the conspiracy, the trial, and the seemingly inexplicable behavior of the leading characters. Context as always is the starting point of interpretation. Burr and Wilkinson, for example, could scheme grandly about gold and glory in the Southwest, because that vast area was a contested and largely ungoverned region open to disputed claims between Spain and the United States. Americans were obsessed with traitors and the crime of treason because loyalty to the new nation was still fragile. If Jefferson was paranoid about secession plots, it was because national unity under the new Constitution remained an unfulfilled promise. For Marshall the unfinished nation translated into uncertainty about the law governing the trial process in federal courts, about the constitutional meaning of treason, and indeed about the authority of the federal judiciary itself.

And finally, because the American nation was still a work in progress, there were conflicting visions of what it should look like when completed – visions, as fate would have it, that were clearly represented by Jefferson, Marshall, and Burr. All three were elite members of the founding generation: Burr as a privileged son of New England, and Jefferson and Marshall as born-to-rule Virginians connected by blood to each other through one of the Old Dominion's first families. And each man could lay claim to the Revolutionary heritage, though none so clearly as Jefferson; no man envisaged so fully the cultural possibilities of independence, or wrote so inspiringly about the meaning of republican liberty. Marshall and Burr were too young to have been leaders in the break with England, but both men fought bravely to achieve the liberty that Jefferson wrote about. All three men could justly claim the mantle of the Revolution, which may help explain why they disagreed so passionately about its meaning.

By the time of the Burr trial their disagreements about politics, law, and the future of the nation were irreconcilable. Marshall and Jefferson parted company during the 1790s over the French Revolution. As minister to France in the 1780s, Jefferson witnessed the revolution there during its early, idealistic phase and came to see it as a continuation of the tradition begun by America's revolution against England. Marshall saw the American Revolution as a constitutional and political movement fundamentally at odds with the social upheaval and violence in Revolutionary France. Marshall liked Edmund Burke; Jefferson liked Tom Paine. As the leading Federalist in Virginia during the 1790s, Marshall championed the nationalist policies of Presidents Washington and Adams. While Marshall was working to strengthen the national government and curtail the democratic tendencies of the age, Jefferson, as Washington's secretary of state and then as vice-president under John Adams, was busy organizing a new political party dedicated to states rights, political democracy, and friendship with France.

The election of 1800 brought the clashing views of Marshall and Jefferson into dramatic focus. Jefferson believed that his election to the presidency was a second Revolution that would reassert the true meaning of the first one that had been vitiated by a decade of Federalist misrule. Marshall was certain that Jefferson's radical theorizing would destroy the republic and the Constitution on which it rested. Lame-duck President John Adams nominated Marshall as chief justice in the hope that he would make the Supreme Court a bulwark against Jefferson's radicalism. Marshall got the message and so did President Jefferson, the latter of whom set out to "eradicate" the spirit of "Marshallism" and reduce the power of the Court. The Burr trial, like *Marbury v. Madison* in 1803 and the case of Burr's co-conspirators Erick Bollman and Samuel Swartwout in 1807, was a battle in this ongoing war over the future of the nation.

By 1807 Aaron Burr was no longer a player whose views on the future counted; he was beyond the pale, a man without a party and possibly without a country. Even before his fall, however, he had never cared greatly who won the ideological contest between Jefferson and Marshall. Burr's indifference might seem strange, since it was his organizing genius that delivered New York and the election to Jefferson and his party in 1800. But in fact, Burr had never belonged to any of the ideological schools of thought that divided the founding generation. Unlike the president or the chief justice, he had no official podium after leaving the Senate. Although he was an astute observer of human nature, he did not philosophize or moralize. Except for his farewell speech to the Senate in 1805, which brought tears to the eyes of his fellow senators, he made no uplifting public addresses. Neither did he write elaborate position papers on the great issues of the day, although he clearly could have done so.

His surviving political correspondence and his lengthy private journals are largely devoid of self-examination and self-justification.[5]

In short, Burr was preeminently a man of action, a role he seems to have envisaged for himself while still a student at Princeton in the 1770s.[6] What separated him most clearly from Jefferson and Marshall and most other leading statesmen of the Revolution was his single-minded, self-centered, and unapologetic ambition. Jefferson wrote eloquently about the universal right to the pursuit of happiness; Burr pursued his own happiness. Probably he would have done so less aggressively had fate had been kinder to his talents: had he received the military promotion he angled for during the Revolution; had he not lost his beloved wife Theodosia in 1794; had he not been undercut by Hamilton at every turn for a dozen years; had the presidency not been denied him in 1800; had he not killed Hamilton in the duel at Weehawken in 1804; or had he gotten the chief justiceship of Pennsylvania, which "he applied for indirectly" shortly before undertaking his western enterprise.[7]

Poor bby

Burr never complained about these setbacks, which rather than quelling his ambition, instead added an element of reckless urgency to his plans to make it big out West – either by driving the Spanish from Mexico or by separating the western states from the Union (depending on whose account one believed). In Burr's universe God helped those individuals – and those nations – who helped themselves. His audacity, arrogance and sense of frustrated entitlement set in motion the unlikely series of events that brought him into Chief Justice Marshall's circuit court, with President Jefferson in hot pursuit.

So here they were, a popular and justly famous president and a uniquely gifted judge locked in combat, each focused on the fate of Aaron Burr, the man who, in the words of John Adams, "must and would be something,"[8] if not the president of the United States than maybe the emperor of Mexico. The conflicting visions of the young nation symbolized by Jefferson, Marshall, and Burr would reveal themselves in the trial and would likely influence its outcome. The lawyers in the case, though less

---

[5] See Gordon Wood, "The Real Treason of Aaron Burr," 143 *Proceedings of the American Philosophical Society*, No. 2 (June 1999), 280–95. Also see ch. 8 in his *Revolutionary Characters* (New York, 2006).

[6] Nancy Isenberg, drawing on Benjamin Rush's letter to John Adams (April 3, 1807), makes the point in her *Fallen Founder: The Life of Aaron Burr* (New York, 2007), 16.

[7] On Burr's frustrated search for success, see Benjamin Rush to John Adams, April 3, 1807, Adams Papers, MHS.

[8] Adams to Rush, June 23, 1807, ibid.

well known to history, were barely less important than the principal players, and they too reflected the partisan and cultural divisions of the age.

Personal character counted heavily in the small world of republican statesmen where all the participants knew one another. And this also was revealed in the texts of the trial report.[9] Not surprisingly, the struggle in Marshall's packed courtroom often verged on chaos, which furnished entertainment for the spectators and copy for the press. Out of the chaos, however, came some sound law suitable for the new nation and for ours as well. The challenge is to understand how politicians, lawyers, and judges created first the chaos and then the law.

[9] Robert A. Ferguson discusses the vulnerability of the legal text to interpretation in *The Trial in American Life* (Chicago and London, 2007), 27.

I

Jefferson and Burr on the Road to Richmond

"I never indeed thought him an honest, frank-dealing man, but considered him as a crooked gun, or other perverted machine, whose aim or shot you could never be sure of."

Jefferson on Burr[1]

"Although I never thought so highly of his natural Talents or his acquired attainments, as many of both Parties have represented them, I never believed him to be a Fool. But he must be a Idiot or a Lunatick if he has really planned and Attempted to execute such a Project as is imputed to him."

John Adams on Burr[2]

"... Mr. Jefferson has been too hasty in his Message in which he has denounced him [Burr] by Name and pronounced him guilty. But if his guilt is as clear as the Noon day sun, the first Magistrate ought not to have pronounced it so before a Jury had tryed him."

John Adams on Jefferson on Burr[3]

Historians looking to illustrate the way judicial lawmaking in the new nation was influenced by chance and contingency, human passions, follies and character quirks might well turn to the treason trial of Aaron

---

[1] Jefferson to William B. Giles, April 20, 1807, Lipscomb and Albert E. Bergh, eds., *Writings of Thomas Jefferson* (Washington, DC, 1903), 11: 191 [Hereafter Bergh, *Writings of Jefferson*].

[2] John Adams to Dr. Benjamin Rush, Feb. 2, 1807, Adams Papers, MHS. The original of this letter is held by the Boston Public Library in the John Adams Manuscript Collection.

[3] Ibid.

Burr. To make the point the story should begin with Aaron Burr and Thomas Jefferson, because it was their mutual feelings of distrust and contempt and their intersecting political aspirations that set the trial in motion and set loose the political passions that influenced the proceedings.

The relationship between Jefferson and Burr began in the late 1790s, when both men were interested for their own reasons in driving the Federalist party of Washington and Adams from office. Whether Jefferson and Madison talked serious politics with Burr in 1791 on their famed botanical trip to New York is not clear. What became clear in the course of the decade, however, was that Burr proved himself to be the man most capable of delivering New York's electoral votes in the upcoming presidential election of 1800. For his pivotal role in forging the New York–Virginia political axis, Burr won a place on the ballot with Jefferson. When New York's electoral votes carried the Democratic Republican party to victory, Burr deserved a real share of the credit.[4]

Whether he also deserved to be president of the United States was another matter. This became a real possibility when it was discovered that Burr and Jefferson were tied for votes in the Electoral College. Before the passage of the Twelfth Amendment in 1804, electoral votes were cast only for the president, with the vice presidency going to the person receiving the second highest vote count. According to the Constitution, a tie in the Electoral College would be settled by a vote in the House of Representatives with each state casting one ballot. Unfortunately for the Democratic Republicans, the Federalists in the House were in a position to determine the outcome of the election; unfortunately for Burr, Alexander Hamilton was the man who would determine who the Federalists would support. Jefferson finally won – but only after thirty-six votes and weeks of backroom politicking that culminated in a permanent rift between Jefferson and Burr, who were now president and vice president respectively.

Looking at their conflicting political styles during the 1790s, a falling out between the two men seemed all but inevitable. Jefferson the republican ideologue objected to the Federalists because they had betrayed the values of the Revolution; his primary role in organizing

---

[4] Burr's success in uniting New York's political factions in support of the new party is treated concisely in Isenberg, *Fallen Founder*, 196–202. Alfred Young's *The Democratic Republicans of New York: The Origins, 1763–1797* (Chapel Hill, 1967) captures the raucous world of New York politics in which Burr flourished.

Thomas Jefferson

the opposition – the same role he had performed in justifying the Revolution against Great Britain – was to supply, and indeed embody, the ideological justification for the new Democratic Republican party.

While Jefferson and Madison were directing party-building operations from on high, Burr was engaged in hand-to-hand combat in New York's vicious political warfare – which is to say he was behaving very much like the pragmatic, nonideological politician he was. Jefferson may have initially considered Burr in New York as he considered James Monroe in Virginia and Albert Gallatin in Pennsylvania, that is, as a subaltern in the struggle to return purity to national politics. Colonel Burr, however, did not see himself as a lieutenant in Jefferson's political army. Not surprisingly Jefferson and his supporters in Virginia began to doubt Burr's ideological commitment and to think of him as a "crooked gun" with a most un-republican-like ambition.

The open rift between Jefferson and Burr – the first step in a series of events that would bring both men into Marshall's Richmond circuit court – occurred when Burr refused to withdraw publicly from the contest for president in the House of Representatives. Jefferson also suspected that Burr was secretly campaigning for Federalist votes in order to become president. As senior in age and reputation, Jefferson had claim on the first office and understandably viewed Burr's perceived refusal to step aside as a breech of personal honor and also as conclusive proof of his inordinate ambition.

In fact, Burr did not court Federalist votes as Jefferson claimed; moreover, Burr did indicate privately that he was not angling for the presidency and advised his party to stand united and not to bargain with the Federalists. He did not, however, announce publicly that he was not a candidate for president. Whether justifiably or not, Burr remained in the race with a clear conscience, with his own sense of honor intact – and with an apparent passive disregard for the outcome. What Burr did take away from the ordeal was an enhanced distrust of Virginia politicians, who heartily returned the favor. Burr also had no doubt he would make a better president than Jefferson; unfortunately he never ceased thinking so.[5]

Burr served as Jefferson's vice president from 1801 to 1805 and by all accounts did so with distinction. Still, while Jefferson never declared open war on his vice president, it was immediately clear when the spoils of victory were being distributed that Burr had no future in Jefferson's party. When Burr killed Hamilton in the duel at Weehawken in the summer of 1804, he became persona non grata among leading Federalists and, indeed, in polite society in general. To recoup his honor and his fortune – and to fulfill his self-perceived destiny as a leader of men – he went west, where in 1805–1806 he appeared to be involved in a filibustering expedition to liberate Mexico from Spanish rule (if one believed Burr) or a military operation to separate the western states from the Union (if one believed President Jefferson).

If Burr revealed a deep truth about himself in the electoral dispute in 1800 and in his western adventure, Jefferson's over-the-top response to Burr's activities was equally revealing. In his message to Congress on January 22, 1807, which appeared the following day in the *National Intelligencer*, Jefferson pronounced Burr guilty of treason for attempting to separate the western states from the Union. The idea of secession, it should be noted, was itself not all that strange to Americans, whose

---

5 See Isenberg, *Fallen Founder*, 196–220 regarding Burr's behavior in the disputed election. On the role that honor played in that election, consult Joanne B. Freeman, *Affairs of Honor: National Politics in the New Republic* (New Haven and London, 2001), ch. 5.

union of states was barely operative, its fragility having been from the beginning a matter of constant concern. Jefferson's version of Burr's activities in the West found traction, in fact, because Burr's conspiracy was depicted by the partisan press as the culmination of western separatism dating from the 1780s.

For Jefferson to warn the American people of Burr's activities was a prudent thing to do for a president charged with protecting the security of the nation. For him to declare Burr guilty of treason without the benefit of a grand jury indictment or a jury trial was another matter altogether. And not only did Jefferson become judge and jury, he also entered the judicial arena in the two major court cases resulting from his initial pronouncement of Burr's guilt. The president's first involvement came early in January 1807 when he personally initiated treason proceedings against Burr's friends Erick Bollman and Samuel Swartwout in the federal circuit court for the District of Columbia in Washington. In Richmond, Jefferson assumed the role of chief prosecutor. The president's involvement in both cases brought him face to face with John Marshall. In Richmond the personal enmity of the two men quickly morphed into a major contest over the meaning of separation of powers in the Constitution.

The President as Judge and Jury: The Question Is Why?

It is easy to join John Adams in condemning Jefferson for declaring Burr guilty of treason without so much as a chance to defend himself in court; the challenge is to understand why the president did what he did. The question is how Jefferson weighed the evidence about Burr's activities in the West during the period leading up to his January 22, 1807 declaration of Burr's guilt. For one thing, Burr's activities were extraordinary in their scope and audacity. What Jefferson heard about them, moreover, pointed to the real possibility that Burr was engaged in a serious criminal conspiracy, that is to say, that he was planning either to wage war against Spain or to separate the western states from the Union – or both. Whether or not Burr had taken concrete action to implement his conspiracy – the central factual and doctrinal issue in the Richmond trial – the president had to take action. When and what action is the question.[6]

---

[6] Malone, *Jefferson the President: Second Term, 1805–1809* (Boston, 1974), 5: chs. 13–15 treats this issue with masterful insight. [Hereafter Malone, *Jefferson*]

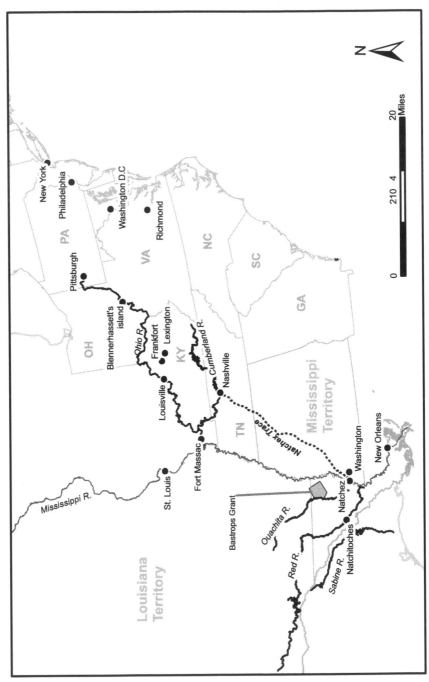

Burr's Western Travels, 1805–1807

Indeed, Jefferson had known of Burr's mysterious travels throughout the West and Southwest since the early summer of 1805. So did most of the nation. In July 1805 the *Philadelphia Gazette of the United States* published several anonymous "Queries" outlining possible explanations of Burr's activities, one of which was an attack on Mexico, another the severance of the Union. These essays were quickly reported in William Duane's Philadelphia *Aurora* and Thomas Ritchie's Richmond *Enquirer*, both administration papers that Jefferson read.[7] By late 1805 and increasingly throughout the following year other newspapers across the nation, ever anxious to increase their circulation, were busy tracking the exploits of the former vice president turned conspirator.

Probably the most influential of the many accounts of Burr's activities appeared in a series of articles in the Frankfort, Kentucky *Western World* during the summer of 1806. Sensationalist to the extreme, these articles, signed "Spanish Pensioner," identified Burr and James Wilkinson, commanding general of the United States Army and governor of the Louisiana Territory, as co-conspirators in a vast plot to drive Spain from the Southwest, conquer Mexico, and lead the western states out of the Union. Given the pervasive anti-Spanish sentiment of the western states and the long history of separatist rumors in the area, the *Western World*'s account found instant traction and spread quickly to newspapers in the rest of the country.

What the rest of the country did not know was that the conspiracy stories in the *Western World* were trumpeted by Kentucky Federalists, who for local political reasons exaggerated the threat of conspiracy in order to make Jefferson's administration look weak for not stopping it.[8] Among those leading the charge in Kentucky were Joseph Hamilton Daveiss (John Marshall's brother-in-law) and Humphrey Marshall (Marshall's brother-in-law and cousin). There is no evidence that the conspiracy stories were written by the two men, but both were politically and financially connected to the *Western World,* had ready access

---

[7] Malone relying on Walter F. McCaleb, *The Aaron Burr Conspiracy*, discusses the "Queries" essay in *Jefferson*, 5: 231–2.

[8] Wilkinson's most recent biographer claims that Jonathan Dayton, former senator from New Jersey and one of Burr's fellow conspirators, supported the paper financially and planted the "Spanish Pensioner" essays in it in the summer of 1806 in order to guarantee Wilkinson's cooperation in the conspiracy by driving a wedge between Wilkinson and Jefferson. See Andro Linklater, *An Artist in Treason: The Extraordinary Double Life of General James Wilkinson* (New York, 2009), 234.

to its editorial pages, and were instrumental in propagating the stories about Burr's conspiratorial activities.[9]

Daveiss, the United States Attorney for Kentucky, also bombarded Jefferson with letters warning him of the dangers posed by the conspiracy. Frustrated by Jefferson's initial inaction, Daveiss on his own twice instigated grand jury proceedings against Burr in the federal district court of Kentucky based on evidence he himself had gathered.[10] His bungled and failed efforts to get an indictment worked to Burr's advantage, and also made the president's subsequent effort to prosecute him look sinister. Jefferson fired Daveiss who retaliated by publishing a pamphlet attacking the president for failing to nip the conspiracy in the bud.[11]

Though Jefferson was aware of the clamorous newspaper chatter about Burr's activities in the West, he did not initially consider them as warranting a response from the government. In fact, on two occasions in late 1805 and early 1806, while the rumors of conspiracy were gathering steam, Jefferson met privately with Burr at the White House.[12] Both men appeared to be play-acting. Jefferson was coldly formal and noncommittal; Burr was arrogantly brash, suggesting at one meeting that a diplomatic appointment to the Court of St. James might be nice – and intimating that if he did not get it, he could do the administration some harm.[13] While Burr's behavior made Jefferson dislike and distrust him more than he already did, there was no indication that he suspected Burr of plotting disunion. Had he thought so, Jefferson could have stopped the conspiracy on the spot simply by putting Burr on warning.

The evidence that began to accumulate during 1806 may have caused Jefferson to wish he had done so. On January 10, 1806, for example,

---

[9] In the *Western World*, Nov. 1, 1806, John Marshall's younger brother Alexander Keith Marshall denied that he and the Marshall family of Kentucky had supported the establishment of the paper in order to defend his father from charges that the senior Marshall had supported the early separatist movement in Kentucky. There is no doubt that the Marshall family had ready access to the newspaper. Humphrey Marshall along with Henry Clay also defended the editors of the paper in a libel case against the governor of Kentucky.

[10] Milton Lomask, *Aaron Burr: The Conspiracy and Years of Exile, 1805–1836*, 126–7, 138–9, 142–9, treats Daveiss's efforts to indict Burr.

[11] Daveiss, *A View of the President's Conduct, Concerning the Conspiracy of 1806* (Frankfort, KY, 1807).

[12] Malone, *Jefferson* 5: 234–37.

[13] Ibid., 236.

Daveiss warned the president in dire terms that a plot to attack Mexico and separate the western states from the Union was being hatched by Burr and Wilkinson. Another piece of information had Burr plotting simultaneously with British envoy Anthony Merry and with Marques de Casa Yrujo, Spain's minister to the United States. Great Britain and Spain were at war and both countries, for different reasons, would have been pleased to know that the western states were ripe for secession. Burr, it would appear, told each side what it wanted to hear – without explicitly implicating himself in any treasonous plot – apparently in order to extort money for his filibustering operation.[14]

The president also received letters from various sources claiming to have heard Burr talk treason. One such report, received by Jefferson on September 15, 1806, came from Colonel George Morgan, an old Revolutionary veteran. By Morgan's account, during a visit to Morgan's home, Burr had belittled the administration and opined (as he had done to Merry and Yrujo) that the growing dissatisfaction of the western states might lead them to leave the Union. Morgan's testimony to that effect at Richmond would be effectively undercut, but the fact remained, as Burr himself conceded at the trial, that over dinner and wine he might have talked some wild talk.[15] If Jefferson read Morgan's letter to mean that Burr held him and his administration in contempt, he was quite right.

General William Eaton, fresh from duty as U.S. Consul in Libya, was more specific about Burr's treasonable intentions. While his testimony, like Morgan's, would be discredited during the trial in Richmond, Eaton's statement of October 20, 1806 that came to Jefferson via Postmaster General Gideon Granger carried real weight. One thing Eaton reported, and was able to support with corroborating evidence, was that Burr, while traveling through Marietta, Ohio, had placed an order for several boats to be built, boats which presumably would be used to transport his troops down river to New Orleans. More damning, although harder to verify, was Eaton's claim that Burr had tried to recruit him as second in command under Wilkinson for a military expedition designed to effect a separation of the western states.[16]

---

[14] Henry Adams, traveling to England and the Continent in 1879–1880, was the first historian to make extensive use of material in the Spanish and British archives. Reading dispatches from Spanish and British ministers to their home offices convinced Adams that Burr was guilty of treason.

[15] For Jefferson's correspondence with Morgan, see Malone, *Jefferson*, 5: 239–40.

[16] Ibid., 240–41.

The cumulative force of this information, especially the communication from Granger and Eaton, alerted Jefferson. News of Spanish aggression against American territory east of the Sabine River and the rumor that Spanish troops under Colonel Herrera might even attack New Orleans were further reasons for concern, since Spanish aggression might precipitate a war with Spain, which in turn would give Burr a legal justification for attacking Mexico.

After emergency consultations with his Cabinet (on October 22, 24, and 25, 1806), Jefferson alerted federal officials in New Orleans and the western states and territories to be on guard against possible illegal activities by Burr and his followers. At the same time he dispatched John Graham, secretary of the Orleans Territory, to the West with orders to gather information on Burr's activities. At one point, Jefferson even ordered gunboats to be ready to repel Burr's "army" should it attack New Orleans by water. These orders were no sooner given, however, than they were countermanded when fresh information from the West dispelled the fear of immediate danger.[17]

These prudent steps taken, little was done until November 25 when Jefferson received a top-secret communication from General Wilkinson, the first of several that would lead to the president's dramatic report to Congress on January 22, 1807, declaring Burr guilty of treason. Wilkinson's communication – a letter dated October 21 and a paper dated October 20, plus an oral message delivered by a special courier – warned Jefferson that an army of eight to ten thousand men, backed by British naval support, planned to attack New Orleans as the first step in wresting Mexico from Spanish rule. Wilkinson did not name Burr, but it was clear that he was the villain in the story. Attacking the city of New Orleans in the Orleans Territory was treason against the United States; attacking Spain, with whom the United States was at peace, was a high misdemeanor. Wilkinson also claimed he had been promised second in command to Burr himself, with the authority to choose his subordinate officers.[18]

Wilkinson's urgent communication prompted Jefferson's first public response to the conspiracy. On November 27, 1806, he proclaimed to the nation that "sundry persons" were "conspiring and confederating

---

[17] Lomask, *Burr*, 2: 178–9; Nathan Schachner, *Aaron Burr: A Biography* (New York, 1937; Perpetua Edition, 1961), 352–4.
[18] Malone, *Jefferson*, 5: 247–51. Also see Lomask, *Burr*, 2: 179–82.

together" in plotting a military expedition against "the dominions of Spain" and, in addition, were "deceiving and seducing honest and well-meaning citizens, under various pretences," to join them "in their criminal enterprises."[19] The president did not mention Burr by name, however, nor allude to any treasonous plan to foment secession. But he did not have to specify either of those things, since the country had been awash with rumors of Burr's traitorous conspiracy for months.

Jefferson's first proclamation contained no reference to any governmental action to contain the threat. This deficiency was rectified five days later in the president's Annual Message to Congress on December 2. Jefferson repeated his earlier warning about the conspiracy, but this time he indicated that the government had initiated measures to suppress the enterprise and bring "its authors and abettors" to justice.[20] No mention of any specific plan to sever the Union was made at this time and Burr was still not mentioned by name.

Why Jefferson's public statements on November 27 and December 2 regarding the conspiracy were so restrained is not entirely clear. One possible explanation was that he was waiting until Burr had taken overt (and indictable) action. Another explanation is that the president and his cabinet did not entirely trust Wilkinson, who had long been suspected of being in the pay of Spain. Newspapers like the *Western World* in fact claimed that Wilkinson was Burr's partner in treason; so did Eaton in his previously mentioned letter of October 22, 1806.

Wilkinson's loyalty was debated at length in the Cabinet meeting October 22, 1806. What Jefferson and his advisors understood was that Wilkinson, as commanding general with troops facing Spanish forces in the disputed territory east of the Sabine River (the border between Spanish Texas and the United States), was in a position to settle the matter of war or peace with Spain. By attacking, or provoking an attack from Spanish troops in the area, Wilkinson could start a war that would legitimize Burr's plans to attack Spain in Mexico, which in turn might encourage disunion in the Orleans Territory and possibly in the western states as well.[21]

---

[19] James D. Richardson, *A Compilation of the Messages and Papers of the Presidents* (Washington, DC, 1900), 1: 404.

[20] Ibid, 406.

[21] Regarding Wilkinson's pivotal role in the Southwest see Linklater, *Artist in Treason*, chs. 22 and 23.

Strange as it may seem, Jefferson and Burr were in competition for Wilkinson's loyalty: Burr needed the general because war with Spain, which Wilkinson could bring about, would legitimize an attack on Spanish Mexico. Wilkinson also possessed an incomparable knowledge of the terrain and the loyalty of American troops under his command – both factors essential to any operation against Mexico or against the government in Washington. With Wilkinson in Jefferson's camp, Burr's plans could not succeed. In addition, Wilkinson might be useful in settling the border dispute peacefully, as a first diplomatic step in establishing American dominance in the Southwest.

Two related developments brought Wilkinson into the president's camp. The first and most dramatic concerned the infamous cipher letter, dated July 29, 1806, that was delivered to Wilkinson on October 8 by Burr's friend and confidant, Samuel Swartwout. Thanks to the literary detective work of Mary-Jo Kline and her associates, historians now know that almost certainly the letter was not Burr's (as Wilkinson would claim) but Burr's fellow conspirator Jonathan Dayton.[22]

Dayton had been senator from New Jersey when Burr was vice president; both left office in March 1805 and both turned their eyes to the West. As a revolutionary war hero and a signer of the Constitution, Dayton was an ideal front man for Burr. Not only was Dayton the contact man with Wilkinson, but he was also Burr's partner in the latter's plan to extort money from Spain to finance his operation. Along with Senator Robert Smith of Ohio and several other prominent western politicians, Dayton joined Burr on the assumption that Burr's objective was to fight Spain.

Dayton's cipher letter, delivered to Wilkinson by Swartwout, was full of high-flown rhetoric about gold and glory in Mexico, and like several others of Dayton's letters to the general, was meant to keep Wilkinson in the conspiracy; it had the opposite effect. What the letter told the general was that Burr's "army" was on the move: according to the letter, what was once a plan now appeared to be a reality and that reality, thanks to Burr's wild talk and sensationalist newspaper coverage, looked every bit like treason against the United States. Wilkinson had a choice to make

---

[22] Mary-Jo Kline, ed. *Political Correspondence and Public Papers of Aaron Burr* (2 vols., Princeton, 1983), 2: 973–86. [Hereafter Kline, *Political Correspondence of Burr*]; Kline's analysis of Wilkinson's alterations of Dayton's letter is the definitive scholarship on the cipher letter; see especially pages 984–6 for her argument that Dayton not Burr was the author of the cipher letter.

and little time to make it. Either he was with Burr and his men or he was against them and for the president.

Knowing what he knew, it was an easy choice. Wilkinson knew that he himself had been associated with western separatism in the past; he knew that he had been identified publicly, in the *Western World* and in other newspapers, as Burr's partner in a treasonous plan to revolutionize the western states. The general also knew by late summer that a war with Spain was unlikely, which doomed any plan to attack Mexico or revolutionize the West. Then, on September 30, 1806, for reasons that remain unclear, Spanish troops retreated from contested territory east of the Sabine River and set up camp on its western bank. On October 23, fifteen days after receiving the cipher letter, Wilkinson and his troops marched into the area abandoned by the Spanish. And on November 5, 1806, the general concluded the Neutral Ground Agreement, which turned out to be the first step in the implementation of Jefferson's plan of peaceful expansion.[23]

In negotiating the Neutral Ground Agreement, Wilkinson had demonstrated his usefulness and loyalty to the administration; what he had to do now was to disassociate himself completely and convincingly from the conspiracy. His solution to the problem was to forward a decoded copy of the cipher letter he received from Dayton to the president – altered to implicate Burr in treason and to remove all traces of his own involvement in the conspiracy. Wilkinson's special military courier delivered the doctored letter to Jefferson on January 18, 1807.

Coming on top of Wilkinson's other warning letters, and those of Daveiss, Eaton, and others, the receipt of the cipher letter prompted Jefferson to take decisive action: thus the previously mentioned report to Congress of January 22, 1807. The president's report, issued in response to a House resolution introduced by John Randolph, was a radical departure from his public statements of November 27 and December 2. Not only did he name Burr for the first time, but he also declared, "his guilt is placed beyond question." Jefferson also praised Wilkinson as a soldier and a patriot, referring specifically to Wilkinson's letter of October 21, which he received on November 25.

According to the president, Burr "contemplated two distinct objects, which might be carried on either jointly or separately, and either one or the other first, as circumstances should direct." One was "the severance of the Union." The second was "an attack on Mexico." Burr

[23] Malone, *Jefferson*, 5: 246.

was no longer just the man who wanted to steal the presidency from Jefferson in 1800, or the man who killed Hamilton at Weehawken in 1804. Now he was an arch traitor to the country that succored him.[24]

The president's report was national news and his supporters across the nation praised him for preventing "the Cataline of the West" from destroying the Union. But why after a prudent and successful policy of keeping Burr under close surveillance, and why after acknowledging that the conspiracy had been completely crushed,[25] did the president take the law in his own hands by pronouncing Burr's guilt to the entire country? Well before January 22, Jefferson also knew there would be no war with Spain – which fact alone doomed Burr's plans.

Indeed, on December 10, Burr's "army," consisting of twenty-five or thirty young men, had already been dispersed by the Wood County militia, operating under the orders of Ohio governor Edward Tiffin. In late December 1806 at the mouth of the Cumberland River, Burr would join with those who fled from the militia and with others who would join the flotilla later, bringing the total strength to no more than one hundred untrained and lightly armed men. If Burr was contemplating treason against the government, he had apparently not bothered to tell his men, who were under the impression that they would fight Spain if there was a war, or if not, that they would settle land along the Washita River that Burr had promised them. Whether Burr ever acquired full title to the so-called Bastrop lands is not clear, but there is no doubt that settling the new West could be used, and in fact was used, during the Richmond trial to explain the "conspiracy."

The situation was puzzling. As John Quincy Adams observed shortly after Jefferson's pronouncement of Burr's guilt, "The projects and transactions of Mr. Burr, are giving rise to an extraordinary course of our public affairs. On the one hand we are assured that his conspiracy is altogether impotent; without means; and without resources – while on the other we adopt the most violent and extraordinary measures to counteract them."[26]

So the question remains: If Burr was never a threat to the Union why did Jefferson pronounce him guilty of treason and lay waste to the

[24] *Messages and Papers*, 1: 412–17.
[25] Jefferson to Wilkinson, Jan. 3, 1807, Ford, *Works of Jefferson* (12 vols., New York and London, 1905), 10: 332–5, especially 333. Also see Malone, *Jefferson*, 5: 260.
[26] John Quincy Adams to Abigail Adams, February 3, 1807, Adams Papers, MHS.

fundamental principles of due process to do so? As with most matters of human motivation, there is no fully satisfactory answer. Jefferson's justification for his decision was contained in the packet of materials documenting Burr's activities over the previous months – those that had prompted his earlier warnings to the nation on November 27 and December 2, 1806. What was new, and presumably the determinative factor prompting the January 22, 1807, charge of treason, was the decoded copy of the cipher letter that Jefferson received from Wilkinson on January 18. Wilkinson obviously sent the letter to give credence to his alarming but unsubstantiated charges against Burr made in the documents of October 20 and 21.

The cipher letter was even more alarming, because it declared as a fact that boats designed to carry Burr's army were being built; that Burr's initial force of five hundred or one thousand men – a "host of choice spirits" to be joined later by "a corps of worthys" led by Burr's son-in-law Joseph Alston – was scheduled to move downriver on November 15, 1806, and take control of New Orleans as the first stage of the campaign against the Spanish forces in Mexico. Burr's army would be protected by the British fleet and by American naval ships under command of Commodore Thomas Truxton. Wilkinson was to be second in command under Burr, with the authority to name his own officers.[27]

Wilkinson's altered and decoded copy of Dayton's cipher letter occupies a complicated and ironic place in the events leading to the treason trial in Richmond and also in the trial itself. Rather than proving Burr's guilt, the letter actually discredited Wilkinson's testimony against Burr, both in the legal proceedings against Burr's friends in the Bollman and Swartwout case in the early months of 1807, and in the grand jury proceedings in Richmond, where Wilkinson himself barely escaped being indicted. It should be noted here too that the letter was not used in the principal treason trial by either the prosecution or the defense – the defense because exposing Burr's friend Dayton as the author of the letter might well implicate Burr; the prosecution because a true account of the letter would embarrass the president for trusting Wilkinson in the first place.

Indeed, the president would have saved himself much grief and embarrassment had he scrutinized Wilkinson's copy of the cipher letter carefully before acting on it. There were obvious reasons for doing so,

[27] For a copy of the cipher letter see Kline, *Political Correspondence of Burr*, 2: 986–7.

starting with the fact that Wilkinson's credibility was already in doubt: witness the cabinet debate of October 22. In addition, the president had information that Wilkinson and Burr were co-conspirators; federal attorney Daveiss and William Eaton alerted Jefferson of this fact. So also did the articles in the *Western World*, which were not just politically motivated fabrications but were also distillations of pervasive rumors already circulating throughout the West. Given the public buzz in the summer and autumn of 1806, the president should have known that Wilkinson, if not actually connected to Burr's operation, was at best an untrustworthy source as to what that operation was.

On its face, moreover, Wilkinson's copy of the cipher letter should have raised a red flag. For one thing – and the point immediately came up in the Bollman and Swartwout trial – the cipher letter, like all of Wilkinson's other letters regarding Burr, had not been attested to under oath. Then there was the letter's un-Burr-like grandiloquence; and more important still was the letter's questionable timing. Wilkinson's copy of the cipher letter that Jefferson received on January 18, 1807 was dated July 29, 1806. If the information in the letter was indeed "urgent" for the security of the nation, why did Wilkinson not send it sooner?

There were other problems and questions. Why, for example, did Wilkinson not include the original cipher letter along with his copied translation? And if Burr wrote the letter, as Wilkinson claimed, why did the letter refer to Burr in the third person? The answer as noted above was that the author of the letter was not Burr but Jonathan Dayton.[28] Indeed, why would either man be communicating to Wilkinson at all about the conspiracy, and why in a code that only Wilkinson could decipher? And why, if Burr planned to wage war, would he bring his daughter and grandson along on such a dangerous enterprise, as the letter claimed?

Granted, the president had other matters to deal with besides Aaron Burr and the cipher letter. But given the fact that Wilkinson was already under "very general suspicion of infidelity,"[29] and given the fact that any threat to the Union had been eliminated by the president's policies (the crux of his report to Congress on January 22), it is hard to understand

---

[28] For the full account of the cipher letter, its reconstruction from contemporary sources by Mary-Jo Kline and her assistants, and the role it played in the hectic summer of 1806, see "Editorial Note," ibid., 973–86.

[29] Malone, *Jefferson*, 5: 244.

why he did not ask some or all of the above questions about the cipher letter. Had he done so, according to Jefferson's leading biographer, the president might well have modified his categorical statement that Burr was a traitor.[30] Indeed, had the president studied the letter closely, it is doubtful he would have trusted any of Wilkinson's statements regarding the conspiracy.

However, if Jefferson had reasons to doubt Wilkinson's credibility regarding Burr, he also had some compelling ones for not doubting him – which is different from really believing him. Scoundrels have their uses, and Wilkinson was the president's scoundrel. As commanding general he had the loyalty of the army; as governor of the Louisiana Territory (an office Jefferson bestowed on him in 1805) he had his finger on local sentiment. He also understood the tangled politics of the Southwest, knew the terrain, and, to put it generously, had long-standing connections with Spanish officials in the region that might prove essential to the administration's diplomacy.

Whatever Wilkinson had conspired to do with Burr in the past, he was now in Jefferson's camp – and this was the one thing that Wilkinson's communication about the cipher letter made indisputably clear. And having Wilkinson on Jefferson's side meant that he was not on Burr's side. Moreover, it must have occurred to the president that Wilkinson could be instrumental in putting Aaron Burr in his place once and for all. Precisely because of his connection to the "conspiracy," the general was in a position to testify against Burr, as long as his own prior involvement could be concealed.

So if Jefferson wanted to expose Burr as an enemy of the republic; if he wanted to educate Americans about what a republican statesman should *not* look like; if he wanted to get even for Burr's role in the disputed election; if he wanted to eliminate Burr, the New Yorker, in order to keep the Virginia dynasty cranking along with Madison in 1808; if he wanted to prevent Burr from disrupting the southwest frontier by bringing about war with Spain, in short, for conducting his own private foreign policy as if he were president – Wilkinson was indispensable.

For his part, the general was quick to see the advantage – or the necessity, to be more accurate – of teaming up with the president. Exposing Burr would go far in discrediting the growing perception that he and Burr were co-partners in a criminal conspiracy. At the same time, Wilkinson could make points with the president for future use, which he did in fact

[30] Ibid., 263–6.

do. He could also collect a payoff from Spain by claiming that he had stopped Burr's invasion of Mexico before it could be launched, which he also brazenly attempted to do. In short, the flamboyant general could escape jail or possibly the firing squad, become a conquering hero without firing a shot, and pocket some Spanish gold for good measure.

Jefferson also garnered some political benefits from his association with Wilkinson, at least in the short run. With his general's "victory" over Spain on the Sabine, the president could turn his full attention to Burr's conspiracy. It was after all Jefferson's duty as president to protect the nation and the imperative, then and always, was to err on the side of safety when security was perceived to be the issue. Even though the nation was not in danger, the president's proclamation of Burr's guilt was perceived by many at the time as a victory for national unity, when that quality was in short supply.

And so, irony of ironies, the president who set out to rescue the lost virtue of the republic was now joined at the hip to one of the most consummate intriguers of the age. Jefferson's reputation now hinged on Wilkinson's credibility. Unless the president admitted publicly that his accusation of Burr was a mistake, he had no choice but to defend Wilkinson before, during and after the trial. The general did not make that an easy chore but Jefferson never flinched.

Moreover, given that Jefferson's reputation was on the line, it was all but inevitable that he would assume control of Burr's prosecution. In fact, the public proclamation of Burr's guilt in the report of January 22, 1807, was the president's opening statement to a jury composed of the American public. The ramifications were immense. Reported and often reprinted in the partisan network of newspapers across the country, reports of the president's proclamation gave instant credibility to the sensationalist attacks against Burr already widely circulating. As Burr would discover during jury selection in Richmond, most of his fellow citizens had joined the president in branding him a traitor to his country.

General Wilkinson Takes Charge

If the president's public pronouncements unleashed a tidal wave of anti-Burr sentiment, they also unleashed his general. The man who had been Burr's partner now became his chief accuser and the government's chief witness. With Jefferson's proclamations to back him, Wilkinson spread the word of Burr's guilt and his own innocence through official and unofficial channels, thus further damning Burr in the court of public opinion.

Wilkinson also warned the president and the nation about the imminent danger Burr and his "army" posed to the city of New Orleans. While still at Natchitoches, the general dispatched urgent messages to city authorities urging them to ready the city's defenses. And on November 25, 1806 (the same day Jefferson received Wilkinson's first warning), Wilkinson arrived in the city to take personal charge of military operations to repel the "invaders." All this was unknown to Burr, who was being feted by the citizens of Frankfort, Kentucky for having escaped the clutches of federal attorney Daveiss.

Ordinarily hesitant in battle, the general now transformed himself into a veritable dynamo of bellicosity. After frightening the populace into a state of panic and bullying civilian leaders into submission, on December 6 Wilkinson with the support of several hundred troops assumed military control of the city. He had already declared Burr a public enemy with a $5,000 reward on his head. Now armed with unlimited power, Wilkinson set out methodically to arrest or otherwise silence Burr's supporters, especially those who might implicate Wilkinson himself in the conspiracy. Local officials who continued to object were ignored, silenced by intimidation, or thrown in jail. When Orleans county judge James Workman issued writs of habeas corpus for the release of some of those illegally held, his order was ignored and he himself was forced from office by Wilkinson.[31]

Among those who felt the brunt of the general's oppression was his former friend Daniel Clark, one of the leading merchants of the city, who later wrote a long and scathing account of Wilkinson's duplicity and tyrannous abuse of power.[32] On January 14, 1807, Wilkinson also staged a dramatic arrest of Burr's friend General John Adair, who came to New Orleans bearing the news that Burr's "army" had evaporated.[33]

[31] Wilkinson's actions in New Orleans (and Jefferson's support of those actions) are discussed in Thomas P. Abernathy, *The Burr Conspiracy* (New York, 1954), ch. 11.

[32] Daniel Clark, *Proofs of the Corruption of Gen. James Wilkinson* (1809). For another contemporary account of Wilkinson in New Orleans, see James Workman, *A Letter to the Respectable Citizens, Inhabitants of the County of Orleans, together with several letters to his Excellency Governor Claiborne, and other Documents relative to the Extraordinary Measures lately pursued in this Territory* (New Orleans, 1807).

[33] John Kendall, *History of New Orleans* (Chicago and New York, 1922), 82; for further details see Lomask, *Burr*, 2: 182–5.

The primitive nature of communication between Washington and New Orleans at the time makes it difficult to know when Jefferson received information about his general's lawless career in New Orleans. Wilkinson began his campaign against Burr immediately on his arrival, several days before formal orders were sent from Secretary of War Dearborn authorizing him to take action, and several weeks before he actually received those orders. It is clear, however, that the president condoned Wilkinson's behavior once he found out. When critics protested the general's reign of terror, Jefferson attributed their objections to partisan motives. Rather than advising Wilkinson to obey the law, Jefferson cautioned him not to offend local political sentiment.[34]

Wilkinson's dramatically staged battle of New Orleans temporarily aided the prosecution, since it appeared to substantiate Burr's guilt in the mind of the public. But the general's greatest service to the president and the prosecution, which now appeared to be one and the same, was his arrest and incarceration of Dr. Erick Bollman and Samuel Swartwout, two of Burr's confederates. Thirty-eight-year-old Bollman, who immigrated from Hannover in 1797, was something of an American hero for his daring attempt to rescue Lafayette from an Austrian prison. In 1805 Jefferson rewarded him by appointing him Indian agent at Natchitoches, where he met Burr and agreed to help him recruit men for what he assumed would be the coming war against Spain. Twenty-one-year-old New Yorker Samuel Swartwout, who turned out to be one of Burr's steadfast friends in his time of need, joined the enterprise in 1804.

Both men figured in the legal proceedings against Burr in Richmond and both testified that he had *not* intended a treasonable separation of the western states. What made them central to the story was the fact they were chosen to deliver the duplicate copies of the cipher letter to Wilkinson in July 1806 – Swartwout by land and Bollman by water. Obviously both men knew of Wilkinson's association with Burr, which is why the general had to silence them. When Swartwout delivered the cipher letter to Wilkinson, the general, pretending to be a friend, pumped him for information. When the young man got the drift of what was happening he headed for the woods, but not soon enough. By Wilkinson's order, he was soon captured, charged with treason, and brought to New Orleans under armed guard.

---

[34] Jefferson to Wilkinson, Feb. 3, 1807, Ford, *Works of Jefferson*, 10: footnote 1, 335–6. Also see Jefferson to Wilkinson, June 21, 1807, ibid., 336–7.

Bollman was arrested in New Orleans and held under explicit orders from Wilkinson, this in open defiance of two habeas corpus writs, one issued by the Supreme Court of the Orleans Territory and another by the federal district court.[35] Both men were held incommunicado without access to legal counsel until they were hustled off under armed guard to Baltimore on their way to Washington for trial. When Swartwout tried to escape – and he escaped death only because his guard's weapon misfired – he was put in chains at night during the remainder of the journey. As if that were not humiliation enough, the commanding General of the Army stole his gold watch.

Upon their arrival in the capital on January 22, both men were imprisoned in the Marine barracks, where they waited for President Jefferson to decide their fate. The first stage of the Burr trial – the trial of Bollman and Swartwout for treason, the "trial before the trial" – was about to begin. The president and the chief justice were also about to meet again.

The President as Prosecutor-in-Chief

Jefferson's reasons for rushing to judgment on Burr, as we have just noted, were a complex mixture of impetuosity, vindictiveness, and self-righteousness, all of which were exacerbated by Burr's arrogance and self-importance. The president's decision to take personal charge of the prosecution in Richmond was more straightforward, stemming mainly from the fact that he had already pronounced Burr guilty and now had to make the case. What makes the president's involvement in the trial so important, aside from the fact that it is unique in the history of the presidency, is that it brought him face to face with John Marshall.

Jefferson's decision to spearhead the prosecution also contributed to Burr's acquittal. At any rate, Burr and his lawyers turned the president's decision to intervene into a major feature of their litigation strategy. The point they drove home whenever they got the chance was that the president of the United States was waging a personal vendetta against an innocent man, and worse still, that he was resorting to the most hated aspect of English treason law to do so.

Luther Martin would famously denounce Jefferson for his interference, as we shall see, and so would the formidable John Wickham. But none

---

[35] Charles Warren, *The Supreme Court in United States History* (2 vols., New and rev. ed., Boston, 1926), 1: 30.

of Burr's counsel skewered the president more tellingly than Benjamin Botts, the youngest member of Burr's defense team. On Wednesday, August 26, well into the final phase of the trial, Botts rose to refute the prosecution's contention that the English doctrine of constructive treason, which the government was using against Burr, posed no danger to the nation. Constructive treason was treason law fashioned over the centuries by compliant judges in the service of English monarchs to eliminate rivals and suppress political opposition. Botts drove home the irony that Jefferson of all people should resurrect that un-republican doctrine in America. Speaking to the jury, the court and the packed courtroom, Botts posed a hypothetical: America does not have a king, but, he asked, what would happen, regarding the doctrine of constructive treason, should we "have a vicious president"? Without directly calling Jefferson "vicious," Botts went on to insist, "the president's interference with the prosecution is improper, illegal and unconstitutional." And further: "If the president enters the lists with the attorney for the United States, if he direct a prosecution to be conducted, he becomes anxious and decisively zealous for the conviction ..." Conclusion? "The same vices and malignant passions which actuate a tyrannical king might actuate a tyrannical president."[36]

Before taking his seat, Botts professed having "no doubt that the president acted from good motives, without sufficiently reflecting on the subject" and that he was sure that if Jefferson were present "he would determine that he had done wrong." It is understandable why, after insulting a popular sitting president, Botts would end on this somewhat conciliatory note. It is also doubtful that he really believed what he said regarding Jefferson's good intentions or his likely recantation. Certainly none of Burr's other lawyers, or Burr himself, expected Jefferson to back off, and like Botts, they deeply resented his active intervention.

Had they known the full extent of the president's involvement, Burr's lawyers would have been even more outraged. Jefferson's point man in Richmond and chief prosecutor in the Burr trial was George Hay, whom he had appointed U.S. Attorney for the District of Virginia in 1803. Forty-two years old at the time of the trial, Hay had practiced law for twenty years, his most notable effort having been his role as

---

[36] David Robertson, *Reports of the Trials of Colonel Aaron Burr*, (2 vols., Phil., 1808), 2: 169–70 [Hereafter Robertson, *Reports*].

defense counsel in the trial of James Callender in 1800, who had been charged with libel under the Sedition Act of 1798. Even more pleasing to Jefferson than Hay's effort in the Callender trial was his 1799 pamphlet repudiating the Federalist Sedition Act in favor of the unlimited freedom of the press as guaranteed by the First Amendment.[37]

Jefferson had a dependable ally in Hay, which helps explain the frank correspondence between the two men during the trial. Not only did Hay keep the president informed, but Jefferson corresponded regularly with him throughout the proceedings – and not just to prop up his chief prosecutor's sagging spirits. Jefferson's letters were in fact instructions about litigation strategy: about the nature of the charges that should be brought, about evidence, about whom to call for witnesses and how to interrogate them. At one point Jefferson administered a firm reprimand to Hay for referring to *Marbury v. Madison*, instructing him "to stop citing that case as authority, and to have it denied to be law."[38]

Jefferson also sent Hay a bundle of blank presidential pardons to be used to elicit damaging testimony from potential witnesses against Burr. One such witness was Dr. Erick Bollman, whose refusal to plead guilty to a crime he never committed (in return for one of those pardons) publicly exposed the president's personal intervention in the trial. Most historians, even those who admire Jefferson most, have been hard-pressed to justify his action – or to account for it.[39]

So why did the president take personal charge of the prosecution and why did he pursue Burr so relentlessly? Walter McCaleb gave a simple explanation in his pioneering work on the Burr conspiracy when he insisted that Jefferson set out to get Burr for his unwillingness to withdraw from the disputed presidential race in 1800. Jefferson never specifically admitted to these vindictive feelings, but such a perceived breach of loyalty between gentlemen counted heavily in a society still governed by

---

[37] Hortensius [Hay], *An Essay on the Liberty of the Press* (Philadelphia, 1799, reprint, 1803).

[38] Jefferson to Hay, June 2, 1807, Bergh, *Writings of Jefferson*, 11: 213. In his letter, the president explained to Hay why *Marbury v. Madison* was not good law.

[39] For Jefferson's instructions regarding the interrogation of Bollman and his reference to the bundle of blank pardons "to be filled up at your discretion," see Jefferson to Hay, May 20, 1807, ibid., 11: 205–6; for a sampling of other of the president's instructions to Hay, see Jefferson to Hay, May 26, 28; June 2, 12, 17, 19, 20, 23; Aug. 20; Sept. 4, 7 (two letters of the latter date), 20, ibid., Vol. 11. Malone discusses Jefferson's intervention in "The President and Burr's Prosecution," *Jefferson* 5: ch. 17.

a code of honor. The president may have been opposed to dueling, but he was inclined to deal with Burr's behavior as a personal affront to be dealt with personally.

Concerning Jefferson's intervention in the Richmond trial, there was also the matter of his detail-oriented, take-charge nature to be considered – witness his plans for Washington City, or his blueprint for the University of Virginia, or his minute attention to the building and rebuilding of Monticello, or the overseeing of his orchards, or his daily recording of the weather. Jefferson had a penchant for detail and a copious mind to match. On top of that, or *because* of that, he found it difficult to delegate authority. On a more practical level, he may well have doubted George Hay's ability to get the job done in Richmond. The administration's failure to convict Justice Chase in the recent impeachment trial was widely attributed to prosecutorial ineptness, and Jefferson was determined not to repeat the same mistake in Richmond.

Jefferson's hands-on approach might also be seen as a compensation for the embryonic state of federal law enforcement institutions. The U.S. Attorney General, a non-cabinet level office created by the Judiciary Act of 1789, was a one-man operation with no regular contact with the federal attorneys such as Hay located in the states. Caesar Rodney, Jefferson's attorney general, had no impact at all on the Burr trial, although he made one cameo appearance. Jefferson also had a point when he complained that communication problems and the geographical scope of Burr's activities in the West made it difficult to gather timely information.[40] Some 140 potential witnesses from various parts of the country were finally identified, but the logistical problems and expense of deposing them or transporting them to Richmond in time for the trial were immense. That an administration elected on a platform promising fiscal austerity, and whose annual expenditures in 1807 were just over eight million dollars, would spend over $100,000 on the trial was a sure sign of its importance in Jefferson's mind.

All this is to say that Jefferson had reasons for keeping a watchful eye on the legal proceedings leading up to and including the Burr trial. These reasons do not, however, adequately account for his personal interference in the habeas corpus trial of Burr's confederates Bollman and Swartwout in Washington early in 1807, or for his micromanagement of Burr's prosecution in Richmond later in the year.

---

[40] See, for example, his complaints to William Branch Giles, April 20, 1807, Ford, *Works of Jefferson*, 10: 383–8.

Jefferson's involvement in the latter trial is particularly striking considering his party's general opposition to overbearing executive power, and also in light of his own pressing duties as president. While directing the trial from the White House, for example, Jefferson had to deal with a rebellion in his own party led by fellow Virginian and previous speaker of the House, John Randolph of Roanoke. The Randolph faction accused the president of having reneged on his campaign promise to curb executive power and reduce the scope of national authority – the very issues that surfaced in Burr's trial. As foreman of the grand jury in Richmond, Randolph could not have failed to see the connection. In any case, Randolph's opposition to Jefferson increased as a result of the trial. Another unresolved issue on the president's agenda was the ongoing contest with Chief Justice Marshall and his Court, an old rivalry that surfaced dramatically in *Marbury v. Madison* in 1803 and was amplified by the administration's unsuccessful impeachment of Marshall's colleague Justice Samuel Chase in 1805.

Adding to the president's domestic woes was the growing threat of war with England, a threat made real on June 22, 1807, in the midst of the trial in Richmond, when HMS *Leopard* attacked the American frigate *Chesapeake* off the coast of Norfolk, Virginia. According to Henry Adams, Americans were united for the first time since the Revolution and were waiting on the president to call them to arms.

Given the foreign and domestic problems, one might have expected Jefferson to leave Burr's prosecution to others. However, rather than detracting from these problems, personally leading the charge against Burr addressed them – at least indirectly. Smashing a perceived conspiracy to destroy the Union and moving manfully to collar the "traitor" would build popular support for the president, which would in turn work to rally the faithful and quell rebellion in party ranks. Abigail Adams even suspected that Jefferson cried wolf regarding Burr because he had been criticized for "countenancing" General Francisco Miranda's filibustering expedition against the Spanish in Venezuela – a project embarrassingly similar to Burr's plan to liberate Mexico.[41]

As for avenging the attack of the *Leopard*, Jefferson chose peaceful economic coercion instead of war. "Calling out the dogs of war" against Burr, to borrow a phrase from Luther Martin's attack on Jefferson

---

[41] Abigail Adams to John Q. Adams, Jan. 16, 1807, Adams Papers, MHS. For Jefferson's involvement see Malone, *Jefferson*, 5: 80–85.

during the trial, was a convenient substitute for *not* calling them out against England.

And what of Jefferson's feud with John Marshall? It is intriguing to speculate that the president pursued Burr in the hope of netting the chief justice along the way. There is no evidence, however, that he had this objective in mind at the outset; furthermore there are good reasons that the president might prefer not to challenge the chief justice on his own turf. By contrast, there is no doubt that once the trial was under way the president did just that. If Jefferson did not set out to get Marshall, neither did he want to be got – as he had been in *Marbury* and in the Bollman litigation preceding Burr's trial. Jefferson may well have intervened in the Richmond trial in order to avoid another bruising by Marshall.

The contest between Jefferson and Marshall reminds us again of the role which character – and character bashing – played in the trial. Fusing legal and political issues with reputation and character, a human tendency in every age, was a pervasive feature of early national political culture where the tradition of *noblesse oblige* and personal honor was still strong.[42] And with Jefferson, even more than for most statesmen of the age, ideological differences readily turned into personal grudges.

So it was not just that Burr refused to withdraw from the presidential contest in 1800, although that alone may well have damned him in Jefferson's eyes. Evidence that Burr was carrying on his own foreign policy as if he were president – by meeting privately with foreign diplomats, and by agitating for a war with Spain, for example – was also a likely reason for Jefferson's reaction. More fundamental still was Burr's failure to share Jefferson's exalted view of the new nation. Well before Burr's conspiracy exposed his "boundless ambition," Jefferson viewed his vice president as an untrustworthy political entrepreneur who was "always at market."[43] Burr had no "moral instinct," at least none that Jefferson recognized; thus before Burr was guilty of treason he was guilty of debasing republican values.[44]

But Burr *was* guilty of treason in Jefferson's mind, at least according to his public pronouncement to that effect. By publicly declaring

---

[42] Freeman, *Affairs of Honor*, makes this point persuasively.

[43] Lomask, *Burr*, 2: 107.

[44] Henry Adams suggested that Burr's lack of "moral sense" and "moral instinct" was one of the main reasons for the hostility of Jefferson and his party toward Burr. Adams, *History of the United States During the Administrations of Jefferson and Madison* (Library of America Edition, New York, 1986), 907.

Burr guilty, Jefferson also committed himself to proving that he had acted rightly. Certainly then, Jefferson's proclamation of Burr's guilt as much or more than anything else explains why he felt compelled to take personal charge of the prosecution, why he found himself beholden to James Wilkinson, Burr's partner in conspiracy turned states evidence, and why he ultimately found himself facing off with the Chief Justice in Richmond.

2

Jefferson and Marshall Square Off

"The worst of precedents may be established from the best of motives. We ought to be upon our guard lest our zeal for the public interest lead us to overstep the bounds of the law and the constitution; for although we may thereby bring one criminal to punishment, we may furnish the means by which an hundred innocent persons may suffer."

Judge William Cranch dissenting, *U.S. v. Bollman et al.*[1]

The legal proceedings against Bollman and Swartwout – Jefferson's personal effort to keep them in jail; the habeas corpus writs sued out on their behalf; their trial in the federal circuit court for the District of Columbia; and their appeal to the Supreme Court of the United States – have been overshadowed by the more dramatic trial in Richmond. What transpired in Washington in early 1807, however, was a dress rehearsal. Lawyers and judges clashed over the definition of treason. Matters of evidence that would ultimately surface in the Richmond trial were vetted. Defense and prosecution lawyers, some of whom would meet again in Richmond, took measure of one another. Finally, thanks to the legal transgressions of General Wilkinson in New Orleans and Jefferson's personal involvement in the Bollman and Swartwout litigation in Washington, the president and the chief justice squared off once again. What happened was a replay of their confrontation in *Marbury v. Madison;* it was also a forecast of what was about to transpire in Burr's treason trial in Richmond.

By the time Jefferson and Marshall clashed in *Bollman,* their intense dislike and distrust of one another was full-blown. It was also

---

[1] 24 Fed.Cas. No.14,622, C.C. Dist.Columbia (1807),1192.

counterintuitive. As descendents of the Randolph family, both were members of Virginia's ruling class. Both shared in the creation of the new nation – Marshall as a soldier in General Washington's Continental Line and Jefferson as a statesman and spokesman of independence. In the partisan 1790s, however, they parted over the meaning of the Revolution they had jointly supported. Jefferson chose to see the Revolution as the dawning of a new era of liberty and political democracy embodied in state and local government. As a moderate Federalist, Marshall emphasized the conservative nature of the Revolution. For him the war against England was a struggle for self-government, not the first stage in a social revolution – in his words "a war of principle, against a system hostile to political liberty."[2] He viewed the national government created by the Constitution as a necessary curb on Jefferson's radical theory of states rights democracy.

With Jefferson's election to the presidency in 1800 and Marshall's appointment as chief justice by departing President John Adams, their ideological and personal differences became a contest between two major branches of government over the Constitution: what it meant and whose interpretation controlled. Jefferson believed that the elected representatives of the sovereign people had the final word; Marshall believed that the law of the Constitution, as interpreted by the federal courts, trumped politics. This had been the issue in 1803 in *Marbury v. Madison* when the president tried to humble the chief justice and his Court and received a law-and-order lecture from Marshall for his efforts. That lecture still rankled when the two men grappled over the constitutional meaning of habeas corpus and treason in the case of Bollman and Swartwout in January 1807.

Jefferson Takes a Stand

The president's intervention in the case followed from his decision to cast his lot with Wilkinson and to defend his law-defying actions in New Orleans. Well before Wilkinson arrived in the city on November 25, the general had decided to distance himself from Burr's conspiracy, as evidenced by the doctored version of the cipher letter he sent to Jefferson. Wilkinson's objective in taking military control of New Orleans, in fact, was not to repel Burr's invading army (which he knew did not exist)

---

[2] Marshall to Edward Everett, August 2, 1826, Charles F. Hobson, ed., *The Papers of John Marshall* (Chapel Hill, NC, 2000), 10: 299.

but to silence those who might testify about his former connection with the man he had just denounced as a traitor. Wilkinson's dragnet caught Bollman and Swartwout, who were shipped off under military guard to Washington for trial.

The president immediately picked up where his general left off. On January 23, shortly after Bollman's confinement in the Marine Barracks in Washington, Jefferson agreed to meet privately with him. Bollman was under the impression that the president wanted objective information about Burr's operation, when in fact the president planned to use Bollman's account to implicate Burr in an attempt to sever the Union. To this end, Jefferson brought Secretary of State James Madison along to take notes.

When the interview was over, Jefferson asked Bollman to put his account in writing, assuring him "on his word of honour" that his remarks would "never be used against himself" – indeed, that his account "shall never go out of his [Jefferson's] hand."[3] The president, as we shall see during the trial in Richmond, did not keep his promise. In any case, what Bollman said in his private interview was not entirely what Jefferson hoped to hear. According to Bollman, Burr's only objective was to lead an attack on Mexico in case of a war with Spain and if that did not transpire, then to settle his men on the Bastrop lands. Bollman even advised Jefferson that such a war would be a great service to the nation.

Bollman's account made a liar out of Wilkinson. Along with the other information in Jefferson's possession linking Burr and Wilkinson, it should have raised serious doubts about having denounced Burr on the basis of the general's communications. In fact, it was not at this point too late for the president to reevaluate and possibly modify the charge of treason Wilkinson had leveled against Bollman and Swartwout and which he himself had leveled against Burr. What Bollman confided to Jefferson and Madison, and to which he would later testify in Richmond, was at worst a conspiracy to violate the Neutrality Act of 1794 by attacking Spain (although in fact Bollman insisted that Burr would engage Spain only if the United States were already at war). In any case there was time to gather more evidence and to resolve the contradictions in Wilkinson's account. The danger of war with Spain was over and with it any threat to the Union that might come from Burr and his small band of supporters, who were now blithely drifting down the Ohio River.

---

[3] Jefferson's promise to Bollman (citing Jefferson to Bollman, Jan. 25, 1807) and Bollman's later account of Jefferson's deception is discussed, in Matthew Davis, *Memoirs of Aaron Burr* (2 vols., Freeport, NY, 1836), 2: 388–91.

Instead of slowing down the juggernaut against Bollman and his companion, however, Jefferson now took personal charge of it. On January 30, 1807, four days before proffering advice to Wilkinson about how to handle the mess he had created in New Orleans, the president personally delivered Wilkinson's affidavit regarding Bollman and Swartwout to Walter Jones Jr., federal attorney for the District of Columbia, ordering him to request the federal circuit court for the District to issue a bench warrant for Bollman's and Swartwout's arrest on the charge of treason.[4]

The request for a bench warrant was itself unusual since it was normally issued only if the prisoners in question had already been indicted. The fact that the President of the United States hand carried Wilkinson's affidavit to Jones was also unusual and advertised the fact that Jefferson had indeed taken charge of the prosecution. Jones followed orders but he went out of his way in his opening statement to the court to make it clear that his motion for a bench warrant was "in obedience to instructions received from the president of the United States..."[5] It is impossible to determine whether he made this statement because he wanted to disassociate himself from the president's aggressive maneuver, or because he wanted to inform the two Republicans on the court (Nicholas Fitzhugh and Allen Duckett) of the president's wishes. Both men were Jefferson's appointees.

Things went badly from the outset, especially when Chief Judge William Cranch, the third man on the court, questioned whether the president's message to Congress of January 22, 1807, which Jones dutifully read, "did in fact announce a levying of war, and whether the court could proceed in any manner upon such information" without violating that part of the Sixth Amendment to the Constitution "which declares that no warrants shall issue but upon probable cause supported by an oath or affirmation."[6] Obviously flummoxed by the question, Jones could only repeat what Jefferson had announced on the basis of Wilkinson's affidavit: that an assemblage of one hundred to three hundred men was descending the river "towards the place of their destination."

He dug himself in deeper by arguing with glaring circularity that this expedition must have been treasonous since the president had called out the militia to suppress it, which he could not have done except in case of

---

[4] See William Cranch's letter to his father, quoted at length in William Draper Lewis, *Great American Lawyers* (8 vols., Philadelphia, 1908), 3: 106–07.

[5] 24 Fed. Cas. at 1189.

[6] Ibid., 1190.

actual invasion or insurrection. Jones's final point was that Jefferson's message to Congress upon which the bench warrant depended "was not offered as evidence upon the trial, but merely as a matter of public notoriety, of which the court might take notice, and prima facie presume the existence of such a state of things for the preliminary purpose of issuing a warrant or other process initiative to a prosecution by indictment."[7]

In short, Jones asked the court to believe that the report to Congress of January 22, "given by the president, in the discharge of his official duty" amounted to an oath within the meaning of the Sixth Amendment.[8] The court had to answer that question before it could reach the main issue, which was whether Wilkinson's affidavit justified the issuance of a bench warrant on the treason charge. On January 24, while the judges were pondering that issue, a Mr. Caldwell of the D.C. bar petitioned the court for writs of habeas corpus on behalf of the prisoners, stating that they had been imprisoned "without just and legal cause, and deprived of the benefit of counsel, or being confronted with the accusers, or of being informed of the nature of their offence; or of the cause of their commitment."[9]

The president now had a major civil rights case on his hands, one that according to John Quincy Adams respected "*the operation of our institutions,*" indeed, "the future prospects of this *Country.*"[10] The issue grew in scope and urgency on January 23, 1807 when Senator William Giles, Jefferson's staunch ally and confidant, introduced a bill in the Senate to suspend the writ of habeas corpus for three months in cases of treason. The bill, along with a special message to the House of Representatives urging it to rush passage of the Senate bill, passed with only James Bayard of Delaware voting against it. There is no written evidence that Jefferson explicitly requested Giles to move his bill, but there can be no doubt that he endorsed it, just as he approved of Wilkinson's action in New Orleans in defiance of the great writ.[11]

The House, with representatives from Virginia leading the charge, defeated the bill 113 to 19. Among those most outraged at the assault on habeas corpus was John Randolph, Jefferson's former Speaker of the House, and Jefferson's son-in-law, John W. Eppes. The heated debate over the bill educated the Washington community, if not the

---

7 Ibid.
8 Ibid.
9 Ibid.
10 John Quincy Adams to John Adams, Jan. 27, 1807, Adams Papers, MHS.
11 Beveridge, *Marshall*, 3: 346–7.

nation, about Wilkinson's tyrannous action in New Orleans and about Jefferson's support of his general. Rufus King probably spoke for many when he observed that the defeat of the bill in the House has "atoned for much imbecility and folly that had before been exhibited."[12] Had the habeas corpus bill passed, the Supreme Court would have been denied the opportunity to review the decision of the circuit court.

That decision came down on January 30, 1807. For the first time in American history, federal judges split along party lines.[13] Jefferson's two appointees (Duckett and Fitzhugh), following arguments of the prosecution on every point, voted to commit the prisoners on the basis of Wilkinson's affidavits as vouched for by Jefferson and supported by the affidavits of General William Eaton, James L. Donaldson, Ensign W. C. Meade, and Lieutenant William Wilson.[14] Federalist Chief Judge William Cranch entered an impassioned dissent.

Even Judges Duckett and Fitzhugh appeared uneasy with their stance. The latter opened his opinion by noting "My extreme indisposition has prevented me from preparing any remarks in support of the opinion which I am called on to give..." But he gave them anyhow.[15] Duckett began by professing his "scrupulous attachment to the right of personal liberty in the citizens of our country," and asked to be judged in this regard by "the whole tenor of his conduct through life" (and presumably not by the opinion he was about to deliver). For good measure, he protested that "no reasons of state, no political motive" had influenced his opinion.[16]

The one point on which both judges agreed – the one that came closest to justifying their decision and the president's as well – was that the hearing was for probable cause only, meaning that there was enough evidence to think that a grand jury might indict the prisoners. Neither judge felt obliged to grapple fully with the question of evidence, although both men gave their reasons for believing Wilkinson's affidavit. As Duckett expressed it in his "short view of the evidence," "the depositions of General Wilkinson prove, unquestionably, the connection of the prisoners with Colonel Burr," and if Burr was "probably" guilty of treason as the president announced, then so were Bollman and Swartwout:

[12] King as quoted in Warren, *Supreme Court*, 1: 303. Also see Levy, *Jefferson and Civil Liberties*, 88–91.
[13] Beveridge, *Marshall*, 3: 346.
[14] "Note" 24 Fed. Cas., 1196.
[15] Ibid., 1194.
[16] Ibid., 1193.

not because they had actually levied war against the United States but because since they knew of Burr's intent, they could be presumed to have been willing to join him in the actual levying of war should that come to pass.[17]

Duckett did not inquire why it was that Bollman and Swartwout should be tainted for delivering the cipher letter to Wilkinson and not Wilkinson as well for having received it, or how it was that the general communicated via a secret code with the alleged traitor. Fitzhugh did concede that the evidence against Burr was circumstantial, and that circumstantial evidence did not meet Article III evidentiary requirements for treason (i.e., two witnesses to the same overt act of levying war). But even so, Fitzhugh went on to declare that Burr's guilt was "established."

Not only did Fitzhugh give credence to Wilkinson's evidence of Burr's guilt (as vouched for by the president), but he went on to argue that the prisoners could be held on the charge of treason because of their association with Burr – this even though the judge acknowledged that the evidence against Bollman and Swartwout supported a charge of misprision (concealment) of treason and not treason itself. His point was that since "there is no intermediate class of offences of a treasonable nature between misprision and treason, it must be treason."[18]

Fitzhugh also accepted Wilkinson's statement – obviously hearsay – that Swartwout, while being secretly interrogated at Natchez, admitted to a treasonable association with Burr. Swartwout denied Wilkinson's account of the matter under oath before the Grand Jury at Richmond and according to John Randolph, who was foreman of the jury, his frank account impressed the jurors.[19] Both Swartwout and Bollman testified that Burr's scheme was not to sever the Union but was directed at Mexico and then only in case of a war with Spain, which he believed was imminent.

Like Duckett, Fitzhugh did not consider the possibility that because the cipher letter was sent by Burr (Dayton) to Wilkinson, the general himself must also have been in on the conspiracy. Nor did he ask why it was that Wilkinson waited so long after receiving the cipher letter to warn the president of the supposedly dire threat to the Union. In short, both judges took Wilkinson's account of Burr and Jefferson's account

[17] Ibid.
[18] Ibid., 1196. Misprision of treason means concealment of treason.
[19] William Cabell Bruce, *John Randolph of Roanoke* (2 vols., New York, 1970), 1: 306.

of Wilkinson at face value. Or less charitably, they believed Wilkinson because Jefferson vouched for his credibility and expected them to follow suit.

If Cranch's colleagues believed Wilkinson because Jefferson did so, Cranch doubted Wilkinson because he doubted the president. Cranch's opinion, moreover, carried unusual weight because of his family connections and no less because of his undisputed ability and integrity. The wife of Cranch's father Richard Cranch was the sister of Abigail Adams, which made John Adams young Cranch's uncle and John Quincy Adams his first cousin. President Adams appointed young Cranch associate judge on the federal circuit court for the District, which was created in February 1801. President Jefferson nominated Cranch as Chief Judge of the circuit court in 1806, a position he held for a record fifty-four years. While serving on the circuit court, Cranch was also the reporter for the Supreme Court of the United States during the early years of John Marshall's tenure, which meant that Cranch reported the Marshall Court's Bollman decision which drew on his own dissent in that case at the trial level.[20]

Cranch was a moderate Federalist like his uncle, but he was also a man widely respected for his integrity and his sound judgment. What Cranch saw in the Bollman proceedings – what others were beginning to suspect and would come to believe during the trial in Richmond – was that the president was carrying on a personal vendetta against Burr.

Cranch divulged his misgivings to his father shortly after the decision of his court in the Bollman case came down. "So anxious was the President to have this prosecution commenced," he wrote, "or, to use his own language, to deliver them to the civil authority, that he came to the Capitol on the day of their arrival and with his own hand delivered to the District Attorney, Mr. Jones, the affidavit of General Wilkinson, and instructed the attorney to demand of the court a warrant for the arrest of Bollman and Swartout [sic] on the charge of treason. When this circumstance is considered, and the attempt made in the Legislature to suspend the privilege of *habeas corpus* on the very day on which the motion was made for a warrant against Bollman and Swartout [sic],... you may form some idea of the anxiety which has attended my dissent from the majority of the Court."[21]

---

[20] See Hagner's "William Cranch" in Lewis, *Great American Lawyers*, 3: 87–119.
[21] Ibid., 107.

Where the majority opinions of Duckett and Fitzhugh for the circuit court were hesitant and weakly reasoned, Cranch's dissent was powerful, persuasive, and prescient. "In times like these," he warned, "when the public mind is agitated, when wars, and rumors of wars, plots, conspiracies and treasons excite alarm, it is the duty of a court to be peculiarly watchful lest the public feeling should reach the seat of justice, and thereby precedents be established which may become the ready tools of faction in times more disastrous. The worst of precedents may be established from the best of motives."[22]

Cranch had equally strong words for Jefferson, whom he feared was taking the law into his own hands. It did not matter, he reasoned, that the president acted "from the best of motives," or from a "zeal for the public interest," a benefit of the doubt Marshall did not extend to his cousin.[23] What *did* matter was that the government – the president and his lawyers – trampled on freedoms guaranteed in the Bill of Rights, namely the right of persons to be secure against unreasonable seizures, and that no warrants shall issue but upon probable cause, supported by oath or affirmation. To secure those rights the Constitution guaranteed the accused the right to the writ of habeas corpus, which Jefferson and Giles sought to subvert.

Judge Cranch might also have mentioned that Bollman and Swartwout – both held incommunicado under constant military guard since their military arrest in New Orleans – had been denied the right to counsel guaranteed by the Sixth Amendment. Strangely, Jefferson's lawyer Caesar Rodney, Attorney General of the United States, objected to the prisoners having access to counsel "on the grounds of humanity." To grant them that right, he argued, "would excite a public prejudice against them, if they should be committed after being heard by counsel." Granting the prisoners the right of counsel at this stage of the proceedings, he added, would usurp "the province of the jury" at the trial stage.[24] Little wonder Cranch was outraged.

Most pertinent for the forthcoming trial in Richmond, Cranch's dissent addressed the questions of evidence in treason trials raised by the prosecution lawyers, by the opinions of Duckett and Fitzhugh, and implicitly by Jefferson's public declaration of Burr's guilt. Cranch homed in on Article III, which stated that conviction for levying war required "two witnesses to the same overt act." The meaning of those words was

[22] 24 Fed. Cas., 1192.
[23] Ibid.
[24] Ibid., 1191.

critical to Bollman and Swartwout, because the president insisted on charging the prisoners with treason solely on the basis of the written testimony of Wilkinson and others. Although Jefferson had already pronounced Burr guilty on such evidence, both Jones and Rodney admitted in the bail hearing that the affidavits "do not show that war had been levied." That defect, they contended, "is supplied by the message [of the president], which, being an official message, was under oath, and proved the treasonable intent of seizing upon New Orleans – and thus that war had been levied."[25] In sum, it was enough that Bollman and Swartwout were, as Wilkinson's affidavit claimed, "confederates in treason" to charge them with treason.

With the help of Charles Lee's argument for the prisoners, Cranch exposed the weakness and dangers of the majority's position. "To a man of plain understanding," he said, "it would seem to be a matter of little difficulty to decide what was meant in the constitution by levying of war; but the subtleties of lawyers and judges, invented in times of heat and turbulence, have involved the question in some obscurity." He did not intend to undertake a full discussion of the matter, he said, but he knew for sure what should be avoided in a republic governed by a written constitution: "It is, however, to be hoped, that we shall never, in this country, adopt the long list of constructive treasons invented in England, by the worst of judges in the worst of times."[26]

Nor should the president of the United States undertake to do so. Cranch stood on solid constitutional ground when he declared: "I can never agree that executive communications not on oath or affirmation, can, under the words of our constitution, be received in a court of justice, to charge a man with treason, much less to commit him for trial."[27] Cranch felt compelled to be "explicit" on this point because "such communications can not be evidence on the trial." For the court to give legitimacy to the president's "communications" at this stage of the proceedings would be to prejudge the question of guilt or innocence; to do so, he concluded, would be "deemed a dereliction of duty."[28] It is "the duty of the judiciary calmly to poise the scales of justice, unmoved by the arm of power, undisturbed by the clamor of the multitude."[29] John Marshall could not have said it more eloquently.

[25] Ibid., 1192.
[26] Ibid., 1193.
[27] Ibid.
[28] Ibid.
[29] Ibid., 1192.

In fact, Cranch was addressing the chief justice and his colleagues on the Supreme Court, who on February 13, 1807, in *Ex parte Bollman* heard the case on appeal on the writs of habeas corpus sued out by Charles Lee, Robert Goodloe Harper, and Francis Scott Key on behalf of Bollman and Swartwout who still languished in jail. Thanks largely to Cranch's dissent, the constitutional issues that would continue to separate Jefferson and Marshall were now identified. Questions concerning the definition of treason and the meaning of "levying war" had been broached, if not definitively answered. And finally, questions of evidence that would perplex the bench and bar in the Burr trial (and generations of historians thereafter) had been vetted.

The Marshall Court Defines Treason – Almost

The process of clarifying the meaning of treason in Article III, Section 3 of the Constitution began during the 1790s. In the crimes act of that year Congress made treason punishable by death. That statute also provided that defendants in treason cases were entitled to a copy of the indictment against them and a list of the witnesses and jurors in the case. The accused was given the right to challenge thirty-five members of the jury panel without cause, and was also granted the right to counsel and the right of compulsory process.[30]

The only federal case law on the treason clause during the 1790s came at the circuit court level in cases arising out of the tax rebellions in western Pennsylvania – the Whiskey Rebellion in 1794 and the Fries Rebellion in 1799. Counsel in *Bollman* would refer to judicial rulings in these cases, but their authority as precedents was limited for several reasons: first, because in the cases from the 1790s, unlike those in the Bollman and Burr litigation, actual (if ineffectual) force was used by the accused; and second, because the objective of the defendants in both the Whiskey Rebellion and the Fries cases was to oppose the execution of a federal statute and not to levy war against the federal government in order to overthrow it.

Bollman, then, was the first time the Supreme Court en banc ruled on the meaning of levying war in Article III and on the evidentiary requirements for conviction.[31] One might logically assume that the decision

---

[30] Richard Peters, ed., *The Statutes at Large of the United States*, 1: 112, 118–19, as cited in Bradley Chapin, *The American Law of Treason* (Seattle, 1964), 84, 142.

[31] On the federal circuit court decisions in the 1790s see Chapin, ibid., ch. 6, especially 85–97.

would be the definitive precedent for future courts regarding the meaning of treason in Article III – and the controlling one in the circuit court trial of Burr in Richmond. Such was not the case, for several reasons. One reason was that the main issue before the Bollman Court, as Marshall made clear, was not whether the prisoners were guilty of treason, but "whether the accused shall be discharged or held to trial."[32] A second reason was that Marshall's opinion on the meaning of treason was open to interpretation.

Before reaching the issue of treason, however, the justices had to decide whether or not the Court had the authority to issue a writ of habeas corpus in a case on appeal from a federal circuit court, which had already ruled in favor of commitment. On February 13, in the first of two opinions, Marshall, with Johnson and one other justice dissenting (Samuel Chase most likely), held that the Court could, by the authority of Section 14 of the Judiciary Act of 1789, issue the writ.[33] Johnson objected to Marshall's broad interpretation of Section 14, and he also noted that he was prompted to dissent because counsel for Bollman and Swartwout had insulted President Jefferson, who not incidentally had appointed Johnson to the Court in 1804 to challenge Marshall's dominance.[34] A second issue, debated at length and decided once and for all, was whether the court could issue the writ if the case had been brought under original jurisdiction. Citing his own opinion in *Marbury v. Madison*, Marshall held that the answer was no.

Arguments on the merits now proceeded, the issue being whether there was sufficient evidence to hold the prisoners for trial on the charge of treason (as the circuit court below had ruled) or whether they should be released. To rule on this question, Marshall had to address the meaning of treason – "levying war" – in Article III of the Constitution. Connected to this issue was the question concerning the admissibility of James Wilkinson's affidavit, upon which the government had relied to hold the prisoners on the charge of treason.

---

[32] 4 Cranch 125.

[33] Marshall's dictum that the writ applied only to federal and not state prisoners, it might be noted, was wrong, as Eric M. Freedman shows in "Milestones in Habeas Corpus: Part I. Just Because John Marshall Said It, Doesn't Make It So: *Ex Parte Bollman* and the Illusory Prohibition on the Federal Writ of Habeas Corpus for State Prisoners in the Judiciary Act of 1789," *Alabama Law Rev.*, No. 2, 51: 531–602.

[34] For Johnson's position see Donald G. Morgan, *Justice William Johnson: The First Dissenter* (Columbia, s.c., 1954), 56–57. The Bollman and Swartwout litigation is discussed in George L. Haskins and Herbert A. Johnson, *Foundations of Power: John Marshall, 1801* (New York and London, 1981), 256–61.

Attorney General Rodney, speaking in favor of commitment, made roughly the same arguments he made in the circuit court below, and his argument continued to be burdened with the same damning admissions. As to whether Wilkinson's affidavit had been taken under oath as required by the Sixth Amendment, Rodney was satisfied that any irregularities that occurred in New Orleans (when the city was under Wilkinson's military rule) were corrected by "the act of congress respecting the authentication of records."

As to whether there was sufficient evidence to indict on the charge of treason, Rodney conceded, "none of the evidence now offered would be competent on the trial; nor even if it appeared in a proper shape, would it be sufficient to convict the prisoners."[35] "The expedition against Mexico would not be treason," he conceded further, "unless it was to be accomplished by means which in themselves would amount to treason." And further: the prosecution "cannot at present say exactly when and where the *overt* act of levying war was committed, but from the affidavits, we think it fair to infer, that an army has been actually levied and arrayed." Finally, he readily acknowledged "that General Wilkinson was interested to make the worst of the story," but that made no difference, since "the declarations of the prisoners themselves are sufficient."[36]

But why trust Wilkinson's account of what Swartwout said after conceding that the general was "interested to make the worst of the story"? The answer, and the legal foundation of the prosecution's case, was that the president of the United States had already declared Bollman and Swartwout (along with Burr) guilty of treason. As federal attorney Walter Jones argued in *Bollman*, "A state of war is a matter of public notoriety, and he [Jones] had considered the president's message as evidence of that notoriety, it being a communication from the supreme executive, in the course of his duty, to that department of government which alone could decide on the state of war."[37] If the president said war had been levied by Burr and his followers, that settled the matter. Nothing was said as to the reliability of the information from Wilkinson that led the president to make his declaration. But obviously Jones was not troubled, since he observed that even if the general was "to be considered as *particeps criminis*...it would be no disqualification of his testimony."[38]

[35] 4 Cranch, 115.
[36] Ibid., 115–116.
[37] Ibid., 118.
[38] Ibid., 119.

Regarding the meaning of treason in Article III, Jones had little to offer, except to remind the court: "Treason is a greater crime in republics than in monarchies, and ought to be more severely punished." Presumably he did not mean that innocent people ought to be punished, or that the specific rules of evidence required by Article III ought to be watered down – but that, like much else in the arguments of Jones and Rodney, is not clear. At one point in the argument over the Court's power to issue the writ, Justice Johnson actually stepped in to help the prosecution, mentioning "such objections as occur to my mind against the arguments urged by the counsel for the prisoners."[39]

If the prosecution was lackluster, the defense lawyers, a solid phalanx of seasoned Jefferson critics, held forth with much learning and even more rhetoric, or as Johnson put it, with a "very unnecessary display of energy and pathos."[40] They expounded on the Court's statutory authority to issue habeas corpus writs. Much was said, and much of it tangential to the case at hand, about the nobility of the great writ and about the glories of the Constitution and the common law that informed it. Robert Goodloe Harper, the brash, brilliant young lawyer from Maryland, celebrated the Supreme Court as the guardian of liberty in the time of troubles – a paean of praise obviously addressed to the president, who as everyone knew had only recently tried to curb the Court's powers.[41]

Praiseful references to Marshall's opinion in *Marbury* were no doubt calculated to raise the president's ire, too, as was Harper's praise of judicial review itself: for the "power of the judiciary to collate an act of Congress with the constitution, when it comes judicially before them, and of declaring it void, if against the constitution, is one of the best barriers against oppression, in the fluctuations of [f]action, and in those times of party violence which necessarily result from the operation of human passions, in a popular government."[42] Even more provocative was Harper's condemnation of the efforts of the "dominant party, flushed with victory, and irritated by a recent conflict," to "shut the mouth of the supreme court."[43]

Political rhetoric aside, the main objective of the defense was to discredit the evidence supplied by Wilkinson to establish probable cause

[39] Ibid., 102.
[40] Ibid., 103.
[41] Ibid., 82–83.
[42] Ibid., 85.
[43] Ibid., 90.

on the charge of treason against the prisoners – the same evidence that would be used against Burr at Richmond. Under particular scrutiny was Wilkinson's copy of the cipher letter, his affidavit regarding his conversation with Swartwout, and affidavits from the other witnesses purporting to validate his account of Burr's treasonous expedition.

Charles Lee led off with "a minute examination" of the prosecution's evidence, concluding that it entirely failed to establish probable cause on the treason charge. What the evidence proved, if it proved anything, was "an intent to set on foot an expedition against Mexico, in case of war between this country and Spain."[44] Lee went on to argue what was now becoming apparent to those who followed the proceedings, that Wilkinson's affidavits were drawn up "to vindicate and justify the illegal seizure and transportation of the prisoners..." Rather than use the courts of New Orleans, which had been open for business, Wilkinson had seized the two men, "by orders of a military office" and sent them two thousand miles away "without any process of law or legal authority" to Washington "to be disposed of by the Executive."[45] Wilkinson's motives as well as his affidavits were now an issue – and so were those of the president.

Francis Scott Key, picking up where Lee left off, focused on the evils of constructive treason, which he accused the prosecution and the president of having invoked against the prisoners. Constructive treasons were those created by judicial interpretations of the statutory language in the great English treason statute of 25 Edward III in 1351 – language borrowed by the drafters of Article III, Section 3 of the Constitution. In one important respect, the treason statute of 1351 was a victory for due process, since before its passage, treason was a matter of interpretation by judges who were administrative arms of the monarchy. While 25 Edward III specifically prohibited judicial constructions of treason, it also defined treason very broadly. Moreover, the statute's prohibition of judicially constructed treason doctrine was often ignored by the courts. Some judicial decisions followed the liberal spirit of the act of 1351, which was to curb the political uses of treason law. Other decisions, however, especially those handed down during the reign of the Stuart kings in the seventeenth century, made treason law into an instrument for repressing political dissent.[46]

44 Ibid., 110.
45 Ibid., 111.
46 An American edition of Joseph Chitty, *A Practical Treatise on the Criminal Law...* (2 vols., Philadelphia, 1819), 2: ch. 5, especially at 35–40, drawing on Blackstone's

While what English judges and treatise writers said about treason over the centuries might seem irrelevant to American lawyers and judges, such was not the case; both regularly turned to English legal history to explain the language of the Constitution. In fact, the Supreme Court justices on circuit in the 1790s treason cases mentioned above uniformly resorted to constructive treason doctrine in charging their juries. Lawyers in the Burr trial would also draw on English judicial decisions with an eye to persuading Marshall to either expand the definition of treason or to narrow it down.

The argument over constructive treason in Richmond actually began in *Bollman*. Francis Scott Key stated the issue precisely: "In England," he said, echoing Cranch's dissent below, "the books speak of two kinds of levying of war – direct and constructive. But there is only one in this country..." When the Framers made "levying war" treason, he said, they meant the *actual* levying of war. "If 100 men conspire, and only 50 actually levy war, the latter only are guilty as principals."[47] Wilkinson's affidavits "do not show any act of treason" or any "assemblage of men, nor military array. There is not a tittle of evidence, that any two men have been seen together with treasonable intent, whether armed or not." As to the affidavits of Meade and Wilson, upon which the prosecution relied to authenticate Wilkinson's account, they "relate only to rumors derived from General Wilkinson, whose business it was, if he could get such rumours there by no other means, to create them himself."[48]

Why the commander of the army should create rumors of secession, civil war, and treason, Key left others to ponder; as well as why, given Wilkinson's reputation for double-dealing, the president did not question the reliability of his affidavit. Harper proceeded to do just that in an argument that would resonate throughout the rest of the proceedings against Bollman and Swartwout and also those against Burr in Richmond: "We object to the translation of the ciphered letter contained in General Wilkinson's affidavits, being admitted as evidence, because General Wilkinson has not sworn that it is a true translation, nor sent the original, with the key, so that the court can have a correct translation made. Nor is it proved, that the original was written by Colonel

---

Commentaries, Comyns Digest, and English case law, lists a dozen offenses that were treasonable in England. Chitty's volumes were widely read by American lawyers and contained additional notes of related American cases by Richard Peters Jr., the son of district judge Richard Peters, who sat in the trial of the Whiskey Rebels.

[47] 4 Cranch, 112.
[48] Ibid., 113.

Burr, or by his direction, nor that the prisoners were acquainted with its contents."[49] In any case, as Luther Martin pointed out: sooner or later Wilkinson would have to testify under oath.[50] When he did so at Richmond, Burr's counsel (which included Martin and Lee) were ready to pounce.

Marshall delivered his opinion on Saturday February 21, 1807, to a packed courtroom full of senators and representatives and other Washington dignitaries. It was a dramatic moment, because as Marshall observed, "there is no crime which can more excite and agitate the passions of men than treason" and "no charge demands more from the tribunal before which it is made a deliberate and temperate inquiry. Whether this inquiry be directed to the fact or to the law, none can be more solemn, none more important to the citizen or to the government; none can more affect the safety of both."[51]

The Bollman case was important to citizens; it was also challenging to the Court. It was important because both the definition of treason and the clarification of federal habeas corpus law related directly to the fundamental liberties of individual citizens. It was challenging to Marshall and his colleagues for several reasons, starting with the fact that the issue had already become politically charged and further, because it was clear to all that what the Court said about treason and about Wilkinson's evidence would influence the trial against Burr once he was apprehended. Adding to the pressure, the Court about to rule for the first time on the constitutional meaning of treason for the first time consisted of only four of six justices. Sitting with Marshall were Justices Chase, Johnson, and Washington, who as it turned out were divided on some of the key issues, including the meaning of "levying war" in Article III.[52]

If and how the divisions on the Court influenced Marshall's opinion is impossible to say, but clearly his definition of treason was not crystal clear. If one goes by what he said he meant to say, it seems certain that he intended to limit the scope of the treason clause so as to depoliticize it. To this end, he made two points. One: "To constitute that specific crime for which the prisoners now before the court have been committed, war must be actually levied against the United States. However flagitious may be the crime of conspiring to subvert by force

---

[49] Ibid., 120.
[50] Ibid., 122.
[51] Ibid., 125.
[52] Justices Livingston and Cushing were the absent members.

the government of our country, such conspiracy is not treason." Two: "To conspire to levy war, and actually to levy war, are distinct offences. The first must be brought into operation by the assemblage of men for a purpose treasonable in itself, or the fact of levying war cannot have been committed."[53]

These holdings freed Bollman and Swartwout, since there was no evidence presented to prove that actual war had been levied or that they had taken part in any treasonable assemblage. But then to the confusion of the prosecution in Richmond and to generations of historians as well, Marshall went on to say, "It is not the intention of the court to say that no individual can be guilty of this crime who has not appeared in arms against his country. On the contrary, if war be actually levied, that is, if a body of men be actually assembled for the purpose of effecting by force a treasonable purpose, all those who perform any part, however minute, or however remote from the scene of action, and who are actually leagued in the general conspiracy, are to be considered as traitors."[54] In other places in his opinion – George Hay would point to several in Richmond – the chief justice appeared to endorse an expansive definition of levying war.

Considering the circuit decisions from the 1790s in which constructive treason doctrine was uniformly accepted, it would not have been surprising if Marshall had followed suit in *Bollman*. Indeed, the foremost proponent of that doctrine in those earlier cases, Justice Samuel Chase, was one of the four justices in *Bollman*.

Nevertheless, a close reading of Marshall's opinion that places the disputed passages in context indicates that he had rejected constructive treason doctrine in defining "levying war" and in its place had set forth a narrow definition of treason "consonant to the principles of our constitution."[55] The prosecution in Richmond, however, reading selectively, argued that Marshall had endorsed enough of the English doctrine to snare Burr – even though he was not present when war was allegedly levied and even though there was no evidence that anything resembling actual war had occurred. What is more, Hay framed his indictment of Burr on that understanding of *Bollman*. Marshall's subsequent clarification of that opinion in Richmond invited his critics to claim that he had not only shifted ground, but that he had done so for partisan political reasons.

---

[53] 4 Cranch, 126.
[54] Ibid., 126.
[55] Ibid., 127.

If Marshall's definition of "levying" war in *Bollman* was open to
a broad interpretation, his ruling on "the testimony which has been
exhibited against the accused" was not.[56] The question was whether
Wilkinson's affidavit regarding Burr's (Dayton's) cipher letter (addressed
to Wilkinson and delivered by Swartwout) was admissible, especially
in the absence of the original cipher letter. The majority of the circuit
court below felt that this issue was not controlling in a probable cause
hearing, but Marshall disagreed emphatically, noting that their decision
had imposed "a long and painful imprisonment" on the accused. As part
of their judicial duty, judges had the obligation to see that the evidence
against the prisoners was weighed by the same "legal" standards as if it
were presented to a trial court and jury.

The problem was that Marshall's colleagues could not agree on
what those legal standards were. Reargument on that point – which
Marshall asked for on February 19 – apparently did not settle the matter either. What the majority did agree on, and what Marshall stated
in his February 21 opinion for the majority, was that there was not
"one syllable which has a necessary or a natural reference to an enter-
prize against any territory of the United States."[57] The justices divided
as to whether Swartwout's account (as reported in Wilkinson's affidavit) indicated that Burr intended to move against the United States.
A majority did agree, however, that there had been no "open assemblage of men" for that purpose.[58] "The mere enlisting of men, without
assembling them, is not levying war." If as Wilkinson claimed, thousands of men were on the march, the evidence would "force itself upon
the public view."[59] Marshall would make the same telling point in the
Richmond trial.

The Bollman decision, rendered by only four justices, who were themselves divided on important issues, was not a conclusive statement of
the law – especially given the fact that Marshall appeared to waffle on
the definition of treason. While he ruled that Bollman and Swartwout
could not be held on the charge of treason, he also held out the possibility that they might be indicted for high misdemeanor, since the evidence
showed that they were "engaged in a most culpable enterprise against
the dominions of a power at peace with the United States." He also

---

[56] Ibid., 128.
[57] Ibid., 132–33.
[58] Ibid.,133–34.
[59] Ibid., 134–35.

noted for a unanimous Court that such a case could not be heard by the Supreme Court but would have to be tried in the district where the crime was committed.

Marshall's decision for the Court, printed only three days after it came down, quickly became the subject of partisan disputation. Indeed, even before the final decision, a correspondent for the Federalist *New York Evening Post* predicted the outcome and speculated on the nature of the divisions among the justices.[60] On February 25, Justice Johnson's dissent denying the Court's authority to issue the writ of habeas corpus was published separately on page one of the *National Intelligencer*. The president, who had been following the proceedings closely, was predictably outraged and assumed that Marshall spoke for the Federalists, or what remained of them, and that he freed Bollman and Swartwout in order to embarrass him personally. Loyal supporters in Congress, with Jefferson's encouragement, also renewed their effort to limit the Court's habeas corpus jurisdiction. Talk of Marshall's impeachment, already rampant after *Marbury*, now intensified.

Obviously the consternation in the president's camp was not because Bollman and Swartwout went free, since they were never the main targets of the prosecution (as Jefferson's offer to pardon Bollman made clear). What troubled Jefferson and his lawyers was that the decision that freed them might also be used to defend Burr when he came to trial.[61] And there was reason for concern. Not only did the cipher letter and Swartwout's interpretation of its contents establish Wilkinson's association with Burr; it also pointed to the conclusion that Burr's plan was not to divide the Union but rather, to wrest Mexico from Spanish control. In fact, Burr would be charged with that crime in Richmond. Fortunately for him as it turned out, the prosecution proceeded to try him first on the charge of treason with its formidable standard of proof. President Jefferson made that call; he did so, one has to think, because he had already declared publicly that Burr was a traitor.

On to Richmond

Bollman and Swartwout were out of jail and two months later Marshall was on his way to Richmond to hold his circuit court where the trial of

---

[60] *New York Evening Post*, Feb. 20, 1807, as cited in Warren, *Supreme Court*, 1: 307.
[61] For Jefferson's position on the impact of the court's decision in the Bollman case, see Jefferson to James Bowdoin, April 2, 1807, Bergh, *Writings of Jefferson*, 11: 186.

the main culprit was scheduled to take place. There was time aplenty for the lawyers on both sides to ponder the lessons of *Bollman*. The government discovered that the evidence against Swartwout and Bollman, much of which they planned to use against Burr, was deeply flawed. They must also have sensed that Wilkinson's various statements were full of contradictions that would not bear scrutiny under cross examination; especially vulnerable, should it be presented in court, was the doctored cipher letter, since it had already been critiqued by the lawyers and discredited by Marshall's opinion. In fact, when called to testify under oath before the grand jury in Richmond, Wilkinson's own involvement in the conspiracy would be impossible to disguise. If Wilkinson went down, the government's case would be in serious trouble.

There was, of course, an outside chance that a friendly jury might disregard the evidence and believe Wilkinson, especially if by some adversarial magic the general's character (vouched for by the president) could be pitted against Burr's (provided it could be sufficiently besmirched). The effort to do just that would be a key element in the prosecution's litigation strategy. Beyond some miraculous resuscitation of Wilkinson's character and the destruction of Burr's, however, the prosecution's best hope was to persuade Marshall to adopt the English doctrine of constructive treason. And the best way to do that would be to convince him that he and his colleagues had already done so in *Bollman*.

The prospect for Burr and his lawyers looked dark, but there were also some rays of hope. On the positive side, two members of Burr's defense team, Charles Lee and Luther Martin, by working together in the Bollman trial, had taken the measure of Wilkinson. They also learned for a fact that the president had made Burr's conviction a personal cause. By dramatizing executive overreach they could simultaneously paint Burr as an innocent victim and play on Marshall's distaste for Jefferson.

What the defense had to contend with, on the other hand, was Marshall's language in *Bollman* that appeared in some places to embrace the doctrine of constructive treason. Secondly, they had to reckon with an aroused public that had clearly followed the president in condemning Burr out of hand. Finally, there was Aaron Burr himself. For all his charisma and legal knowledge, he had operated so close to the edge of the law that he might well have crossed the line – or at the very least, might be perceived as having done so by the jurors in Richmond. Whether they would take kindly to his aristocratic aloofness was a further question.

Both sides understood that public opinion would play a crucial, possibly even a determining role in the Richmond trial. They also understood – and Burr most emphatically since his life was on the line – that the president not only had the law enforcement agencies of the government at his command but that he was also the commander-in-chief of public opinion. The challenge for the defense was to remake Burr's public image and to expose the president's vendetta against him. Whether John Marshall would respond favorably to their arguments – or restrain their aggressive attack on the president – remained to be seen. In either case, the chief justice himself was destined to be one of the characters in the battle over character that was about to unfold.

3

Legal Theater in Richmond

Aaron Burr Front-and-Center

"The Drama under rehearsal at the Richmond Theatre, first reported to be a Farce, is now said to be of a new species of Melo-Drama."

Virginia Argus, June 17, 1807

"...I want the jury, this audience and all the world to know and be impressed with what are the rights of the accused."

Edmund Randolph[1]

"...two thirds of our speeches have been addressed to the people..."

George Hay to Jefferson, June 14, 1807[2]

While the president was mobilizing the nation against him in late 1806 and early 1807, Burr was setting his plans in motion in the West. Intimations of trouble came when he was twice presented to federal grand juries: first in November 1806 in Kentucky for a conspiracy to revolutionize the western states; and then in February 1807 in the Mississippi Territory, this time for fomenting secession. Both grand juries refused to indict, but Burr's luck ran out in Mississippi. When district judge Thomas Rodney, the father of Jefferson's Attorney General, got word of Jefferson's proclamation, he ordered Burr to appear in court for further interrogation. Burr, aware at last that the president was out to get him, bade a hasty farewell to his young followers and headed for the woods – a wanted man with a reward on his head. He was arrested near the tiny town of

[1] Robertson, *Reports*, 2: 384.
[2] *The Thomas Jefferson Papers Series 1. General Correspondence, 1651–1827*. Lib. Cong.

Wakefield in the Mississippi Territory, taken under armed guard to Fort Stoddard and thence for several hundred miles through the southwest wilderness to Richmond, where he arrived in the evening of March 26.

Things looked bleak. He had been branded a traitor by the president he helped elevate to office and with whom he served ably as vice president for four years. A combat officer of the Revolution who served with distinction, he had been hunted down and collared like a common horse thief. He was down and out, exhausted and bedraggled. Rather than leading a victorious army into Mexico City, he entered Richmond under armed guard – the object of idle curiosity (at best) or outright hatred. On March 30, he stood before John Marshall in the Eagle Tavern for arraignment, charged with betraying the country they both fought to create. The first act of "the far famed trial" was about to unfold.

At the request of U.S. Attorney for Virginia George Hay, who was chief prosecutor in the case, the arraignment proceedings on March 30 and 31 were transferred temporarily to the hall of the House of Delegates to accommodate the mob of eager spectators – and no doubt to capitalize on popular hostility toward Burr. The principal trial, which began on August 3, would also be held in the House of Delegates. Lawyers on both sides adjusted to the fact that they were playing to the crowd.

On April 1, Marshall, sitting as examining magistrate, committed Burr for a high misdemeanor, for organizing a military action against Spain in violation of the Neutrality Act of 1794. Burr was then bailed and free to move about the city, which permitted him to charm the ladies (which he succeeded in doing) and attempt to neutralize the popular hostility against him (which he failed to do). Preliminary proceedings began with the summoning of the grand jury panel on Friday, May 22, the regular opening day of the federal circuit court. Grand jury proceedings continued off and on for the better part of a month, ending on June 24, when the jury brought a true bill indicting Burr for both treason and high misdemeanor.

Arraignment and bail hearings, though technically prefatory to the main event, were in fact opening salvos in the trial. The grand jury proceedings were even more indicative of what lay ahead. While the lawyers argued about treason doctrine and evidence, they took measure of one another and unveiled their litigation strategies. Not surprisingly, since it was thought to be the first line of defense against governmental tyranny, the jury (grand and trial) loomed large in their calculations. Predictably both sides lavished praise on "the people's panel." Both also knew from experience that jury behavior was unpredictable – and susceptible to manipulation by sitting presidents, respected judges, and clever lawyers. The challenge was obvious. The prosecution needed to fuel the anti-Burr sentiment ignited by Jefferson's proclamations, Wilkinson's campaign, and partisan newspaper coverage. The defense had to overcome or at least neutralize popular prejudice against Burr – and perhaps win legal points with Marshall in the process. Both prosecution and defense played to the crowd and the jurors by mixing high-toned law-talk with high-flown rhetoric. The result was legal theater, along with some dazzling courtroom advocacy; in fact the two were inseparably entwined.

Let the "Sovereign People" Be Entertained – and Educated

By one account Richmond's regular population of some six thousand nearly doubled in anticipation of the trial. For ordinary folk who flocked to the scene – whether they were lucky enough to see the action up close or hear about it secondhand in the streets or taverns – the long trial was a rare escape from the drudgery and boredom of hard labor, an opportunity to visit distant relatives, to exchange gossip with neighbors and friends, or to rub shoulders with the well-born and the up-and-coming. The prospect of seeing a blueblood like Burr brought low was no doubt a titillating prospect to many. And if that did not do the trick, they could drink, carouse, and bet on the ponies – or perhaps follow the example of one of the government's key witnesses, General William Eaton, who it was rumored bet $5,000 that Burr would be found guilty. For some real titillation, one might even catch Eaton in Arab costume (and his cups) doing wild things with "young women of dubious virtue" in one of Richmond's taverns.[3] Burr's trial was a Virginia court-day writ large – very large.

And the grander sorts were as intrigued as were the common folk. "So great was the number of distinguished persons claiming seats within the bar," wrote James Parton, "that the lawyers of twenty years' standing were excluded from their accustomed places, and thought themselves fortunate to get within the walls." By Parton's count, "Including witnesses, jurymen, and lawyers, there were no less than two hundred persons in Richmond who had some official connection with the trial."[4] According to one young girl who witnessed the fracas, the crowd soon

---

[3] Noel B. Gerson, *Barbary General* (Englewood Cliffs, NJ, 1968), 254–6 discusses Eaton's wanton behavior that was used to discredit his testimony at the trial.
[4] Parton, *The Life and Times of Aaron Burr* (14th ed., New York, 1861), 458–9.

divided into partisan rooting sections, with the preponderance of the ladies on Burr's side of the courtroom.[5]

Most of the leading actors, excepting Burr and Luther Martin, were also Virginians either by birth or choice. Many were related by blood or marriage, and almost all of them were known to one another and to the attentive public. Familiarity bred both contempt and admiration. Ongoing rivalries, especially among the lawyers, took on new meaning in the heat of battle. For many the reputation of Virginia itself was on the line, especially since two of her first statesmen, Jefferson and Marshall, were set to do battle.

Regardless of its Virginia flavor, the trial was a national event. People imbued with a "wonder-seizing appetite" came from all over America to see the action.[6] Those who could not make the scene could read about it in their local newspapers, whose editors got their accounts free of charge (and free from copyright) from leading papers like the Philadelphia *Aurora* and the Richmond *Enquirer* – both of which had reporters on the scene.

What made the Burr trial truly national, however, was not the national audience, but the great issues at stake – and the national figures who symbolized those issues. Marshall and Jefferson were not just Virginians; they were the Chief Justice and President of the United States. What separated them was not just personal animus, but profound differences over the separation of powers, the nature of constitutional interpretation, and the meaning of nationhood itself. Treason was not just an important constitutional question to be settled; it was also an issue inseparably bound up with those nation-defining qualities of allegiance, duty, and patriotism.

These were matters of supreme importance, moreover, that ordinary citizens as well as elites could grasp and discuss. One might even suggest that Richmond in the summer of 1807 provided its own version of Jürgen Habermas's "public sphere" – the civic space open to citizens for rational discourse without the intrusion of state bureaucracy or social class.[7] To be sure, the "state" was present to channel the public debate in Richmond, and social class still counted heavily in opinion making.

---

[5] For the account of the young girl's story entitled "Magnetism of Aaron Burr," see *Omaha World Herald* (published as *Sunday World Herald*), Jan. 22, 1905, Vol. XLIII; Issue 114; p. 23. Omaha, Nebraska.

[6] Beveridge, *Marshall,* 3: 441, quoting Edmund Randolph.

[7] Jürgen Habermas. *The Structural Transformation of the Public Sphere: An Inquiry Into a Category of Bourgeois Society* (Cambridge, MA, 1989).

Aaron Burr

Even so, when the people in Richmond, rich and poor and all stops in between, debated the latest article on the trial in the *Enquirer,* when they crowded round to hear street-corner orators like young Andrew Jackson defend Burr and assail Jefferson, when they argued about the meaning of treason or the character of Aaron Burr, when they compared the bombast of Martin to the eloquence of Wirt – when they did all these things freely and voluntarily and with gusto, they were educating themselves to be citizens of the new nation. The grand jurors were part of the scene, too, which was fitting and proper since it was their duty to speak for the sovereign people.

The catalytic focus of this civic education project in Richmond was the enigmatic figure of Aaron Burr. It was not just his notoriety as the killer of Hamilton, nor the mystery of his western "conspiracy" that generated debate. It was also the fact that he appeared to represent virtue gone wrong: a Lucifer-like inversion of republicanism itself, one rooted not in public service but rather in an unrestrained, unapologetic pursuit of personal wealth and glory. How much Burr was really different from many others of his class in this regard is a good question, but he was perceived to be not just a traitor to the republic but a challenge to all it stood for. The trial was Burr's chance to prove otherwise: to the nation, to the spectators in the House of Delegates, and most importantly, to John Marshall and the jurors who would decide his fate. Whatever else it was, the Burr treason trial was also a moment of republican reckoning.

Burr as Master Strategist

The adage that a man who tries his own case has a fool for a client was decidedly not true for Aaron Burr. The absence of a printed edition of Burr's legal papers makes it difficult to document his professional career with precision, but there is no doubt that he was one of New York's leading lawyers. He was not a lawyer's lawyer, not a master of common-law pleading, not a source of arcane legal wisdom, but like John Marshall, he knew what he needed to know and had a reputation for getting the job done. Unlike Marshall, whose practice had been almost exclusively appellate, Burr excelled as a trial lawyer, with a special gift for parsing complex factual situations, weighing evidence, and most of all for persuading juries by the force of his well-cultivated courtroom persona. These professional qualities served him well in Richmond.[8]

In addition to being a seasoned trial lawyer and a savvy politician, there were other reasons that Burr was uniquely qualified to manage his own defense. To start with, it was his own life that was on the line – a fact that concentrated his mind wonderfully. Also, Burr was the only lawyer in the courtroom who really knew what Burr the western adventurer had been up to. While Burr left no written record of his litigation strategy, it seems clear from the proceedings that he was the master strategist. Indeed, according to Harman Blennerhassett, who followed the trial closely while awaiting his own day in court, Burr felt free to alter "the notes of his counsel." He said of Burr that he "for the most

[8] Lomask, *Burr*, 1: ch. 5, especially the discussion of Burr's performance in *People v. Weeks* (1800), a case that has many of the same challenges as his own trial.

Benjamin Gaines Botts

part marks out the course they pursue on his defense."[9] It is a good guess too that from the very beginning Burr planned his enterprise in the Southwest with a lawyer's knowledge of what the law allowed – or what someone who knew the law could get away with.

In addition to knowing the legal landscape better than anyone, Burr also had knowledge about Jefferson's mode of operation – and that was useful knowledge since the president was directing traffic in Richmond. Marshall

[9] Blennerhassett's Private Journal, Aug. 19, 1807, in William H. Safford, *The Blennerhassett Papers, Embodying the Private Journal of Harman Blennerhassett* (Cincinnati, 1864), 342. [Hereafter Safford, *Blennerhassett Papers*].

Edmund Randolph

was harder to figure, however, because he was not given to showing his hand; in this regard he resembled Burr himself. The bad news for Burr was that Marshall was a Federalist who considered Hamilton a great man, and who greatly feared the new political party system that Burr helped create. The good news for Burr was that Marshall distrusted Jefferson as much as he did. It counted for something – a great deal perhaps – that unlike Jefferson, Burr and Marshall were comrades-at-arms during the Revolution. For Marshall there was a strong presumption that soldiers who fought for the nation – Marshall and Burr wintered with Washington at Valley Forge and shared the field at the battles of Monmouth Courthouse and Brandywine – would not set out to destroy what they fought to create.

Luther Martin

Burr's first strategic decision was to choose his defense team. Not surprisingly, all of them had serious doubts about Jefferson and his administration, and all were either friends or admirers of John Marshall. All of them, excepting Burr and Luther Martin, were also Virginians either by birth or adoption – which made sense since Virginia lawyers were at home with Virginia juries; and since, according to Section

John Wickham

29 of the Judiciary Act of 1789, Virginia law governed federal trial procedure.

Each of his co-counsel also had something special to offer. Edmund Randolph – governor of Virginia, framer of the Constitution, and U. S. Attorney General and Secretary of State in Washington's administration – was the oldest and most widely known of Burr's lawyers. True to his social status and reputation as a statesman, Randolph was also inclined to pomposity. Blennerhassett classified him as a warm Democrat, but he was above rank partisan politics, a fact that made his harsh criticism of the government's case more telling.[10] According to Blennerhassett, Randolph's effectiveness was only half of what it once was, but even so his arguments at Richmond were marked by learning and gravitas.[11]

Charles Lee, like Randolph, was a longtime professional friend of Marshall's. He had been attorney general of the United States under

---

[10] Ibid., 278.
[11] Ibid., 399–400.

Washington and John Adams. Like Marshall, he was a Federalist with a record of opposing Jefferson – most notably in 1803 as sole counsel in *Marbury v. Madison,* and in 1805 as one of the lawyers who defended Justice Chase in his impeachment trial before the Senate. Lee was also one of the lawyers in the Bollman case, which meant that he knew the terrain and the players. For Marshall he had high regard and the feeling was mutual. Although his role in the Burr trial was limited, he added heft and reputation to the defense.

John Wickham was not an actor on the national stage by choice. He was, however, one of Virginia's finest lawyers with a command of English and American sources and a gift for logical analysis much like that of Marshall's. He could be intimidating, even arrogant, in dealing with opposing counsel, but his unique talents were widely acknowledged and admired by his fellow lawyers. Indeed, four years before facing Wickham in the Burr trial, Wirt praised him for his learning, his style, and for his tactical ability to choose his ground wisely – and to abandon it with "an astonishing versatility" when occasion demanded.[12] Congenial southern gentleman though he was – Wirt once referred to him as "the courtly Wickham" – he was also adept at throwing *ad hominem* punches when it served his cause.[13] Hay was his favorite target in the Burr trial but Wirt also took some hits, which Wirt then returned in kind.

The indisputable master of invective was neither Wickham nor Wirt, however, but Luther Martin of Maryland. Martin stepped onto the national stage as Maryland's representative to the Philadelphia Convention of 1787, first as a champion and then as an opponent of the Constitution. Talent and ambition carried him quickly to the head of the Maryland bar and for many years he served as state attorney general. In 1805 he joined Lee to defend Chase in the impeachment trial, and the two were together again in the Bollman trial. Martin hated Jefferson as much as he loved his friend Burr; with Burr's beautiful daughter Theodosia he was positively smitten. His prodigious law learning and total recall ("old law ledger" they called him), mixed with some down-home rhetoric and a few shots of brandy ("old brandy bottle" they also called him), provided some of the most intellectually impressive and dramatic moments of the drama-packed trial.

12 William Wirt, *The Letters of the British Spy* (Reprint with Introduction by Richard Beal Davis, Chapel Hill, 1970), 217–19; Wirt's essays appeared in the *Virginia Argus* in 1803 and in book form later that year.
13 Wirt to Judge Carr, April 7, 1816, in John P. Kennedy, *Memoirs of the Life of William Wirt* (2 vols., Philadelphia, 1849), 1: 406.

Benjamin Botts and John "Jack" Baker completed Burr's defense team. Botts, the youngest of Burr's lawyers, made up in legal agility and audacity what he lacked in age and reputation. Judging by his learned and feisty arguments in Richmond, he was destined for great things in the profession. Tragically, he died in the great Richmond theater fire of 1811 at the age of thirty-five. Baker was better known for his congeniality and sense of humor than for his lawyering – for "his influence out of doors," as Harman Blennerhassett quaintly put it.[14] Burr probably retained him because of his likely popularity with Virginian jurors (since he was a Democrat with "a good heart"), and perhaps to keep the other side from signing him up. A newly minted New York lawyer and future literary star named Washington Irving was also on hand, not to argue in court but to provide pro-Burr copy for his brother's New York newspaper.

The prosecution, with federal attorney Hay nominally in charge, was outmatched as well as outnumbered. As a stalwart supporter of Jefferson and soon to be son-in-law of James Monroe, Hay was closely connected to the state's Democratic-Republican establishment. He was also a close friend of John Randolph of Roanoke (who, after his break with the administration, was no longer a member in good standing). Hay was a competent lawyer with considerable experience in Virginia's federal circuit court, most notably as one of the lawyers who defended James Callender in his seditious libel trial in 1800. Hay's two pamphlets *On the Liberty of the Press* (1799 and 1803), inspired by the Federalist Sedition Act of 1798, advocated a definition of freedom of the press remarkably liberal for the time and far in advance of Jefferson himself.[15] As chief prosecutor in the Burr trial, however, Hay was out of his depth. Self-doubt made him hesitant, often apologetic, and especially sensitive to personal affronts from his more able opponents, which only invited them to ratchet up their insults. He became more despondent and more prone to mistakes as the trial wore on.

Unfortunately, Hay was not greatly aided by Alexander MacRae. Like Hay, he was an avid supporter of Jefferson and, as Lieutenant Governor of Virginia at the time of the trial, was expected to garner popular support for the prosecution. On rare occasions he found a groove, but according to Burr's son-in-law Joseph Alston, his performance was often "so flat, that it nearly cleared the house."[16] Caesar Rodney, President

---

[14] Safford, *Blennerhassett Papers*, 426.
[15] Leonard W. Levy, *Emergence of a Free Press* (Chicago, 2004), 311–15.
[16] As reported by Blennerhassett in Safford, *Blennerhassett Papers*, 360.

William Wirt

Jefferson's attorney general, made only one half-hearted, almost apologetic appearance for the prosecution before withdrawing entirely. The impression he left in his wake was that prosecuting Burr for treason was a doomed enterprise.

The government's mainstay, if one does not count the president, was William Wirt. Young, handsome, ambitious and brilliant, Wirt at thirty-five already displayed those qualities of forensic greatness that would carry him to the top of the United States Supreme Court bar, a place of distinction he clearly coveted and very much deserved. Born in Maryland, he studied law in Virginia and became a passionate champion of the Old Dominion, though not of the radical states rights element that would soon gain control of Virginia. As the trial wore on and Hay wore down, Wirt emerged as the government's answer to Wickham and Martin. Where Martin went at it hammer-and-tong with spit flying (literally), Wirt's delivery, as befit a diligent student of Hugh Blair's famous book on rhetoric, was self-consciously measured, ornate and smooth as silk. No lawyer at Richmond was more adept at playing to the crowd or the jury. He was more professional than partisan, but he was partisan nonetheless. He took the job to please the president, and also with an eye on making a name for himself. Wirt was essentially a kind, humorous, and companionable gentleman, but he relished the competition for distinction that was so much a part of Virginia's legal culture at the time.[17] For him, John Wickham was the man to beat.

Working against that prospect was the fact that Wirt and Hay were stuck with the case Jefferson handed them, which meant that they were stuck with James Wilkinson as their chief witness. Their main strength, another gift from the president, was that most everyone in the country, and certainly the partisan crowd in Marshall's courtroom, thought that Burr deserved to hang.

"A Piece of Epic Action"

Given the importance of public opinion, it was inevitable that Burr's trial often resembled a theatrical performance, a "piece of epic action," in Wickham's words, or a bad "Melo-Drama," as the pro-administration *Virginia Argus* called it. If there is any doubt that both sides played to the gallery, one has only to note the innumerable references to public opinion in the trial transcript.

C. W. Jefferys's vivid painting of the trial tells the same story. In his rendition, the hall of the House of Delegates resembled a makeshift Elizabethan theater where the spectators were all but inseparable from the lawyer-actors in the pit. Chief Justice Marshall is a barely distinguishable figure in the distant background. At the center of the painting is an impassioned lawyer haranguing the jury and the spectators; perhaps he is Wickham praising Burr seated on his right, or maybe it is Wirt delivering his famous depiction of Burr as the serpent in the republican Garden of Eden. We do not see the sand boxes that were installed to catch the flying tobacco juice, but we can feel the ambient energy of the crowd. To harness that energy to their cause was the challenge facing both sides; for Burr it was a matter of life or death.

---

[17] Kennedy, *Memoirs of Wirt*, 1: 348–9.

English history is replete with examples of governmental manipulation of public opinion in order to shape the outcome of state trials. Jefferson, as we have seen, had peculiar reasons for following suit. For the defense to strike back, however, as Burr and his lawyers did at Richmond, appeared to signal a new departure in the "noble science of defense," to use William Wirt's reference to the tactics of his opponents.[18] In any case, theatrical persuasion was a key element of Burr's strategy and that of the government as well. Educating the public, as Wirt emphasized in his *Letters of the British Spy*, required lawyers to master the art of fine speaking. Written first as a series of essays in the *Virginia Argus,* Wirt's slim volume challenged a new generation of Virginians to reverse their state's declining influence in the affairs of the nation; not surprisingly, Wirt looked to his own profession, and of course to himself, to lead the way. Among those singled out as model republican lawyers were several men who would figure prominently in the Burr trial.

Heading the list was Chief Justice John Marshall, but Wickham and Randolph were also prominently mentioned. Wirt praised Wickham as the best all-around lawyer "at the bar of Virginia," although he also tossed in a couple of barbs, which Wickham apparently noted with some annoyance. Randolph on the other hand took a drubbing, all the more hurtful because of his much cherished reputation, and also because Wirt's criticism appeared to be well founded. Randolph carried his bruised ego and a desire for retribution into the Burr trial. Because Wirt's essays were widely read, and because they emphasized the oratorical qualities of advocacy, they were, without his knowing it, advance billing for the adversarial fireworks in Marshall's courtroom in which he himself would star.[19]

Burr of course was most interested in a favorable verdict, not in making a reputation for himself. But he knew from his experience in New York, and from his experience with federal grand juries in Kentucky and the Mississippi Territory, that appearance, even play-acting, counted heavily with juries. Burr was a genius at presenting himself. As he once boasted to his daughter Theodosia, he could even "play the fool" when the situation demanded, adding, "No one can do it better."[20]

---

[18] Robertson, *Reports*, 2: 57–58. Wirt was referring specifically to the defense's motion to suppress all evidence not relating to the levying of war on Blennerhassett's island.

[19] Chapter 7 in Wirt's *Letters of the British Spy* treats Marshall, Randolph and Wickham.

[20] [Burr] *The Private Journal of Aaron Burr* (2 vols., Rochester, NY, 1902), 2: 440.

Theodosia Burr

In Richmond, Burr played the innocent but unbowed victim of Jefferson's wrath. When Theodosia planned to join him in Richmond, he coached her about the supporting role she was expected to play. "I beg and expect it of you," he wrote on June 24, 1807, "that you will conduct yourself as becomes my daughter, and that you manifest no signs of weakness or alarm." And again on July 6, 1807: "Remember, no agitations, no complaints, no fears or anxieties on the road [to Richmond], or I renounce thee." Theodosia got the message and performed her part brilliantly;[21] with such a noble daughter it was hard to think of the father as the despicable traitor he was charged with being.

Toward the end of the trial, Burr became increasingly irritable and depressed, but for the most part he never deviated from the character he

[21] Mark Van Doren, ed., *Correspondence of Aaron Burr and His Daughter Theodosia* (New York, 1929), 221, 224.

wished to present to the public and the court, "unshaken," Washington Irving observed, in "his serenity and self-possession." Burr was clearly in command, but his strategy was to let his lawyers do most of the talking and most of the heavy legal lifting. By remaining in the background, he thereby dramatized those decisive moments when he stepped into the spotlight. As an actor and legal strategist Burr was impeccable.

The array of legal talent in the Burr trial was impressive. Here were Virginia's finest lawyers, and Maryland's, too. The president and the chief justice were both trained in the law, and so were some key members of the grand jury and the trial jury when they were finally sworn. The only real outsider was Burr. The key players knew they were being watched and judged – by the "the jury, this audience and all the world," as Randolph dramatically proclaimed. Almost certainly counsel on both sides were familiar with Wirt's essays touting the unique responsibilities of republican lawyers.

They also knew one another – strengths, weaknesses, virtues, warts and all. Most had crossed professional swords and had been pegged in the professional pecking order based on proven ability or the lack thereof. Richmond lawyers moved in the same social circles too, and Wickham, Botts, and MacRae, along with Marshall, were in fact neighbors in the "Court End" of town.[22] Civility prevailed at the outset, but as the trial wore on tempers frayed and egos showed. When Wickham roughed up Hay, Hay took it as a personal affront and lashed out. When Luther Martin got bombastic and abusive, opposing counsel ridiculed him as a Maryland interloper, and gave him a dose of his own medicine. Lawyers on both sides, young, old, aspiring and established, played to the crowd and then blamed each other for doing so.

Party passions in Virginia greatly intensified the clash of professional egos. Burr of course was the catalyst and his presence, after Jefferson branded him as a traitor, was enough to mobilize many patriotic Virginians. When the Federalists took up Burr's cause, as they did after Jefferson expelled him from his party, partisan warfare assumed a deeper ideological cast. It may have been true, as Marshall said, that Federalism in Virginia was nearly dead – a "small & oppressed minority." Nevertheless, Federalism, even in its moribund state, stood for everything the party of Jefferson hated. And this was particularly true when it came to the federal judiciary, and most especially true when it came to Federalist Supreme Court justices on circuit who presumed to

[22] Norma Lois Peterson, *Littleton Waller Tazewell* (Charlottesville, 1983), 11.

tell Virginian lawyers how to practice Virginia law. A case in point, one that threatened to haunt Marshall in 1807, was the sedition trial of James Callender at the May term in 1800 of the federal circuit court in Richmond, Justice Samuel Chase presiding.

On the face of it there was little similarity between Burr who was charged with plotting secession, and Callender, who was charged with publishing scurrilous articles about President Adams in violation of the Sedition Act of 1798. Several things, however, made the Callender case relevant. One thing concerned the authority of the trial jury to rule on the constitutionality of the Sedition Act. Not only did Chase deny the jury this authority, but he even prohibited Callender's lawyers from arguing the question. When Wirt persisted, Chase called him a "young gentleman" and ordered him to sit down. Chase also dismissed several of Hay's arguments out of hand.[23]

Chase's most damning error in the eyes of Virginia's Republican law-yers – one that figured in his impeachment in 1805 and prefigured Marshall's decision on evidence in the Burr trial – occurred when he prohibited John Taylor of Caroline from testifying on the grounds that because his testimony was relevant to only one of the several charges against Callender, it was likely to prejudice the jurors regarding the remaining charges. Chase then proceeded to prejudice them himself by didactic instructions that all but determined the jury's decision to convict, which it dutifully did.

Before it was over, Callender's lawyers, including Wirt and Hay, in a fine bit of legal theater, picked up their papers and stormed out in pro-test. Chase departed Richmond as public enemy number one. Not sur-prisingly, many inveterate court-haters feared that Burr's trial would be a reprise of Callender's, with Marshall playing the role of villain.

Marshall of course was not Chase. Wirt himself made the point in his *British Spy* essay. John Randolph was even more forceful during Chase's impeachment trial, when he damned Chase's behavior in the Callender trial by contrasting it with Marshall's fairness and integrity as a trial judge.[24] Still, for many, Marshall's Federalism was reason enough to

[23] For an incisive analysis of the Callender case and of Justice Chase's confrontation with Virginia lawyers and Virginia legal culture, see Stephen B. Presser, *The Original Misunderstanding: The English, the Americans and the Dialectic of Federalist Jurisprudence* (Durham, NC, 1991), ch. 8.

[24] James F. Simon, *What Kind of a Nation: Thomas Jefferson, John Marshall, and the Epic Struggle to Create a United States* (New York, 2002), 210–11; Randolph com-pared Chase in Callender to Marshall on circuit in a capital felony case involving Thomas Logwood charged with counterfeiting.

doubt his impartiality, and on top of that were his opinions in *Marbury* and *Bollman*. It can hardly be doubted that the president's loyal followers in Richmond and elsewhere were hoping that Hay and company would make Marshall atone for Chase's sins, especially if doing so would hang a villain like Burr. Marshall understood, as he confessed to Richard Peters, that by "obeying the public will instead of the public law" he could not only make it "less serious" to himself, but also dampen down Jefferson's campaign to humble the Supreme Court.[25]

Burr's Grand Juries: Some Early Lessons

Reading the arguments of counsel in the legal proceedings connected with the "conspiracy" reminds one of how much American lawyers were still indebted to the English legal inheritance, and how readily they deviated from it when necessity called. The institution of the grand jury, perhaps the most venerable of Anglo-American legal institutions, was a case in point. As with the law itself, American circumstances had by 1807 already left their mark. In England grand juries, like the common-law courts themselves, made up a part of the King's administrative system. In the long struggle leading to the break with England and during the Revolution itself the grand jury, now backed by the authority of the sovereign people, was celebrated as the first line of defense against governmental tyranny.

Fifteen years of experience under the new government, however, had modified this idealistic picture considerably, particularly for veteran trial lawyers like those in the Burr trial. For one thing, the grand jury process was complicated by the constitutional settlement itself, notably by the absence of a guarantee of the right of indictment by grand jury in the original document. The Fifth Amendment, which was ratified in late 1791, rectified this omission by providing, "No person shall be held to answer for a capital, or otherwise infamous crime, unless on a presentment or indictment of a Grand Jury." Section 29 of the Judiciary Act of 1789 confused the issue, however, by providing that the grand jury process in the federal courts (like Marshall's in Richmond) should, in the absence of specific congressional legislation, follow that of the state in which the trial took place. Because state laws governing juries were often unsettled, and because they varied from one state to another, lawyers and judges had to settle matters on the spot. As prosecutions for the

---

[25] Marshall to Richard Peters, Nov. 23, 1807, Hobson, *Papers of Marshall*, 7: 165.

violation of the Sedition Act of 1798 proved, federal prosecutors backed by Supreme Court justices on circuit were hard for juries to resist.

As a seasoned trial lawyer, Burr knew all about the unpredictable (and thus malleable) behavior of juries. The Callender trial drove home the same lesson too, as did the federal government's successful prosecution of other cases under the Sedition Act. More directly relevant for Burr, however, was his personal experience with federal grand juries in Kentucky in early November 1806, and in the Mississippi Territory in early February 1807.

In Kentucky, Burr was pursued by a crusading federal attorney named Joseph Hamilton Daveiss, who hated Burr for killing his namesake and hated Jefferson for being a democrat. By charging Burr with high misdemeanor (for planning to attack Spanish forces in Mexico) and intimating treasonable intent to foment disunion, Daveiss could get back at Burr and also indirectly make the Federalist case that Jefferson was a feckless leader who had failed to act decisively against Burr's threat to the Union.

Daveiss's first move was to request a warrant from federal district judge Harry Innes ordering Burr to appear before a grand jury. Innes, who was allied with the Democratic-Republicans in Kentucky, correctly refused to issue the warrant, on the grounds that it was based solely on hearsay evidence.[26] On hearing that he had been charged, however, Burr voluntarily returned to Frankfort and insisted on a grand jury hearing to clear his name. This grand jury had to be dismissed because Daveiss's chief witness failed to appear. Daveiss also weakened his case by relying heavily on the sensationalist and unsubstantiated attack on Burr in the Frankfort *Western World,* a Federalist newspaper in which he had a personal interest. Nor did it help Daveiss's cause that his associate in the *Western World* was Humphrey Marshall, a cousin and also a brother-in-law of the chief justice.[27] It should also be noted that the editors of the *Western World,* John Wood and Joseph Street, later disavowed their accusations of Burr and proclaimed his innocence.[28]

[26] For an analysis of the exchange between Daveiss and Judge Innes regarding Burr, see Mary K. Tachau, *Federal Courts in the Early Republic: Kentucky 1789–1816* (Princeton, 1978), 138–45.

[27] In addition to Tachau's *Federal Courts,* I have consulted the account of the Kentucky proceedings in Lomask, *Burr,* 2: 142–49. Regarding the concerted activities of the Marshall clan, see Blennerhassett's statement in Safford, *Blennerhassett Papers,* 465–6.

[28] For Wood's denunciation of Daveiss and "the whole Marshall party" in Kentucky, see Safford, *Blennerhassett Papers,* 372.

After his grand jury victory, Burr assumed that the matter was over, only to be informed that Daveiss planned to present him a second time. Although he could have easily proceeded down river, Burr returned again, this time in the company of a promising young lawyer-politician by the name of Henry Clay. Daveiss's chief witness again failed to appear, and to cover his mistake, Daveiss insisted on interrogating the remaining witnesses in the privacy of the grand jury room, in effect turning the grand jury into a trial jury without the presence of defense lawyers.[29]

Daveiss's move was defeated and with it his effort to get an indictment. Not only did the grand jury fail to indict, but the citizens of Frankfort threw a lavish celebration in Burr's honor. The following day the Frankfort *Palladium* praised Burr for "the calmness, moderation, and firmness which have characterized him through life."[30] Being cool under fire, projecting an image of innocence and confidence – and choosing the best local lawyer that money could buy or fame and friendship could entice – were some of the lessons Burr took to Richmond.

When Burr appeared before the federal grand jury in the Mississippi Territory in early February 1807, his situation had changed and so had the lessons to be learned. By then news of the president's proclamation (along with the articles in the *Western World*) had turned public opinion strongly against him. Wilkinson, now in control of New Orleans, had put a price on Burr's head and dispatched agents to arrest him. His credit was gone and many of his followers as well. Thanks to the president, the charge against Burr in the territorial court was not high misdemeanor (as it had been in Frankfort) but high treason. To add to his woes, federal judge Thomas Rodney (the father of Caesar Rodney, Jefferson's attorney general) was convinced by the president's proclamation that Burr was a danger to the Union. His charge to the grand jury was all but an explicit order to indict.[31]

Fortunately for Burr the grand jury was not in an obedient mood. Not only did the jurors refuse to bring in a true bill, as Rodney ordered them to do, but they also declared, "after due investigation" that Aaron Burr

---

[29] As Mary Tachau notes in *Federal Courts*, 143, the interrogation of witnesses before the grand jury by the prosecution is now common practice in England and the United States, but it was not permitted, or at least was not common practice, during this period. The argument between Daveiss and Henry Clay over the right of the prosecution to interrogate witnesses before the grand jury is reported in the *Western World*, Dec. 18, 1806.

[30] *Palladium* of Nov. 13, 1806 as cited in Lomask, *Burr*, 2: 145.

[31] Lomask, *Burr*, 2: 216–18.

"has not been guilty of any crime or misdemeanor against the laws of the United States, or of this Territory, or given any just occasion for the alarm or inquietude to the good people of this Territory." And even more forcefully, they berated acting governor of the Territory, Cowles Meade, for "unnecessarily" taking military action against Burr and his property when "no resistance had been made to the civil authorities." Finally, for good measure, the jurors condemned Wilkinson's tyrannous behavior in New Orleans and suggested to the president that he should bear some responsibility for his own law-breaking activities, which threatened to "sap the vitals of our political existence."[32]

As recollected from the Richmond jail, these victories might have bolstered Burr's spirits. By contrast, it surely occurred to him and his lawyers that grand juries composed of frontiersmen who hated Spain and distrusted eastern politicians were vastly different from the one in Richmond that would likely be composed of well-informed Virginia gentleman who instinctively distrusted New Yorkers. The jury independence that worked for him in Kentucky and Mississippi could easily work against him in Jefferson's Virginia.

Also to be calculated was the unpredictable power relationship between judge and jury. And here the behavior of Judge Rodney was a cautionary tale. Instead of heeding his grand jury, Rodney gave the jurors an arrogant law-and-order dressing down for refusing to indict a scoundrel like Burr, as the president wanted them to do. He then took matters into his own hands by ordering Burr's detention – and after he escaped, his arrest. John Marshall was not, of course, Thomas Rodney; nonetheless, the power that judges had over juries, no less than the unpredictable behavior of juries themselves, obviously could hurt as well as help Burr.

So it was that lawyers in Richmond, defense and prosecution alike, approached the grand jury hearings with a sense of urgency engendered by past experience. By Virginia law, the grand jury panel consisted of twenty-four freeholders to be summoned by the federal marshal, from which sixteen would finally be chosen. No one knew what the final shakedown would be, but the jurors, whoever they were, were certain to feel the pressure of the anti-Burr sentiment swirling about in Richmond. The prosecution aimed to capitalize on this sentiment, which meant pressing home the heinous nature of Burr's crime and the heinous nature of Burr himself. Burr and his lawyers had to slow down the government's

---

[32] Ibid., 217–18.

juggernaut, or at the very least, establish a toehold of doubt in the minds of Burr-haters.

Accordingly, opinion-shaping issues of law and character surfaced during arraignment when Burr appeared before Marshall in the Eagle Tavern on March 30. Hay's first move, as noted above, was to request that all proceedings be held in the hall of the House of Delegates in order to accommodate the crowds, a sure indication that mobilizing public opinion was high on his agenda. Hay put Burr's honor on the line too when he argued that the New Yorker would flee from "justice" if bail were not sufficiently high.

Wickham and Randolph responded by attacking Wilkinson's affidavit as "vague, weak, and unsatisfactory" and "abounding in crudities and absurdities." Striking what would become a dominant theme, they presented Burr as an innocent victim of executive power, a law-abiding man of honor without friends in a hostile territory. In narrating the events that brought him to Richmond, Burr spoke passionately to the same point.[33]

Attorney General Rodney for the prosecution then addressed "the numerous and attentive audience" in a speech that seemed to support Burr. Rodney was "embarrassed" to charge a former vice president with treason – a gentleman "esteemed for his transcendent talents, and whom he once considered as his friend, and treated as such in his own house…" The attorney general was confident that Burr would get a fair trial, but he also acknowledged that the government had thus far failed to produce evidence that war had actually been levied. If Burr should be acquitted, he concluded, "it would give no man more heartfelt pleasure than himself."[34] Rodney clearly did not want blood, which may explain why this was his one and only appearance for the prosecution.

On April 1, Marshall brought the commitment phase to a close. After vetting the affidavits of Wilkinson and Eaton, he ruled, ominously for the prosecution, that after several months they had failed to produce sufficient evidence that war had actually been levied. Accordingly, he committed Burr for high misdemeanor only, which of course raised the question of bail, which reintroduced the question of Burr's character.[35] Hay started the fracas by insisting that the $10,000 suggested by Marshall was not enough, noting sardonically that "certain gentlemen of

[33] Robertson, *Reports*, 1: 4–8.
[34] Ibid., 1: 3, 10.
[35] Ibid., 1: 11–18.

this place" had already stepped forth to keep him "from the humiliation of an imprisonment."[36] Wickham did not take kindly to "the spirit" of Hay's insinuations, claiming that "gentlemen of great respectability" would gladly come to the aid of "a gentlemen in distress" but for the fear that they might be branded "enemies of their country" if they did so."[37]

Hay retorted that a hundred thousand dollars would be easy for Burr to raise, intimating that a large sum might be needed to secure his presence if the charge of treason were brought, apparently forgetting that treason was not a bailable offense. Burr answered Hay by reminding the court and the packed house that he could not make bail himself because the president by executive order had ordered the seizure of all his property.[38] The matter of bail was settled when Burr's fellow counsel vouched for his character by coming up with $10,000.

Grand jury selection began on Friday, May 22. Taking nothing for granted and trusting no one, Burr nit-picked every step of the way, starting with the technical misstep made in summoning the panel. What bothered him was that the marshal struck one name from the original list of twenty-four and substituted another. This switch prompted both sides to display their learning on the disputed point in Virginia law. Botts for the defense said he did not mean to impugn "the honourable character" of Major Joseph Scott, the federal marshal in charge of selecting the panel, but did so anyway. Wickham said the same and did the same. When Scott rose to defend his reputation, Wickham berated him again for the interruption.

Marshall finally intervened to cool tempers, which permitted Burr to ask the question that was really on his mind: if the marshal struck one juror and substituted another, who was the other and why was the first juror struck? When it was established that no sinister motives were involved, Burr, with a nudge from Marshall, acquiesced in the change.[39]

Burr then demanded and got the right to challenge the panel for favor – a process that quickly confirmed the partisan nature of the jury pool. William Giles was the first to be struck, for the obvious reason that he had already gone on record as to Burr's guilt. At Hay's suggestion, Giles agreed to withdraw but not before defending his "public conduct" and predicting that the "true character" of Burr's transactions and Burr

---

[36] Ibid., 13.
[37] Ibid., 19.
[38] Ibid., 20.
[39] Ibid, 1: 31–38.

himself would be exposed. Marshall permitted Giles to excuse himself and was no doubt secretly relieved, since he was Jefferson's point man in the Senate where he spearheaded the movement to suspend the writ of habeas corpus. Giles was also one of the Marshall Court's most vociferous critics.[40]

Wilson C. Nicholas, another loyal Jeffersonian, also agreed to withdraw. After apologizing for shirking his patriotic duty, he claimed that Burr and his supporters would have waged a clandestine campaign to destroy him had he not withdrawn. How they would have done this, he did not say. Like the other honor-obsessed gentlemen on the Richmond stage, Nicholas begged the crowd to judge his reputation and character "on the general tenor of my life."[41] For some reason, he seemed to think that he himself was on trial. Dr. William Foushee, one of Richmond's most respected public citizens, was also excused after admitting that his mind was irrevocably settled as to Burr's guilt.

Burr thus succeeded in getting rid of two troublemakers, but not before they succeeded in maligning his character. With Major Joseph Eggleston he recouped some lost ground. Eggleston wanted off the panel and seemed certain to get his wish, since he admitted that he thought Burr guilty of treason and had "expressed his opinion in public company." When queried by Marshall, however, he also admitted that further evidence might change his mind.[42]

Burr's response was good theater and great psychology. He would gladly accept Eggleston, he said, even though he was predisposed against him. Why? Because he was candid gentleman enough to admit his biases and fair enough to keep an open mind. Eggleston was the best he could hope for, but he also asked the court "to notice, from the scene before us, how many attempts have been made to prejudge my cause." Marshall refused to excuse Eggleston.[43]

One of the last to be named was John Randolph of Roanoke. Marshall designated him foreman, which prompted Randolph to make an uncharacteristically brief speech stating that he did not wish to serve because he had a "strong prepossession" as to Burr's guilt. He also had serious doubts about Jefferson, which Marshall no doubt appreciated. Since Randolph had not gone public with his feelings about Burr, and since he

[40] Ibid. 40–41.
[41] Ibid., 42.
[42] Ibid., 43–44.
[43] Ibid., 44.

admitted that further evidence might change his mind, Marshall refused to excuse him.[44] After a few desultory words from counsel, the grand jury panel of sixteen, with Randolph as foreman, was sworn. Marshall charged them regarding "the nature of treason, and the testimony requisite to prove it."[45]

In his charge to the grand jury of the circuit court for the district of Pennsylvania in 1800, Justice Samuel Chase bemoaned the fact "that persons in good Circumstances, and of some Education" were reluctant to serve as grand jurors.[46] Such was not the case in Burr's trial. The "people's panel" did not represent a cross section of the people of Virginia, but it did represent a cross section of the social, professional elite that had monopolized state and national offices in Virginia for decades. Several were prosperous planters and slaveholders and all of them appeared to be men of substantial property. John Ambler, known as "The Duke," was one of the richest men in Virginia, with connections by blood and association to Virginia's leading families. He was a close friend and business associate of Marshall, whose wife Polly was Ambler's cousin and whose sister Lucy married Ambler after the death of his wife in 1787.[47]

Significantly, five of the jurors were lawyers or had once studied law. The most prominent of these was Littleton W. Tazewell, who studied law under John Wickham and who remained his lifelong friend. In the course of his long career Tazewell served in the Virginia legislature and in Congress, taking Marshall's place in 1798 when Marshall became Adams's Secretary of State. He later served as governor and U.S. senator. On the Richmond grand jury, the well-placed Tazewell found himself in "a circle of intimates" that included James Barbour, Joseph C. Cabell, John Mercer, Robert B. Taylor, John Ambler, and foreman John Randolph. Wirt and Wickham, the two main adversaries in the trial, were also two of Tazewell's closest friends; Hay too was a longtime acquaintance. As a grand juror, Tazewell approached the case with an open mind, but became progressively distressed by Wilkinson's contradictory testimony and even more so by Jefferson's continued reliance on his general.[48]

---

[44] Ibid., 44.
[45] Ibid., 46.
[46] Chase's charge is found in Maeva Marcus, ed., *The Documentary History of the Supreme Court of the United States* (New York, 1990), 3: 409.
[47] Jean Edward Smith, *John Marshall: Definer of a Nation* (New York, 1996), 101.
[48] See Peterson, *Littleton Waller Tazewell*, 43–48.

Several other jurors had distinguished records of public service, and several also had connections with Jefferson's party, although none appeared to be rabidly partisan. Judging from the voir dire interrogations, they had followed the controversy surrounding Burr's activities, and on the basis of what they read and heard, were predisposed against him. Several, including John Randolph, also acknowledged that they would change their opinions if the evidence warranted it.

Randolph was a formidable presence on this formidable panel. As Jefferson's Speaker of the House and later as leader of the Tertium Quid faction that split from the administration, he was the only member of the panel with a national reputation. Although Randolph was not a practicing lawyer, he had studied law briefly with none other than his cousin Edmund Randolph.[49] While not given to sustained, systematic thought, as his mismanagement of Chase's impeachment trial revealed, Randolph possessed a nimble mind and an incomparable command of invective. He was a states rights purist who admired Marshall as much personally as he disliked his constitutional philosophy. He was also a friend of George Hay, an admirer of John Wickham, and a relative of both Marshall and Jefferson. The trial would deepen his friendship with the chief justice and hurry the final break with Jefferson. Randolph had little respect for Burr, whom he referred to once as "this troublesome little man."[50] Nonetheless he perceived Wilkinson to be a charlatan and a scoundrel, and because Wilkinson was to be the government's primary witness, Randolph's role as foreman of the grand jury was a plus for Burr.

Theater as Legal Strategy

Late in the trial, Luther Martin mockingly referred to the whole thing as "Much Ado about Nothing." Looking at the period between the swearing in of the grand jury on May 22 and its indictment of Burr on June 24 – a period covering 260 pages in Robertson's *Reports* – one might be tempted to agree. What gave the period a sense of unreality was the fact that a sworn grand jury could not get on with its work, because the prosecution refused to present any of their witnesses until Wilkinson arrived to testify. The problem was that Hay had no way of knowing

---

[49] Randolph showed no real zeal for the study of law, perhaps because his mentor showed no zeal for teaching it; Randolph left before finishing his apprenticeship. See Bruce, *John Randolph of Roanoke* 1: 74–75.

[50] Ibid., 301

when the general would arrive. Each time Wilkinson failed to appear as promised an apology and a new promise were required. Each additional promise raised the level of expectations and the heat of the rhetoric. Sensing Hay's dilemma, the defense lawyers, who had previously stalled the process with technical objections of their own, now demanded that Burr be given his constitutional right to a speedy trial.

Marshall was on the spot too, and confessed not knowing what to do with an idle grand jury. What he did was adjourn the jurors from June 3 to June 11, which prompted Washington Irving to observe that "hostilities" had been suspended so the jurors "might go home, see their wives, get their clothes washed, and flog their negroes."[51] What the jurors actually did with their time off is unclear, but since they were not sequestered, it is a good guess that they followed the proceedings in court even if they did not attend its open sessions.[52] What they heard from friends and neighbors that were present, and what they could have read in the *Enquirer,* was a unique mixture of law and theater featuring Jefferson, Burr, and Marshall.

Hay raised the curtain on the drama by asking the court to confine Burr on the charge of treason based on the "evidence formerly introduced, and on additional testimony to be now brought forward."[53] As opposing counsel were quick to point out, Hay's motion in essence asked Marshall to temporarily usurp the function of a sworn grand jury. It was also a clever stratagem. Not only did it buy some much needed time, but it also gave the government another opportunity to diminish Burr's character without formally presenting evidence to support their accusations.

Whether deliberate or not, Hay's motion put Marshall in the political hot seat. If he ruled to commit Burr, he would give credence to the government's contentions about his guilt and also his character. If he denied the motion, he would appear to be siding with Burr. This is in fact what Jefferson assumed he would do out of spite and what Wickham pleaded for him to do in the name of justice.

By treating Hay's motion as a procedural matter, Marshall escaped the dilemma as best he could. At the same time, he gave the government an unusually personal dressing-down for its shabby tactics noting, "The court perceives and regrets that the result of this [Hay's] motion may

---

[51] Washington Irving to Peter Irving, June 4, quoted in Schachner, *Burr,* 414.
[52] Marshall asked them to withdraw but there is no evidence of formal sequestration. Robertson, *Reports,* 1: 50.
[53] Ibid., 51.

be publications unfavourable to the justice, and to the right decision of the case." As regards the latter: "No man, feeling a correct sense of the importance which ought to be attached by all to a fair and impartial administration of justice, especially in criminal prosecutions, can view, without extreme solicitude, any attempt which may be made to prejudice the public judgment, and to try any person, not by the laws of his country and the testimony exhibited against him, but by the public feelings, which may be and often are artificially excited against the innocent, as well as the guilty."[54]

Jefferson no doubt read these words as a challenge (and a reprise of *Bollman* and *Marbury*), but Marshall avoided a direct confrontation by recognizing Hay's right to make his motion. The resulting debate opened the floodgates of abusive rhetoric. Botts fired the first volley for the defense with a law-packed, meandering lecture on the duties of the grand jury that Hay's motion would usurp; he then apologized to the court for being so long-winded.[55] Hay then explained that he wanted Burr confined so he would not flee, which of course he would do rather than confront the courageous and noble Wilkinson.

Wickham responded by denouncing Wilkinson, this time intimating that he was conspiring with the prosecution to stall the proceedings. Turning from the puppet to the puppet master, Wickham blasted the president for mobilizing "the press, from one end of the continent to the other" in order to excite prejudice against Burr.[56] "Should government, hereafter, wish to oppress any individual; to drag him from one end of the country to the other by a military force; to enlist the prejudices of the country against him; they will pursue the same course which has now been taken against Colonel Burr." He then demanded that Marshall "stand between the innocent [man] and his pursuers," that is to say, the president and his general.[57]

Wirt now rose to defend his colleague and bash Wickham. As for the latter's statement that Hay's presentation was "good poetry" but lousy law, Wirt replied: "It may be an episode, sir: if the gentleman pleases, he is at liberty to consider the whole trial as a piece of epic action, and to look forward to the appropriate catastrophe." Turning a bit "epic" himself, Wirt then accused Burr of shrinking from the evidence, a charge expressed in language that painted the colonel as a coward as well as a

---

[54] Ibid., 81.
[55] Ibid., 51–54.
[56] Ibid., 55–57.
[57] Ibid., 57–58.

traitor. And why he asked, should Burr "turn from defending himself to attack the administration?" And why should his lawyers attempt to "convert this judicial inquiry into a political question...between Thomas Jefferson and Aaron Burr"?[58]

Whether it was Burr's lawyers or Jefferson's involvement that made the case political is a good question, but clearly law and politics were inseparably connected. That connection deepened dramatically when, on June 9, Burr asked Marshall to issue a subpoena *duces tecum* to the president, ordering him to produce Wilkinson's "letter of the 21st October, with accompanying papers, and also authentic orders of the navy and war departments."[59]

Burr's motion mixed sound law with political savvy. On the simplest level, it built on commonly accepted state criminal procedure that allowed defendants access to information essential to their defense, a point even the prosecution conceded. Burr had good reason to think that Marshall would agree. However, even if Marshall did not agree, or even if the president refused to reply to the court's subpoena, the point was clear for all to see: that Burr was the innocent victim of a vindictive president. The matter of evidence was broached, too, which enabled the defense to savage Wilkinson, just as he was about to make his long-awaited appearance. And it worked, too. When Marshall issued the subpoena on June 13, he unavoidably moved into the president's line of fire, which meant that the chief justice and Burr were in the same boat. Useful company indeed.

The subpoena motion also dramatized the fact that the president himself was on trial. The man chosen to drive the point home was Luther Martin. The Marylander's style set him apart from the other two great lawyers in the trial: Wickham, who appeared to soar above the fray while being fully engaged in it, and Wirt, whose soaring rhetoric was always self-consciously proper. In contrast, Martin was down-home, rough-hewn, and unrestrained. He was also a passionate friend of Burr and his daughter Theodosia. Fresh from defending Justice Chase in the impeachment trial in 1805, he was an equally passionate hater of Jefferson. He was also a great trial lawyer, a street fighter with a copious legal mind and a quiver of poison arrows that he now let fly at Jefferson.

One of those arrows carried an American message delivered in a distinctive American idiom, the first of several more to come. The legality

---

[58] Ibid., 58–65.
[59] Ibid., 114.

of the subpoena motion, which Martin discussed with learned references to English authorities and American practice, was his segue to Jefferson's un-republican behavior. "Surely these gentlemen," he said, referring to Hay and company, "do not intend to represent the president as a kind of sovereign, or as a king of Great Britain. He is no more than a servant of the people."[60]

And what did this humble servant do? "He has assumed to himself the knowledge of the Supreme Being himself, and pretended to search the heart of my highly respected friend. He has proclaimed him a traitor in the face of that country, which has rewarded him. He has let slip the dogs of war, the hell-hounds of persecution, to hunt down my friend."[61]

So much for the author of the Declaration of Independence and the self-appointed defender of American liberties. As for James Wilkinson, the president's chief hell-hound: why shouldn't the defense have access to his letters to the president regarding Burr's alleged treachery? Perhaps the general was "not as pure as an angel." Before you buy his story – this to the grand jury and the assembled worthies – remember "that this man has already broken the constitution to support his violent measures; that he has already ground down the civil authorities into dust; and subjected all around him to a military despotism."[62] No wonder Jefferson dubbed Martin "an impudent federal bull-dog" and suggested to Hay that, "as *particeps criminis* with Burr," he might be prosecuted for "misprision of treason at least."[63]

In the debate over the subpoena, nearly everyone had something to say. Hay insisted that Burr's motion was intended to confuse the grand jury but promised the papers anyway, providing the defense could establish their relevance, which of course they could not do without first seeing them. Wirt brassily lectured Marshall on the intricacies of Virginia law concerning subpoenas and reminded one and all that Burr was on trial and not Jefferson.[64] He also insisted that he had no truck with "state secrets," while also insisting on the president's right to preserve them.

[60] Ibid., 127.
[61] Ibid., 128.
[62] Ibid., 129.
[63] Jefferson to Hay, June 19, 1807, Bergh, *Writings of Jefferson*, 11: 233–36, especially 235. To be *particeps criminis* means to be an accomplice in the crime; misprision of treason means having knowledge of treason and failing to report it to the proper authorities.
[64] Robertson, *Reports*, 1: 139.

Wirt wound up his bravura performance by accusing Burr's lawyers of playing to "bystanders" and to Marshall's prejudices by issuing "these perpetual philippics against the government." He wanted a fair trial, he claimed, but he also wanted the judges "for their own sakes" to "compel a decent respect to that government of which they themselves form a branch."[65] Unfortunately the horse was out of the barn, the horse being lawyer Martin's personal attack on the president. Marshall's critics took due notice of his failure to stop Martin. What they did not notice was his strenuous effort to persuade *both* sides to stop grandstanding and settle the matter of evidence by agreement.

The heated debate over the subpoena lasted four days and consumed sixty-five pages in Robertson's *Reports*. When Marshall finally ruled in favor of Burr's motion and issued the subpoena, Wirt and his colleagues concluded that the chief justice had given up all pretense of fairness.

Given Marshall's defiant justification of his authority to issue the subpoena, and his several personal jabs at Jefferson, it is easy to see why his critics might have thought the worst. The immediate issue in the subpoena debate, however, was not about Jefferson and Marshall, nor even about the constitutional meaning of separation of powers. Rather, the subpoena debate first and foremost concerned Burr's right to a fair trial – that is the right of the defense to know the evidence relied on by the prosecution so they could prepare their defense in a timely manner. What Burr demanded, in anticipation of Wilkinson's long-awaited personal appearance, was Wilkinson's letter of October 21 and the accompanying paper dated October 20 – the documents mentioned specifically by Jefferson in his public pronouncement of Burr's guilt on January 22, 1807.

It might seem surprising that Burr did not also request the original cipher letter in his motion for the subpoena. If Jefferson denied having the letter, it would look bad; if the letter were forthcoming it could be used to prove definitively Wilkinson's duplicitous efforts to cover up his own involvement in the conspiracy by falsely accusing Burr. The original letter, however, would also put Dayton directly on the firing line, which Burr was unwilling to do. It was also true that establishing Dayton's authorship of the letter would not help Burr all that much, since it could easily be argued, and perhaps proven, that he had told Dayton what to say to Wilkinson.[66]

---

[65] Ibid., 144–5.
[66] See Kline's account in *Political Correspondence of Burr*, 2: 986.

In any case, Wilkinson's role in doctoring the cipher letter would come up during his grand jury interrogation; so also would the contradictions between Wilkinson's testimony and that of Bollman, Swartwout and other witnesses.

The Grand Jurors Speak

The argument over the subpoena provided some lively theater. But the dramatic climax came with the long-awaited appearance of General Wilkinson and his face-off with Colonel Burr. Anticipation had been building with each postponement and with each newspaper account of the general's seemingly interminable progress from New Orleans to Richmond. He was, after all, the commander of the army, the hero who drove the Spanish from American territory, that is, if you believed his account. He was also the president's man and the prosecution's best hope. As Edmund Randolph sarcastically put it, "he is in reality the *Alpha* and *Omega* of the present prosecution" whose job was "to support by his deposition the *sing-song* and the ballads of treason and conspiracy, which we have heard delivered from one extremity of the continent to the other."[67]

The general made his grand entrance into Marshall's court on June 15, dressed to the nines in an ornate uniform, reputedly of his own design. Accounts of his confrontation with Burr differ widely. Writing to Jefferson, Wilkinson recounted, "my eyes darted a flash of indignation at the little traitor, on whom they continued fixed until I was called to the Book; – here, sir, I found my expectations verified – this lion-hearted, eagled-eyed Hero, jerking under the weight of conscious guilt, with haggard eyes in an effort to meet the indignant salutation of outraged honor; but it was in vain, his audacity failed him. He averted his face, grew pale, and affected passion to conceal his perturbation."[68]

Washington Irving told a different story: "Wilkinson strutted into court…swelling like a turkey-cock." Burr "did not take notice of him until the judge directed the clerk to swear General Wilkinson; at the mention of the name Burr turned his head, looked him full in the face with one of his piercing regards, swept his eye over his whole person from head to foot, as if to scan its dimensions, and then coolly resumed his former position, and went on conversing with his counsel as tranquilly as ever. The whole look was over in an instant; but it was an

---

[67] Robertson, *Reports*, 1: 155.
[68] Wilkinson to Jefferson, June 17, 1807, as quoted in Schachner, *Aaron Burr*, 420.

General James Wilkinson

admirable one. There was no appearance of study or constraint in it; no affectation of disdain or defiance; a slight expression of contempt played over his countenance."[69]

It is hard not to join Dumas Malone in choosing Irving's account as "the truer picture." David Robertson, who witnessed the encounter firsthand, however, split the difference, observing in his *Reports* that Wilkinson's "countenance was calm, dignified, and commanding; while that of colonel Burr was marked by haughty contempt."[70] The two persons

[69] Ibid.
[70] Robertson, *Reports*, 1: 197, asterisk note.

who did not split the difference regarding the general were Thomas Jefferson, who stuck by him (and was stuck *with* him) to the bitter end, and John Randolph, who held him in utter contempt. Unfortunately for Wilkinson, Randolph was foreman of the grand jury that had the responsibility of assessing his evidence, as well as his character.

After sitting in the wings for weeks, the jurors were thoroughly saturated with information. As well-informed gentlemen, several of whom were lawyers, the jurors were acquainted with Marshall's Bollman opinion, with its telling critique of Wilkinson's cipher letter. They also had a chance to ponder Marshall's rather confusing definition of treason in that case. Indeed, according to Blennerhassett, two members of the grand jury, after they were discharged, admitted that "they mistook the meaning of the Chief Justice Marshall's opinion as to what sort of acts amounted to treason," and probably would not have indicted Burr had they understood it correctly.[71] In addition, while waiting for the prosecution to present its witnesses, the jurors had ample opportunity to keep abreast of the ongoing proceedings in the court; and during the formal adjournment in June they no doubt got an earful from friends and neighbors.

When the grand jury finally went to work, it interrogated no fewer than twenty-nine witnesses, chief of whom were Wilkinson, Swartwout and Bollman.[72] The stipulations governing grand jury interrogation of the witnesses were debated in open court, starting with Bollman. As mentioned earlier, Bollman had already volunteered his account of Burr's expedition to Jefferson and Madison, an account that presented Burr as a patriot whose objective was to march against Spanish possessions in the Southwest in the event of war. In return for his candid statement, Jefferson promised Bollman that his account, recorded by James Madison at the president's request, would in no way be used against him in Richmond.

Thus Bollman's surprise when Hay offered him a presidential pardon for the crime of treason – which crime, by Bollman's account to Jefferson, no one committed. He refused Hay's offer with a simple: "No. I will not, sir."[73] A surreal debate followed on the question of whether, because he had been pardoned (even if he did not accept the pardon), Bollman could refuse to testify before the grand jury on grounds of self-incrimination.

[71] Entry of Aug. 8, 1807, Safford, *Blennerhassett Papers*, 314.
[72] Robertson, *Reports*, 1: 330.
[73] Ibid., 191.

Hay insisted that Bollman "could not possibly criminate himself" because the president's pardon "will completely exonerate him from all the penalties of the law." Martin responded that Bollman could not be expected to accept a pardon, which was an admission of guilt, for a crime he did not commit.[74]

Bollman was "sent up to the grand jury without any particular notification," but the debate exposed the fact that the president had granted a pardon simply to elicit testimony against Burr. Not discussed was the fact that Jefferson had reneged on his promise to Bollman that the information he had voluntarily given in good faith would not be used to charge him with any crime. Most likely the jurors discovered the truth during their own interrogation of Bollman. In any case, the president left Bollman twisting in the breeze. Or as Martin preferred to see it: "the man, who did so much to rescue the marquis la Fayette from his imprisonment" would not "abandon his honour through a fear of unjust persecution."[75]

On June 15, Wilkinson himself, "the alpha and the omega" of the prosecution, was sworn and sent to the grand jury, "with a notification that it would facilitate their inquiries if they would examine him immediately."[76] The "notification" was of little effect because of another prolonged debate over whether Wilkinson could, as Hay insisted, bring personal papers with him when addressing the grand jury, in order to prove that he was not involved in the conspiracy.

The defense's main objection, although it tended to get lost among the various contested points, was that allowing Wilkinson to bring the personal papers to the grand jury would permit him to use their contents not only to exonerate himself from involvement in the conspiracy, but also to convict Burr. At one point, Botts cheekily argued that if Hay's request regarding the papers were accepted, Jefferson himself – the other "zealous prosecutor" in the case – might introduce "very improper papers, which he might hope to convey to the multitude abroad, through the channel of the grand jury."[77]

Marshall's brief opinion of June 18 attempted to give something to both sides, but the paper in question – a letter in German from Burr's private secretary to Bollman – was not admitted because the secretary,

---

[74] Ibid., 191–2.
[75] Ibid., 196.
[76] Ibid., 197.
[77] Ibid., 199.

a Mr. Willie, could not be forced to authenticate the letter because to do so would be to incriminate himself.[78]

During the tedious debate over this matter, news arrived from the president regarding Marshall's subpoena ordering him to produce Wilkinson's letter of October 21, 1806, plus other documents related to Burr's defense. In Jefferson's letter of June 17 to Hay, which Hay presented to the court, Jefferson claimed that he had given Wilkinson's letter to Attorney General Rodney, who was on his way to Richmond. Jefferson also stated that he had not replied to Wilkinson's other letters. Copies of the other papers requested, two letters from the secretary of war, he said, were in the mail. As for the possibility that Marshall might order him to testify in person, Jefferson was "persuaded the court is sensible, that paramount duties of the nation at large, control the obligation of compliance..."[79]

To no one's surprise, Jefferson did not make a personal appearance to explain why he had charged Burr with treason and pronounced him guilty. Neither would the jurors hear Wilkinson's account by way of Willie's testimony. The jurors did, however, have enough evidence to indict Burr for treason and high misdemeanor, which they did on June 24. Burr could hardly have been surprised; and in fact, there was some reason for Burr to take heart, because the wording of the jury's true bill explicitly charged him with levying war on Blennerhassett's island on December 10, 1806. The fact that Burr was not present on Blennerhassett's island on that date would prove to be a serious problem for the prosecution; more serious still was the fact that nothing resembling war had been levied.

Another bit of good fortune came when it became public knowledge that the grand jury fell only two votes short of indicting Wilkinson for misprision (concealment) of treason, and high misdemeanor.[80] Later in the trial, three of the grand jurors were called to testify about what happened to influence the grand jury's action. Particularly telling, according

---

[78] Ibid., 243–5.

[79] Ibid., 255.

[80] The source of the leak was juror Munford Beverley. A letter written by John Brockenbrough, another juror, which appeared in the *Virginia Gazette*, July 11, identified Beverley as the leaker, and noted that he, Brockenbrough, had not voted to indict Wilkinson for high treason, since no vote on that subject was taken. On the vote to indict for misprision of treason, Brockenbrough voted not to indict. He did not challenge the fact that the vote for indicting Wilkinson on that charge was seven for and nine against. Beverley tells his side of the story in the Richmond *Virginia Gazette*, July 11; his response was reprinted in the *Western World*, Aug. 13, 1807.

to one juror, Littleton Waller Tazewell, were the contradictions between Wilkinson's account of his interview with Swartwout upon his delivery of the cipher letter and Swartwout's own testimony regarding that event. Tazewell admitted being predisposed to doubt Swartwout, "yet the very frank and candid manner in which he gave his testimony, I must confess, raised him very high in my estimation, and induced me to form a very different opinion of him, from that which I had before entertained."[81]

Other grand jurors apparently felt the same way. But whatever their reasons, the main point was that the grand jury nearly indicted the government's primary witness. According to jury foreman John Randolph, the vote to indict Wilkinson failed "upon certain wire-drawn distinctions," but none of the jurors "pretended to think him *innocent*."[82]

Although the exposure of Wilkinson's duplicity did not prove that Burr was innocent – and indeed may have suggested that both men were involved in a criminal conspiracy – it did mean that Wilkinson's testimony had been seriously discredited. During the remainder of the proceedings – including Burr's trial for high misdemeanor after the principal treason trial ended on September 1, and also the probable cause hearings before Marshall as to whether Burr should be bound over for trial for activities in Kentucky or Ohio after December 10 – the defense hammered Wilkinson for lying under oath and tampering with evidence – and hammered Jefferson for continuing to defend him. In Martin's blunt words, "We mean to shew that General Wilkinson is identified with the government, and the government had declared they would justify him."[83]

The reaction to the public disclosure about Wilkinson's close call before the grand jury was instantaneous. Munford Beverley who voted to indict Wilkinson, for example, was accused of rank partisanship in

[81] Carpenter, *Trial of Burr*, 3: 306.
[82] Randolph to Joseph H. Nicholson, June 25, 1807, Nicholson Mss. Lib. Cong., as quoted in Bruce, *John Randolph of Roanoke*, 1: 303–304. Also see Randolph's account of the grand jury proceedings in *Annals of Congress*, Jan. 11, 1808; Session of 1807–1808, p. 1397, as cited and quoted in Adams, *History*, (Library of America), 919.
[83] Carpenter, *Trial of Burr*, 3: 257. At one point during the trial after the trial, Burr's lawyers moved to interrogate Littleton Tazewell and other members of the grand jury as to Wilkinson's close call. Violating the secrecy of the grand jury was an extraordinary request, but Marshall allowed it (ibid., 289) over Tazewell's objections (ibid., 242) given the fact that it went to the credibility of Wilkinson's further testimony against Burr in the ongoing proceedings against him. Grand jurors John C. Brockenbrough and Joseph C. Cabell along with Tazewell did testify as to the grand jury's interrogation of Wilkinson. ibid., 356–9.

the Fredericksburg *Virginia Herald* of June 30, 1807. Beverley responded
in the Richmond *Gazette* of July 11 with a defense of his vote and his
character, along with a breakdown of the grand jury vote on Wilkinson;
Beverley's letter was reprinted in the Kentucky *Western World* of August
13.[84] The general himself rushed off a self-serving letter to the president
condemning the jurors for dishonoring his heroic service to the country
by exposing Burr.[85] To make certain that prospective jurors in the principal trial put the proper spin on the information, Burr's lawyers moved to
attach Wilkinson for obstruction of justice. Marshall denied the motion
on June 27 and set August 3 for the jury trial.[86]

For all practical purposes, the first phase of the trial was over, although
there was one last exchange of fire over where Burr should be confined
as an indicted traitor. It was finally determined that he would be moved
from his comfortable quarters near the Capitol to refurbished rooms on
the third floor of the Virginia penitentiary. Thanks to the indulgence
of the court and a friendly jailor, the "emperor of the penitentiary,"
as William Duane dubbed Burr, would have a constant supply of fresh
produce and ready access to family, friends and legal counsel.[87] By all
accounts Burr remained upbeat about the trial, and with some reason.

Serious problems remained, however, the most serious being Marshall's
ambiguous definition of levying war in *Bollman* that appeared to countenance the English doctrine of constructive treason, and which among
other things suggested that war could be levied without the actual out-
break of hostilities. If Marshall were to rule positively on these points in
Richmond, as the prosecution would urge him to do, Burr's major line of
defense would be breached.

An additional concern for Burr was the possibility that a hostile jury
might have the last word, no matter what Marshall ruled. In fact, as
Burr's lawyers would soon discover, most of the potential jurors thought
he was guilty as charged. If the prosecution could tap this well of prejudice by hammering away at Burr's character, which they attempted to
do, he could be in trouble. How much trouble would depend in large
part on how much hammering John Marshall would allow.

---

[84] Those who voted to indict Wilkinson, in addition to Beverley himself, were John
Randolph, Littleton Tazewell, Robert B. Taylor, James Garnett, William Daniel, and
John Brockenbrough.
[85] Wilkinson to Jefferson, June 29, 1807, *Thomas Jefferson Papers Series 1. General
Correspondence*, Lib. Cong.
[86] Robertson, *Reports*, 1: 354–7.
[87] Duane as quoted in Malone, *Jefferson*, 5: 331.

4

Treason Law for America

The Lawyers Grapple

"To a man of plain understanding it would seem to be a matter of little difficulty to decide what was meant in the constitution by levying of war; but the subtleties of lawyers and judges, invented in times of heat and turbulence, have involved the question in some obscurity."

Judge William Cranch, dissenting in *Bollman*[1]

"A degree of eloquence seldom displayed on any occasion has embellished a solidity of argument and a depth of research by which the court has been greatly aided in forming the opinion it is about to deliver."

John Marshall, Opinion delivered on August 31, 1807[2]

Although the Court's second decision in *Bollman* (the first having dealt only with the question of whether it could issue a writ of habeas corpus) and *U.S. v. Burr* are regularly cited as foundational rulings on American treason law, the decisions taken singularly and in tandem are difficult to unscramble. Take *Bollman* for example. It was the first treason case to be decided by the Supreme Court, in contrast to the circuit court decisions in the 1790s. This fact alone entitles it to the prominent place it occupies.[3] Nevertheless, several factors detract from its authority as a precedent. For one thing, the defendants, Bollman and Swartwout, were only indirectly connected with Burr's enterprise, which meant that

---

[1] 24 Fed. Cas., C.C.D.Columbia (Jan. 30, 1807), No. 14,622, at 1192–3.
[2] Robertson, *Reports*, 2: 401.
[3] James Willard Hurst, *The Law of Treason in the United States: Collected Essays* (Westport, CT, 1971). When Joseph Story defined treason in his famous *Commentaries on the Constitution of the United States* (5th ed., 2 vols., Boston, 1891), 2: 579, he quoted Marshall in *Ex parte Bollman* not Marshall in *U.S. v Burr*.

the facts did not allow counsel to argue the doctrinal questions fully. In addition, the decision was rendered by only four justices, who were themselves divided over some of the key issues. Whether for this reason or not, Marshall's opinion, while it freed the prisoners, was not clear as to the meaning of "levying war" in Article III, Section 3. Therefore, rather than guiding the arguments in *U.S. v. Burr* in Richmond, the Bollman opinion became the central point in dispute.

As an authoritative statement of treason doctrine, *U.S. v. Burr* has its own disabilities, the main one being that the chief justice on circuit was speaking as a trial judge. As a result, his doctrinal pronouncements, as he admitted several times in the course of the trial, were technically bounded by the Supreme Court's decision, and by his own opinion for the majority, in *Bollman* (despite its ambiguity). The result was that lawyers on both sides in Richmond put their own spin on Marshall's Bollman opinion and of course urged him to say that he had said what they said he said. The chief justice thus got a unique opportunity to clarify – his critics said reverse – his earlier opinion, but his colleagues on the Supreme Court never had a chance to put their official imprimatur on his gloss.[4]

Disabilities aside, Marshall was in a unique position to shape the law of treason. For one thing, district judge Cyrus Griffin was a silent partner on the bench (Jefferson called him a "cypher" and "a wretched fool");[5] for another, Marshall did not have to accommodate the ideas of his fellow justices, even though he wrote them requesting advice on certain points of law. Also, in shaping his doctrinal thinking, Marshall was aided by some of the finest lawyers in the country who in turn were aided by the unique factual complexity of the case (which helped them ask the right questions), and a rich body of relevant legal sources from both sides of the Atlantic (which helped them answer these questions).

Together, then, Marshall and the lawyers were educating themselves and their fellow citizens about American treason law. Their interpretive

---

[4] Marshall wrote to Justice William Cushing asking him to consider some of the legal questions in the case; in the same letter he also asked Cushing to pass the letter on to Justice Bushrod Washington. Both men probably responded, but their replies have not been found. Marshall to William Cushing, June 29, 1807, Hobson, *Papers of Marshall*, 7: 60–62.

[5] Jefferson to James Madison, May 25, 1810, Ford, *Works of Jefferson*, 11: 140. Jefferson no doubt had the treason trial in mind when he condemned Griffin for failing to provide "any counterpoint to the rancorous hatred which Marshall bears to the government of his country, & from the cunning & sophistry within which he is able to enshroud himself."

starting point was the bare bones wording of Article III, Section 3. What the Framers themselves thought about what they wrote had to be inferred mainly from the document itself, since the Philadelphia Convention debates were not yet in print. The republican principles established in 1787 and 1788, however, were still fresh and highly relevant to the debate over treason in Richmond.[6] Equally relevant were the two great English treason statutes that the Framers relied on: 25 Edward III dating from 1351 and the Treason Trials Act of 1696, the source of the two-witness rule in the Constitution. Illuminating those statutes were several centuries of English decisional law, which was in turn supplemented and parsed by the great English legal writers, especially those of the seventeenth and eighteenth centuries.

The lawyers in the Burr trial also drew on the arguments of counsel and Marshall's ruling in the recent Bollman litigation, reports of which circulated widely in the press. Relevant too were the previously mentioned circuit court opinions of Justices Paterson, Iredell, and Chase from the 1790s. Much more to the point was the position of Supreme Court Justice James Wilson. In his charge to the federal circuit court grand jury in Virginia in May 1791, Wilson categorically repudiated the entire concept of constructive treasons. He amplified his argument in his law lectures at the College of Philadelphia in the winter of 1791–1792. As "the preeminent legal scholar of his generation," his liberal ideas on treason found their way to Richmond in 1807 – if not directly, then through Edmund Randolph, who served with Wilson at the Philadelphia Convention, and who joined him on the Committee of Detail that framed the treason provisions in Article III.

All this is to say that treason and treason law were familiar – if as yet unsettled – themes to lawyers, politicians, and the general public in the beginning of the nineteenth century. Many had been traitors themselves, as was Marshall himself when he took up arms against Great Britain in the summer of 1775. As for legal and political materials on treason, counsel at Richmond had access to a wealth of information from both sides of the Atlantic. The pragmatic, nonideological way they mixed and matched old law, new law, and current politics to fit the needs of the new republic affords a rare glimpse of the way lawyers and judges went about making law in the early national period.

---

[6] Two members of Burr's defense team, Edmund Randolph and Luther Martin, were members of the Philadelphia Convention and their respective state ratifying conventions. Randolph was joined in the latter by thirty-three-year-old John Marshall.

Twelve Men Good and True

Given all the high-level law talk and the low-level "Melo-Drama," it is easy to forget that Aaron Burr's life was on the line. According to the prevailing adversarial model, another legacy from England, Burr's fate rested in the hands of twelve impartial jurors sworn to apply the law set forth by the judge to the agreed-upon facts. For several reasons, such a model fails to capture the jury's actual role in Burr's trial. The first problem, which became clear during voir dire, was that truly impartial jurors were in short supply. The second problem, which surfaced during witness interrogation, was the stubborn indeterminacy of the facts themselves. Or to be more specific, the facts became facts according to the legal meaning given to the words "levying war" in Article III.

Relating the generalities of doctrine to the generally messy facts on the ground is of course a perennial challenge in every criminal trial. The challenge was doubly difficult in Richmond, not only because the facts were complex, but also because the doctrine that would determine their relevance, that is, the meaning of "levying war" had not yet been settled. As a result both sides, first the prosecution and then the defense, directed their arguments about those key words not just to Marshall, but over Wickham's objection, directly to the jurors.[7] The implication and Wickham's objection was that the jurors, in addition to ascertaining facts, might also have a say about the law.

The situation was confusing not just because the lawyers used facts to clarify doctrine and doctrine to establish facts, but also because they couched their arguments, as Judge Cranch predicted, in abstruse legal language. There was also the hotly disputed ideological dispute about the role of the jury in matters of law. As champions of the sovereign people, Jefferson and his supporters, including the prosecution in Richmond, liked jury-power. Conservatives like John Marshall, on the other hand, were inclined to question jury competence, especially when jurors ventured beyond their traditional fact-finding role.[8]

---

[7] As Robertson noted, counsel for the United States attempted to give a definition of "levying war" to the jury. However, Wickham contended that defining treason was a matter of law, and as such was the duty of the court alone. Robertson, *Reports*, 1: 584.

[8] F. Thornton Miller, *Juries and Judges Versus the Law: Virginia's Provincial Legal Perspective* (Charlottesville, 1994) is the standard work on juries in the Old Dominion; for an insightful introduction to the role of the jury in criminal trials, see Robert A. Ferguson, *The Trial in American Life* (Chicago and London, 2007), 52–56.

In Richmond, ideological differences over the role of the jury translated directly into a dispute over adversarial tactics. That is to say, the prosecution played to jury-power at every opportunity because they knew that popular opinion and most of the jury pool had already settled on Burr's guilt. Any doubt about this prejudice was removed during the jury selection process, which began in earnest on August 10. The jury pool included twelve from Wood County, which included Blennerhassett's island where war was allegedly levied, and thirty-six from "the body of the district of Virginia."[9] Burr opened the proceedings by asking the jurors to disqualify themselves if they had already judged him guilty. Hay responded by insisting that perfect neutrality, given the notoriety of the case, was impossible. In fact, most of the potential jurors readily admitted, some quite vociferously, that they had followed the case in the newspapers and were sure that Burr deserved to hang.[10]

Only when Burr retreated from the standard of perfect impartiality were twelve jurors finally selected. The best he could hope for, he conceded, were jurors who admitted their bias, but who also indicated a willingness to consider the evidence with an open mind.

It would appear that Burr got even more than he hoped for. At any rate, Edmund Randolph in reporting to Blennerhassett on August 18, called the jury "an excellent one," with the exception of Richard E. Parker who, though "a worthy, honorable man," was also a "violent Jeffersonian partisan."[11] The good news was that Edward Carrington made the final jury list. Carrington, a former U.S. marshal, mentioned that he had followed the case for twelve months, which meant that he was familiar with the Bollman opinion as well as the preliminary proceedings in Richmond; he also admitted that he "had formed an unfavorable opinion of the views of colonel Burr." That Carrington objected specifically to Burr's "views" and not to his character must have been encouraging to the defense. What really mattered, however, was Carrington's acknowledgment that his "opinions were not definitive." Burr had special reason to be pleased that Carrington was chosen foreman of the jury, not the least because he was John Marshall's brother-in-law and close friend.[12]

---

[9] Robertson, *Reports*, 1: 361–2.

[10] For the interrogation of the potential jurors, the debate about the role of the jury, and Marshall's rulings on these issues see ibid., 366–430.

[11] Safford, *Blennerhassett Papers*, 339.

[12] For voir dire and the lawyers' discussion of the jury process see Robertson, *Reports*, 1: 370–430; Edward Carrington's response to questions is found at ibid., 380.

If Hay and his colleagues hoped for a jury that might defy the judge if necessary, then Carrington's presence must surely have dampened their hopes. Luther Martin, on the other hand, was elated. "He thanked God," as he reported to Blennerhassett, that in addressing this jury, "he should not now labor under the lock-jaw, which had hitherto restrained him before Democratic juries."[13]

Fashioning Law to Fit the Facts

Hay's statement to the jury on August 17 was the opening move in the legal chess game that followed. Even with jury opinion on his side, Hay faced serious obstacles. One such was the damage done to the government's case by Wilkinson's earlier appearance before the grand jury. Jefferson's credibility, on which jury opinion rested, also suffered, since he had rushed to public judgment on the basis of Wilkinson's uncorroborated information – a point that the defense would hammer home.

Hay's main problem, however, was not Wilkinson's self-destruction or Jefferson's judgment, but the fact that nearly all of the government's witnesses (the most important of whom was now William Eaton) were prepared to testify only to what Burr *intended* to do and not what he and his followers had actually done.

This gap in the evidence brought the prosecution to the meaning of "levying war" in Article III. Not only was Burr absent when war was supposed to have been levied, but there was little evidence that the two dozen young men who were present had levied anything that resembled war; also there was no evidence indicating that they had been informed of Burr's "treasonable" plans, if such they were. The fantastic notion, attested to by Wilkinson, Eaton, and Colonel Brown, that Burr could transform this motley band into a fully supplied, equipped, and disciplined army capable of taking New Orleans by force and then driving the Spanish from Mexico, was not something the prosecution was prepared to prove. It defied common sense, as John Adams observed, to think that a savvy operator like Burr, even considering his frustrated ambition and inflated sense of himself, could seriously contemplate such a plan. To have done so, he would have had to have been, in Adams's words, an "Idiot or a Lunatick."[14]

---

[13] Safford, *Blennerhassett Papers*, 406.

[14] John Adams to Benjamin Rush, Feb. 2, 1807, Adams Papers, MHS; original held by Boston Public Library.

Hay had a steep hill to climb. He began hesitantly and even apologetically, as when it admitted that he had made mistakes, which itself was yet another mistake. He assured the jurors that the prosecution was not motivated by personal malice, a gratuitous denial that only called attention to Burr's claim that it was. He also professed his sincere concern that Burr receive a fair trial, but then, in a blatant appeal to jury prejudice, demanded that he should get no favors because of his privileged social status. If the former vice president turned out to be the villainous traitor the partisan press and the president made him out to be, then so be it.

On this point, Hay urged jurors not to hesitate to convict on the evidence, even if they had already concluded that Burr was guilty without having seen it. "A juryman may entertain a belief," he declared, "founded on what he has heard out of doors, which would not be warranted by the legal evidence before him in court, on which alone he ought to decide; but if the belief once exist in his mind, from the evidence, that the prisoner has committed the crime alleged, he is then guilty of treachery to his God, to his country, and to himself, if he do not pronounce a verdict dictated by that belief."[15] Buried in Hay's muddled syntax was a direct appeal to the jurors not to be confined by the evidence that he had just said should guide them.

Hay's main objective, however, was to interpret "levying war" in Article III so as to embrace the events of December 10 on Blennerhassett's island. At the same time, he had to snare Burr, even though he was not present on the island when war was supposedly levied. His first move was to argue that "common sense and principles founded on considerations of national safety certainly require, that the crime of treason should be completed, before the actual commission of hostilities against the government."

In other words, if the government had to wait until traitors were in a position to wage war, it might be too late to stop them. Hay then reformulated the issue, insisting that it was not an overt act of levying war that had to be proven but "an overt act of treason." As he put it, "an assemblage of men, convened for the purpose of effecting by force a treasonable design, which force is intended to be employed before their dispersion, is treasonable; and the persons engaged in it are traitors."[16]

[handwritten margin note: A fun paradox in Law]

---

[15] Robertson, *Reports*, 1: 434.
[16] Ibid., 435.

Rather than relating the facts to the law, Hay made the law conform to the facts. Unfortunately the law he relied on was a version of the much-feared English doctrine of constructive treason that held that conspiring to commit treason was treason and that everyone associated with the conspiracy was guilty.

Hay sensed the problem and in fact admitted that the doctrine of "constructive treasons" had produced "much oppression" in Great Britain. But such oppression, he insisted, could never happen in America where there were no tyrannical kings to abuse their authority. Here the government is based on "the will of the people" and "the people know so well their rights, and how to support them. I believe no danger from this consideration, is ever to be experienced here. It may serve as a topic of declamation, but the apprehension of real mischief from this source, is absolutely visionary."[17]

Hay no doubt got some kudos from Jefferson for going after Burr. The problem was that Hay's expedient embrace of constructive treason doctrine was at serious odds with republican (and Republican) ideology, which held that the Constitution was designed to limit the power of the national government, especially that of the executive branch. Both as a perpetual critic of English jurisprudence and a self-proclaimed keeper of the republican flame, Jefferson might have been expected to hew the republican line. Instead he operated on the premise that the end justified the means. Thus, in justifying Wilkinson's law-defying actions in New Orleans, including "the arrest deportation" of Bollman and Swartwoat, could Jefferson declare, "On great occasions every good officer must be ready to risk himself in going beyond the strict line of law, when the public preservation requires it..."[18]

In fact, national security linked to executive authority was the prosecution's strongest argument for using the doctrine of constructive treason. National security was also an argument a jury could understand and appreciate. And not coincidentally, the doctrine of constructive treason was in addition the best available justification for Jefferson's precipitous public accusation of Burr and his all-points-bulletin for his arrest.

National security was a policy argument, however, not a legal one. What the prosecution needed was a legal justification for the broad definition of treason they needed to bring Burr to the gallows. Resort to

---

[17] Ibid., 444.
[18] Jefferson to Governor William C. C. Claiborne], Feb. 3, 1807, Bergh, *Writings of Jefferson*, 11: 150–51.

English legal history was one solution to their problem, as we shall see. But the prosecution's main source for the hated doctrine was not English law, which was not dispositive in American courts, but Marshall's opinion for the Supreme Court in *Bollman*. Hay and company, as noted previously, found enough of the doctrine of constructive treason in that opinion to catch Burr. More to the point, they framed their formal indictment of him on their interpretation of that opinion.

There were problems, however, starting with the fact that Jefferson took Marshall's *Bollman* opinion as a personal rebuke, which it was. The president surely winced, too, when he read Hay's celebration of the Supreme Court's interpretive authority, declaring that *Bollman* was "pronounced after great deliberation" and that "no other tribunal within the United States ought to support a doctrine contrary to the principles of that decision..."[19] Hay strayed even further from Republican constitutional orthodoxy when he justified the Court's interpretation as absolutely necessary, since "without *supplemental interpretation*, the law would be a dead letter."[20] Hamilton or Marshall could not have said it better.

To defend the Supreme Court's authority at the very moment the president was trying to dismantle the Court was not the main problem. More serious from a practical point of view was the fact that Marshall's allusion to the doctrine of constructive treason in *Bollman* was far from clear. Hay conceded as much, noting that the prosecution's definition of treason "is not literally that which is furnished by the decision of the supreme court of the United States [in the Bollman case]..." But, he continued, "it is substantially the same, and is given in conformity to what I understand to be the spirit of that decision."[21]

To make this point to the "gentlemen of the jury," he quoted Marshall's opinion: "*if a body of men be actually assembled for the purpose of effecting by force, a treasonable purpose, all those who perform any part, however minute, or however remote from the scene of action*, and who are actually *leagued in the general conspiracy, are to be considered as traitors*: but there must be *an actual assembling of men*, to *constitute a levying of war.*"[22]

Then, speaking directly to Marshall: "The construction which I have thus given, comes within the words and meaning of the decision of the supreme court, pronounced by yourself. The same idea is expressed in

[19] Robertson, *Reports*, 1: 435. Italics appear in Robertson's *Reports*.
[20] Ibid., 445.
[21] Ibid., 435.
[22] Ibid., 436.

perhaps ten or fifteen other parts of this decision."[23] Several additional short quotes, also from Marshall's *Bollman* opinion, followed, all of them purporting to establish the proposition that the mere assemblage of men with the intent of carrying out a design to overthrow the government constituted treason and "would," in Marshall's words, "certainly be an overt act of levying war."[24]

Hay then supplied an additional gloss by observing, "In the definition which I have just examined, no notice is taken of arms or military weapons; nor have I stated, that any actual force or *hostility* has been employed, for the purpose of effecting treasonable designs; because I think neither of them essential, according to the constitution and the laws of this country."[25]

It is puzzling that Hay quoted Marshall to support the prosecution's interpretation of *Bollman*, since Marshall would have the last word on what he meant by what he said. Perhaps Hay really believed what he argued. But in any case, his primary objective was to persuade the jury to adopt his interpretation of "levying war." To give them something more to chew on, he asked them to consider some "sound principles of common sense and national policy" – matters, he admitted, that lawyers do not always attend to. "Let us suppose a case," he said (drawing obviously on the extravagant testimony of Eaton and Colonel Brown) of "four or five thousand" unarmed men waiting outside the capital "with a deliberate, preconcerted design" to march on the city and take possession of the "ten or fifteen thousand" guns in the public arsenal and then "disperse the legislature, and usurp all the powers of the government." Would they not be traitors, even though "good honest citizens and brave soldiers" would "disperse the conspirators" before they could "carry their treasonable purposes into effect"?[26]

Then rhetorically: was this any different from the band of men who assembled on Blennerhassett's island with the intent to head down river, join up with Burr, gather recruits as they went along and then attack New Orleans and "get arms with the aid of the Spanish minister"? Nowhere did Hay attempt to show that Burr's followers knew anything about his treasonable plans. Presumably by recruiting the men, even under false pretense of settling the Bastrop claim, Burr's constructive guilt was transferred to them.

[23] Ibid.
[24] Ibid.
[25] Ibid., 437.
[26] Ibid., 452.

The point of Hay's hypothesizing was to show that treason thwarted was still treason even though Burr's "army" had not been armed and had not assembled in force. To bolster his doctrinal point, Hay expounded on the connection between 25 Edward III and Article III, and cited Foster's Crown Pleas, and the opinions of Justices Chase and Paterson in the Fries trial for support. Hay did not mean to say that the "able and learned framers of our constitution" had drawn only on English law, but rather "that the English authorities and definition of those terms should be much respected." His point was "to shew that the decision of the supreme court on this subject, in the *case of Bollman and Swartwout*, is not an innovation, not a new doctrine, but is an exact counter-part of, and taken from, the decisions of the English judges."[27]

If Marshall had endorsed the doctrine of constructive treason as Hay claimed, or to be more precise, if the jury believed Hay, the prosecution was more than halfway home. By Hay's reckoning, it would not matter that the events on Blennerhassett's island were unwarlike. Neither would it matter that Burr was absent on December 10, when his followers assembled on the island. Moreover, if intent to commit treason amounted to actual treason, then the various affidavits bearing on that subject would be relevant and admissible. And so most probably would be the testimony of the dozens of government witnesses waiting to testify about what Burr intended to do but had not yet done – and about the kind of evil character he was.

Point Counterpoint

Near the end of his opening statement, and before he confessed to being "too much exhausted" to say more, Hay protested that it was not up to him "to anticipate the defense which will be made for the accused." In fact, it was up to him and his fellow counsel to do just that. In any case, he then went on to "presume" to "speak of the defense he [Burr] had made," which was to claim that "his scheme was peaceful and agricultural." Such a claim focused the trial on the question of intent, which was precisely what the prosecution wanted.

To forestall that possibility, Burr rose to object "to this order of examining the witnesses."[28] Eaton's testimony, he insisted, should go no further than his written affidavit, that is, it should be related only "to what happened at Washington." Burr's point was that no witnesses, including

[27] Ibid., 439.
[28] Ibid., 452.

Eaton, could be heard regarding intent. This is to say, the defense insisted that the overt act of treason had to be proven before the corroborative evidence connecting the defendant to the crime could be considered. No body; no murder. As Burr's lawyers insisted, "it would be ridiculous to inquire into the causes or circumstances of the killing, till the death were proved." To admit corroborative evidence before the material fact in the trial was proven would be "irregular, irrational and illegal" as "every prosecutor, learned in criminal law" knows.[29] Indeed, to "begin at the wrong end of the prosecution," to make such an elemental mistake regarding trial procedure, must have been due to "inadvertence, want of experience" on the part of the prosecutor.[30]

To thus educate and embarrass Hay, and to arrest the introduction of further irrelevant evidence, the defense "argued with great ingenuity and at considerable length," citing Marshall's ruling at Burr's bail hearing, copious English authorities, Justice Iredell's ruling at the Fries trial, and other American precedents. The gauntlet was down.

Wirt picked it up with a characteristic combination of learning and bombast designed to redeem Hay's reputation from the "manifest disrespect" shown him, and to put Burr's lawyers back on the defensive. "I defy, said Mr. Wirt, the gentlemen to produce a single example, from all the English authorities, from the whole history of their jurisprudence, where the attorney general, or the counsel for the crown, has been arrested in the introduction or arrangement of the evidence, by the counsel of the defendant, and put on a different course. I defy them to produce a single example, of any interference with the course adopted by the prosecutor."[31]

Wirt demanded the right to tell the whole story as it happened: to develop "this conspiracy from its birth to its consummation," to unravel "the plot from its conception to its denouement," to trace "Aaron Burr step by step as he advanced and became more bold, till the act was consummated, by the assemblage on Blennerhassett's island." Any attempt to suppress evidence was premature, because it denied the prosecution the right to state its case in a manner "consistent with universal practice in prosecutions, both in our own, and every other civilized country." The prosecution demanded the right to present their case to the jurors

[29] Ibid., 452–3.
[30] Ibid., 453.
[31] Ibid., 454.

as a narrative like the "history of the late revolution," as a tale with a beginning, middle, and end, one with heroes and villains.[32]

Much more to the point, Wirt wanted to introduce evidence aimed at proving intent, because intent to commit treason was inseparable from the act of treason. As he explicated: "Can there be an overt act of treason without an intention to commit it? Can any assemblage, however large, armed or arrayed, however disorderly and tumultuous, commit an act of treason without intending it? And ought not their intention be proved?" Moreover, and above all, the jury had the right to hear all the evidence, including the matter of Burr's intent, if the prosecution should choose to introduce that first. If the court should agree with Burr's objection, it would prevent the jury from hearing all the evidence. "The court has no such powers. The only power which the court possesses is, not to direct the order in which the evidence shall be introduced, but to instruct them on the law..." And just in case Marshall missed the lecture: "The court cannot withhold from them any evidence touching the issue. Will the court stop us? Will the court or the jury decide on the issue?"[33]

Linked

That point was the central issue that Marshall addressed on August 31. Until then he listened patiently to the torrent of talk unleashed by Wirt's response to Burr's objections about evidence. The first question to debate concerned the order in which evidence could be introduced: whether witnesses and evidence concerning intent could be introduced before that concerning the overt act, or whether the overt act had first to be considered and proved.

Wirt, now the prosecution's mainstay, initiated the debate with a discussion of *The Trial of Hardy*, an English treason trial that he admitted was "not directly applicable to the case now before the Court."[34] His point, which he bolstered further by citing American precedents as well as other English case law, was to show that the prosecution was free to argue intent whenever it chose to do so and that "A *jury must give a verdict on all the evidence collectively...*"[35]

Charles Lee, newly arrived on the defense team, countered Wirt's argument by demanding that "*an open deed of war,*" as stated in the indictment, had first to be proved. Luther Martin then responded to Wirt's impressive foray into English law with some impressive and

[32] Ibid.
[33] Ibid., 457.
[34] Ibid., 455.
[35] Ibid., 457.

equally irrelevant citations of his own. And after demonstrating to his
own satisfaction that the law of evidence prevented Wirt from talking
about intent, he proceeded to talk about intent himself. Burr's intentions
"were most meritorious," predicated as they were "on principles of an
honorable war, and only to be carried on in the event of his country
being engaged in it, and with a view to the emancipation of millions
[of Mexicans] who are now in bondage." Martin could only hope and
pray that his hero Burr may "not meet the fate that Washington himself
would have met, if the revolution had not been established." After citing
more English law, he ended by urging the court to stop Hay from proceeding further "til he prove some overt act."[36]

On August 18, after two days of acrimonious argument, Marshall
settled the order in which evidence could be presented. His brief ruling
aimed to cool tempers and move the case forward. He also saved himself
some grief and counsel some time by making it clear that his earlier rulings made during arraignment and bail hearing no longer applied, since
"at that time, no indictment was found, no pleadings existed, and there
was no standard, by which the court could determine the relevancy of
the testimony offered..."[37] He also soothed bruised egos among counsel
by noting, "the argument on both sides appears to be, in many respects,
correct." He then proceeded to give something to each side in a statement so complex that both sides probably thought that they had been
vindicated.

Marshall agreed with the prosecution that the "levying of war, is
a fact, which must be decided by the jury." But he also reminded the
jurors, "The court may give general instruction on this, as on every other
question brought before them" so that "the jury must decide upon it as
compounded of fact and law." In his view, intent to commit the act and
the act itself were so intertwined that the attempt to separate the two
in regard to the order of evidence presented would be impossible. As he
explained, "The overt act may be such as to influence the opinion, on
the testimony afterwards given, respecting the intention; and the testimony respecting the intention, may be such, as to influence the opinion
on the testimony, which may be afterwards given respecting the overt
act."[38] Since treason and the intent to commit it were connected, and
since, as Wirt had argued, it was impossible to talk about both things

---

[36] Ibid., 467.
[37] Ibid., 469.
[38] Ibid., 471.

simultaneously, the court "must permit the counsel for the United States to proceed to shew the intention of the fact, or order to enable the jury to decide upon the fact, coupled with the intention."[39] Score one for the prosecution.

Their victory was far from complete, however, and it clearly did not detract from the court's final authority to determine the admissibility of evidence. In Marshall's words: "But it is proper to add, that the intention which is considered as relevant at this stage of the inquiry is the intention which composes a part of the crime, the intention with which the overt act itself was committed; not a general evil disposition, or an intention to commit a distinct fact. This species of testimony, if admissible at all, is received as corroborative or confirmatory testimony." In other words, the prosecutor is "at liberty to proceed according to his own judgment" but the court is free to exclude the evidence he presents if it "does not appear to be relevant."[40]

Witnesses Testify About Intent

Marshall's ruling meant that the law of evidence would be applied and clarified witness by witness, after arguments from both sides, and according to his determination. The first to appear for the government was General Eaton, described by one insightful historian as a combination of Lawrence of Arabia and James Bond.[41] After Wilkinson's dismal showing, Eaton was the government's best hope. Known as the "Lion of Dern," Eaton was widely acclaimed for leading the military expedition that humbled the rulers of Tripoli, who had sanctioned depredations by the Barbary pirates against American shipping in the Mediterranean. For his efforts, Jefferson appointed Eaton consul at Tunis. He left that office under a cloud, however, and showed up in Washington in the winter of 1806–1807, claiming that the government had failed to reimburse him for expenditures incurred in the line of duty. It was during this period – Eaton could not recall the exact date – that Burr contacted him regarding his western scheme, presumably because of his military experience, and no doubt because of his presumptive disaffection from the administration.

[39] Ibid., 470.
[40] Ibid., 472.
[41] Buckner F. Melton Jr., *Aaron Burr: Conspiracy to Treason* (New York, 2002), 93.

As Eaton told the court, he was initially attracted to the enterprise because he was impressed with Burr's military reputation and "the distinguished rank he held in society." He assumed that Burr's military plans were premised on a war with Spain, and as such had the tacit backing of the administration.[42] Further conversations, however, convinced him that Burr's project was not only illegal but contemplated "a central general revolution" that involved the overthrow of the government in Washington, and an attack on New Orleans, as the first step in wresting Mexico from Spain and separating the western states from the Union.

According to Eaton's self-serving account, he continued his connection with Burr in order to elicit further evidence of his guilt before informing President Jefferson of the imminent threat to the Union. Jefferson had good reason to doubt Eaton's warning, especially since by his own testimony, Eaton had suggested to the president that the dreaded revolution could be averted simply by "the removal of Mr. Burr from this country" – perhaps by a diplomatic posting to "Paris, London, or Madrid."[43] When Jefferson took no action, Eaton returned home to Massachusetts "and thought no more of colonel Burr, or his projects, or revolutions…" Only, he said, when he was informed that Burr had contracted to have boats built, did Eaton express further concern to the president, this time by letter.

Eaton admitted that he had no written evidence from Burr or anyone else to support his story.[44] No matter. His account made its way into the popular press and the general made his way to Richmond as a principal witness for the government. Before he testified, however, he discredited himself by drinking, gambling, and wild behavior on the wrong side of town – and by conveniently settling his disputed account with the administration. According to Blennerhassett, who kept his finger on the pulse of Richmond, Eaton had "dwindled down in the eyes of this sarcastic town into a ridiculous mountebank," one "despised by Federalists" and "mistrusted by the Democrats."[45]

Cross-examination was short and brutal. Eaton could not remember important dates, and did not seem to recollect where he was at various times in his own narrative. Asked to state what he did to interrupt Burr's treasonous project, he could only say that he made a public toast

[42] Robertson, *Reports*, 1: 474.
[43] Ibid., 478.
[44] Ibid., 479.
[45] Safford, *Blennerhassett Papers*, 315–16.

to the United States: "palsy to the brain that should plot to dismember, and leprosy to the hand that will not draw to defend our union."[46] He could not recall if the toast was actually drunk, where it had been made, or how it got into the newspapers. Pressed on the matter of the money received from the administration, he bristled, before admitting that he had received "about 10,000 dollars" shortly before the trial.[47]

Burr concluded his cross-examination with pointed questions about the details of the "revolution" he allegedly plotted. Eaton had no details and nothing but his own recollection of their conversations. When Burr asked if Eaton had recommended him as ambassador, Eaton could only say that he did so, "as you were a dangerous man" and because he "thought it was the only way to avert a civil war."[48] At no time, either in his written letter to Jefferson in October 1806 or during his testimony, did he make any effort to connect Burr to the events on Blennerhassett's island. Without being asked, he stated: "Concerning any overt act, which goes to prove Aaron Burr guilty of treason, I know nothing."[49]

Eaton's testimony was only slightly less disastrous for the prosecution than Wilkinson's had been. Indeed, his outbursts of temper, for which he apologized, his forgetfulness, the contradictions between his written affidavit and his oral testimony, not to mention the sheer extravagance of his accusations, may actually have helped Burr.

While revealing his own naiveté and cupidity, however, Eaton also inadvertently attested to the New Yorker's gargantuan ambition, predatory instincts, and his cold and calculating willingness to exploit those who trusted him. Therfore, concerning the important matter of character, assuming the jurors could read between the lines of Eaton's testimony, Burr may well have lost some ground.

The testimony of Commodore Truxton, the government's next witness, would lead one to surmise that Hay and company had not bothered to question him before putting him on the stand. In any case, the first thing out of his mouth after admitting that he had been in court when Eaton testified, was, "I know nothing of overt acts, treasonable designs or conversations, on the part of colonel Burr." At this point, according to reporter Robertson, Hay "*seemed* to doubt whether the evidence of the commodore applied to this charge," and was "indisposed to examine

---

[46] Robertson, *Reports*, 1: 480.
[47] Ibid., 483.
[48] Ibid., 484.
[49] Ibid., 473.

him."[50] Wickham jumped on Hay's embarrassing indecision by insisting that the commodore tell his story, which he proceeded to do.

According to Truxton, Burr knew that he had been passed over for promotion by the administration, a slight Burr promised to rectify if Truxton would assume command of the naval operations in the planned attack on Mexico. Reportedly, Burr spoke openly of "an expedition to Mexico, in the event of a war with Spain, which he thought inevitable." When Truxton insisted there would be no war, Burr replied that his expedition would then proceed down river and settle a large tract of rich land on the Washita River. If war with Spain should occur later, " he would be ready to move." In any case, according to Truxton, Burr claimed that the Washita settlers-to-be were "respectable and fashion-able people" who would create "a charming society" which would dou-ble in two years.[51]

On cross-examination by Martin, and later under questioning from one of the jurors, Richard Parker, Truxton admitted that "all his conver-sations respecting military and naval subjects, and the Mexican expedi-tion, were in the event of a war with Spain."[52] Pressed by Burr, he also acknowledged, "I never heard you speak of a division of the union" – a fact, according to Truxton, that differed sharply from accounts in the newspapers.[53]

Further questions from Burr implanted two other exculpatory notions in the minds of the jurors: first, "that private enterprises by individu-als, are lawful and customary in cases of war" – a proposition that was true;[54] and, second, that Burr had operated on the assumption "that the Mexican expedition would be very beneficial to this country."[55] Among the spectators at the trial was a young lawyer named Winfield Scott who agreed, and who four decades later would lead a triumphant American army into Mexico City.

On the question of intent, the government had taken a beating. Eaton, like Wilkinson before him, did more damage than good. And what Truxton said under oath seemed to confirm what Bollman had volun-teered to Jefferson before the trial, which was that Burr planned to lead an extensive military and naval operation against Spain in Mexico, and

---

[50] Ibid., 485.
[51] Ibid., 487–8.
[52] Ibid., 490.
[53] Ibid., 489.
[54] Ibid., 491.
[55] Ibid., 489.

this only in case of a war with Spain. Although Eaton accused Burr of planning to march on Washington and seize New Orleans, his most concrete testimony comported with the accounts of Truxton and Bollman as to Burr's intentions.

Burr was not home safe, but he had given the jury a plausible argument that his activities in the West in 1805 and 1806 were legal and perhaps even patriotic. The fact that Jefferson knew of these activities, that he had condoned them until his public pronouncement of Burr's guilt, and that he had done nothing to nip them in the bud, all strongly suggested that Burr the lawyer had carefully planned – at least initially – to stay within the limits of the law even while he was pushing those limits to the utmost.

Concerning the "War" on Blennerhassett's Island

From the beginning of the trial the Constitution was the elephant in the room. Prosecutors and defense counsel, court and jurors, all knew that sooner or later the events on Blennerhassett's island and Burr's relation to those events would have to be assessed in relation to the treason provisions in Article III. Had war been levied or had it not?

Peter Taylor, who had worked for the Blennerhassetts as a gardener for three years, was the first to testify on this question. He was a plain man who clearly relished his moment in the spotlight; according to Thomas Boylston Adams, he was also a "rogue" or a "blockhead."[56] Much of Taylor's story occurred in October 1806, when he was dispatched by Mrs. Blennerhassett to warn her husband that the "people got much alarmed" and to tell him and Burr not to return to the island; "if you come up our way, the people will shoot you."[57] Taylor also recounted what Blennerhassett said to him about Burr's expedition: how "we are going to take Mexico; one of the finest and richest places in the whole world," and how Theodosia "was to be the queen of Mexico, whenever colonel Burr died."[58]

As to the crucial events on the island, however, Taylor had little to say that signified war: there were four boats, "about thirty" men, some of whom had rifles, some muskets. Taylor helped load the boats, carrying "half a bushel of candles and some brandy" and some other boxes of

[56] Thomas B. Adams to John Q. Adams, Jan. 24, 1808, Adams Papers, MHS.
[57] Robertson, *Reports*, 1: 493.
[58] Ibid., 494.

Harman Blennerhassett's mansion

which he knew nothing. That was all, except that he remembered that Aaron Burr was not present to lead the young men who were supposedly headed down river to drive the Spanish from North America.

The real issue, however, was not what Burr's men intended to do once they departed the island, but what they did while they were there. Before the prosecution returned to that issue, the matter of intent surfaced again, this time during the interrogation of Colonel George Morgan and his sons, General John Morgan and Thomas, who was studying law at the time. Burr continued to remonstrate against this kind of testimony, but Marshall permitted it because its relevance, he said, could not be determined in advance of hearing it.

The gist of the Morgans' testimony concerned their conversations with Burr on August 21, 1806, or thereabouts. The brothers and their father recalled that Burr had talked openly about "the weakness and imbecility of the national government" and boasted "that with two hundred men, he could drive congress, with the president at its head, into the river Potowmac."[59] Allegedly Burr also predicted that the separation of the trans-Allegheny states from the rest of the union "must take place inevitably, in less than five years."[60]

[59] Ibid., 502.
[60] Ibid., 497.

On cross-examination by Burr, General Morgan admitted that his father had recently suffered a serious fall, and that he "was old and infirm; and like other old men, told long stories and was apt to forget his repetitions."[61] Burr also planted the idea in the jurors' minds that the conversations in question took place during dinner and in the presence of several other people, including the colonel's wife and were "jocular" in nature.[62]

After the Morgans, all the government's witnesses were queried as to the events of December 10 with an eye to proving an overt act of levying war. Those events, it will be recalled, took place after the nation had been alerted by the president's proclamation, and after warrants for the arrest of Blennerhassett and Comfort Tyler had been issued by the governor of Ohio. The Wood County militia too was on it way.

Witnesses testified as to the hectic scene: how provisions were hurriedly loaded on the boats, how bullets were being "run" (molded), how the men were armed (lightly it appeared), and whether all of them had rifles (not all did). The only event remotely approximating the levying of war occurred when Edward Tupper, recently appointed brigadier general of the Ohio militia, arrived on the scene. As Jacob Allbright, the government's witness, reported: "Tupper, laid his hands upon Blannerhassett, and said, 'Your body is in my hands, in the name of the commonwealth.' Some *such words* as that he mentioned. When Tupper made that motion, there were seven or eight muskets leveled at him." After a few words were exchanged one of the men said he would "*as lieve as not*" shoot the general. "Tupper then changed his speech, and said he wished him to escape safe down the river, and wished him luck."[63] According to Allbright, Tupper then advised Blennerhassett to stay and stand trial.

Allbright's account of the encounter between General Tupper and Blennerhassett and his men, wherein guns were leveled and threats made, was the only direct testimony bearing on any "warlike" events that might have constituted levying war. Allbright's testimony was immediately challenged on the grounds that it contradicted his written affidavit.[64] When Burr asked him whether he had stated in writing "that the men who raised their muskets against general Tupper, were not in earnest," Allbright admitted that his written account of events "was a piece of my

[61] Ibid., 504.
[62] Ibid., 503.
[63] Ibid., 509.
[64] Ibid., 512–13.

opinion. I did not know whether they were in earnest; as there was no quarrel among them, and no firing afterwards."[65] Additional witnesses for the government failed to explain how war could have been levied if there had been no quarrel and no shots fired in anger.

Rather than war there was chaos, "nothing but *hub-bub* and confusion" according to one eyewitness,[66] as Blennerhassett, Comfort Tyler, and their companions scrambled to load their boats before the authorities arrived to arrest them. Every witness agreed that the man who recruited the men and who contracted for the supplies and boats was not present. Ironically, the closest thing to violence occurred on the morning after the expedition departed, when the Wood County militiamen – called to action by Ohio Governor Tiffin and fortified with whiskey and peach brandy – arrived on the scene, charged through Blennerhassett's elegant gardens, invaded his wine cellar, ransacked his house, and terrified his wife.[67]

Blennerhassett's wife would remember the invaders bitterly as "Wood county rabble." Rabble they may well have been, but by scrambling Burr's little band they effectively ended the conspiracy. Jefferson, ever the localist, had hoped all along that the westerners would settle up with Burr without the help of national military intervention; that is pretty much what happened December 10, 1806, on Blennerhassett's island.[68]

John Wickham Struts His Stuff

The prosecution had gone with its strength, but none of their witnesses had given credible testimony proving overt acts of war. Rumor was that the government had more than a hundred witnesses waiting to do better. If that was a bluff, Burr called it. On August 20, he and his lawyers demanded that "the prosecution should produce all the evidence which they had, relative to the overt act, before they attempted to offer any collateral testimony...", that is to say, evidence not directly connected to the levying of war on Blennerhassett's island.[69] "Too much irrelevant evidence," they said, had already been submitted, and besides, they reminded the court again, Burr was in Kentucky when the alleged overt acts were said to have been committed.[70]

---

[65] Ibid., 512.
[66] Mr. Edmund P. Dana, ibid., 529.
[67] Parton, *Burr*, 436–8, describes the scene in vivid detail.
[68] On this point see Malone, *Jefferson*, 5: 257–9.
[69] Robertson, *Reports*, 1: 526.
[70] Ibid., 529.

Hay responded by accusing his opponents of "attempting thus to arrest the inquiry" and "prevent the public from seeing and knowing what had been done, and which ought to be known…" For the prosecution, the jury had become "the public." Hay demanded yet again "that the whole evidence should be submitted to the jury, whose province it was to decide whether, according to the exposition of the law by the court, there had been war or not…" The prosecution, said Hay, conceded that the court had a right to instruct the jury as to the law – to "explain what in law constituted an overt act" – but "it could not stop the prosecution [from examining witnesses], and say to the jury, that no overt act was committed…" Moreover, he added, "the question was not, *where* the accused was when the treason was committed, but whether he *procured it* or *had a part in it?*"[71]

The determinative issues were now on the table: the question of evidence and the authority of the jury as related to that of the court. And basic to all else: what was the constitutional definition of treason? And this question called forth contending theories of interpretation: whether the words in Article III were self-evident, as Judge Cranch had insisted; or whether their meaning could be extracted only by reading them through English authorities; or, alternatively, whether Marshall's opinion in *Bollman* settled the matter, and if so how.[72]

These questions called forth a dazzling display of legal learning and oratory that reveals a great deal about the law-making role of lawyers in the early republic: counsel's unapologetic disregard of ideological consistency (as when Jefferson's lawyers embraced the hated doctrine of constructive treason); the frankly pragmatic tactics (as when both sides wrapped their legal arguments in American patriotism and republican ideology); the mixture of law and theater (as when Wirt waxed melodramatic over Blennerhassett in order to discredit Burr in the eyes of the jury); the ungentlemanly no-holds-barred style (as when both sides got personal and ugly); and the ad hoc mixture of constitutional and common-law language and theory. All these factors mark the trial as a uniquely revealing moment in the history of American trial advocacy. Certainly what emerged at the end of the process, as Marshall sifted and sorted his way through the arguments, was a distinctively American version of English treason law.

Wickham launched the great debate on August 20 in an argument that lasted two full days. There had been other memorable speeches

---

[71] Ibid., 530.
[72] Wickham sets forth the interpretive issues clearly at ibid., 534.

during the proceedings, as when Martin unleashed his thunderbolts against Jefferson, or when Wirt made his debut as the trial's most flamboyant orator. Wickham, too, had already lived up to his reputation as Virginia's leading trial lawyer. In terms of logical clarity, comprehensive scholarship, and intellectual force, however, his August 20 speech carried his reputation, and the debate, to a new level.

Where Hay had been cumbersome and apologetic, Wickham was eloquent and cocksure. How much he spoke from written notes in delivering his speech is not clear, but the fact that Robertson put some of his argument in quotes suggests that Wickham wrote out part of it. MacRae also commented on Wickham's "volume of notes."[73] In any case, his commanding argument set the agenda for the remainder of the trial. Wickham's fellow counsel, even the venerable Randolph, paid tribute to Wickham's effort and often simply expanded on the points he set forth. Hay also acknowledged the intellectual force of Wickham's presentation in the process of admitting his own inadequacies. Wirt got it right when he said of Wickham's opening statement and the strategy behind it that it was "a bold and original stroke in the noble science of defense. It marks the genius and hand of a master."[74] Marshall agreed.

Wickham's battle plan was to foreclose every line of attack available to the prosecution.[75] His first and main point was to discredit the English doctrine of constructive treason, "the foundation on which the prosecution must rest." Such a doctrine, he declaimed, was "incompatible with our republican institutions, and utterly inconsistent with every idea of civil liberty." It was not just the fate of Aaron Burr that the English doctrine put in jeopardy, but also that "of every citizen of the United States, and of future generations." Burr's cause was "the cause of every member of the community and of posterity."[76]

Having linked the prosecution and Jefferson's administration to English tyranny, Wickham turned to the prosecution's resort to "artificial rules of construction" (specifically their use of "the common law and usages of the courts in construing statutes") to engraft English treason doctrine onto the Constitution. "This instrument is a new and original compact between the people of the United States, embracing their public concerns in the most extensive sense; and is to be construed, not by the

---

[73] Robertson, *Reports*, 2: 30.

[74] Ibid., 57–58.

[75] For Wickham's argument see Robertson, *Reports*, 1: 532–96; Wirt on Wickham, ibid., 2: 56–135.

[76] Ibid., 1: 532–3.

rules of art belonging to a particular science or profession, but, like a treaty or national compact, in which the words are to be taken according to their natural import, unless such a construction would lead to a plain absurdity, which cannot be pretended in the present instance."[77]

Wickham's commonsense approach to constitutional interpretation made the prosecution's reliance on English law look sinister; it also played to Marshall's well-known Federalist sympathies. The Constitution, declared Wickham, was a document emanating from the American people, designed to protect their liberties, and written in plain language they could understand. "The words of the constitution, *'levying* (or making) war,' are plain and require no nice interpretation..."[78] It was simple: "no person can be convicted of treason in levying war, who was not personally present at the commission of the act, which is charged in the indictment as constituting the offence." To convict there must be two witnesses to the overt act. When it comes to the matter of treason and the proof thereof, the Constitution was self-explanatory. "If I be correct in this, there is an end to all further inquiry."[79]

Wickham knew of course that there would be further inquiry. Accordingly, he set out to refute the prosecution's interpretation of English precedents, which he had just declared to be irrelevant. After "diligent and painful research" into the relevant English cases, treatises and parliamentary acts covering several centuries, he concluded that there were no valid precedents for trying someone for levying war who was not present when war was levied. Judicial holdings to the contrary – that is, those cases from the lawless reign of James II and the hand of judges like "the execrable Jeffries" – were not good law and should not be cited as such.[80]

Equally problematic were the prosecution's efforts to enlarge the constitutional definition of treason by reference to common-law analogies and rules of interpretation.[81] Even Congress could not enlarge the definition of treason, for the simple reason (shades of *Marbury*) that any such attempt "would be void" as a violation of the supreme law of the Constitution.

Regarding Article III, then, the Constitution was clear and controlling; moreover, "It explains itself."[82] History "ancient and modern" and

---

[77] Ibid., 533.
[78] Ibid., 533–4.
[79] Ibid., 533.
[80] Ibid., 535–7.
[81] Ibid., 548–50.
[82] Ibid., 553.

the "great volume of human nature before them" taught the members of the Philadelphia Convention to oppose tyrants by way of "constitutional sanction." The Founders "knew that when a state is divided into parties, what horrible cruelties may be committed even in the name and under the assumed authority of a majority of the people, and therefore endeavoured to prevent them."[83]

There were still other matters to be considered, other mistakes of the prosecution to be exposed, other justifications to be refuted, and other avenues of retreat to be cut off. Wickham took another full day to complete the job. In one telling argument, he exposed the contradiction between the specific wording of the indictment and what the prosecution was trying to prove. Having indicted Burr for levying war on Blennerhassett's island, they could not, Wickham insisted, then proceed to treat him as an accessory before or after the fact and call it treason.

They could not do so without first trying and convicting Blennerhassett, Tyler, and Smith, and all the others who supposedly did levy war on Blennerhassett's island. But these men were innocent, too, Wickham asserted, because no war had been levied. Not a single witness, let alone the two required by the Constitution, had presented credible evidence of an overt act of war. Hay's earlier statement that no military action was necessary was refuted by English law and by citations to the opinions of Justices Paterson, Chase and Iredell in the treason trials of the 1790s.[84]

All of these matters brought Wickham to Marshall's opinion in *Bollman,* which the prosecution claimed had endorsed the doctrine of constructive treason. Wickham had some work to do here. In fact, he conceded that some of Marshall's language seemed to endorse the hated doctrine, but he went on to argue that a reading of the *entire* opinion went the other way.[85] Moreover, he concluded, the constitutional meaning of treason was not argued by counsel in *Bollman* and was not relevant to the determination of that case. So whatever Marshall said on the matter was mere dictum.

Wickham was masterful, the conductor of the orchestra who also wrote the score. He set forth the strategic points that his co-counsel would amplify. He insulted the professional competence of opposing counsel to throw them off balance, although he denied any intention to

[83] Ibid.
[84] Wickham's argument on the indictment at ibid., 557–96.
[85] His analysis of *Bollman*, ibid., 585.

"ridicule" and disclaimed "all personal allusions."[86] Further, he assailed the motives and morality of the government's position, which he also denied doing.

Was it really possible, he asked, that "the gentlemen on the other side" would "seriously contend for doctrines, that will expose all the people of this country more to the dangers of constructive treason, to greater oppression and hardships, than the people of any other country have ever been subjected to?" Impossible. "The records of this trial will be a monument of an attempt to establish principles that must infallibly introduce slavery." That cannot be. Even if the president were willing "to conduct the prosecution on principles that would destroy the liberties of their country," would his lawyers go along? Surely not Virginia's finest. But if they should persist in doing so – and here Wickham looked to his friend Marshall – the doctrine of constructive treason "will never be sanctioned in this country."[87]

Edmund Randolph echoed Wickham's argument, and like Wickham implored Marshall personally to look to his judicial duty and to his reputation: "Amidst all the difficulties of this trial," he said, "I congratulate your Honour, on having an opportunity of fixing the law, relative to this peculiar crime, on grounds which will not deceive, and with such regard to human rights, that we shall bless the day on which the sentence was given..."[88] This from a pillar of the legal community – the man who had supported and befriended Marshall since the 1780s, who secured his entrance into the legal profession, and who joined forces with him to secure the ratification of the Constitution in 1788. In this trial, as in the Old Dominion itself, nearly everything was personal, and therefore a matter of personal honor.

All Power to the Jury: Wirt to the Rescue

MacRae launched the counterattack for the prosecution, focusing first "on the strange manner in which this defense has been conducted" and especially on the tendency of Burr "to quit his situation as an accused" and become a "public accuser" of the "meritorious" Wilkinson, "the savior of his country." Before tackling Wickham's legal arguments, the Lieutenant Governor of Virginia berated "the gentleman from Maryland"

[86] Ibid., 585, 596.
[87] Ibid., 596.
[88] Robertson, *Reports*, 2: 12.

for pledging his personal devotion to Burr as evidence of his innocence. As a "duty to himself as well as to truth and justice," MacRae then challenged Wickham's interpretation of English treason law. And finally, he undertook to justify the wording of Burr's indictment by arguing that the prosecution had merely followed Marshall's Bollman opinion, which endorsed the doctrine of constructive treason.[89] MacRae had performed creditably, but when he sat down, Wickham was still the man to beat.

On August 25, William Wirt took on the job. His argument, or rather his command performance, was nearly as long as Wickham's and, in its own way, equally impressive. First came the obligatory caveat, how he aimed only at justice for the accused, and how he "would not plant a thorn, to rankle for life in my heart, by opening my lips in support of a prosecution which I felt and believed to be unjust." Niceties aside, the truth to be shown was that Burr's motion to suppress evidence was "a mere manoeuvre to obstruct the inquiry." Worse still, it would give the court a power it did not have and would "wrest the trial of the facts" from the jury where it rightfully belonged.[90]

Wirt promised all-out war, fought of course by the gentlemanly rules governing republican lawyers. He would take Burr out of "the drawing room" where Wickham had put him and return him to "the hall of justice" where he would be exposed as the scheming traitor he was. Wirt promised to treat his great adversary "with candour," which Wickham did not display in his own arguments. Wirt would "keep no flounces or furbelows ready manufactured and hung up for use in the millinery of my fancy..." There would not be "a squib or a rocket in every period."[91]

Promises and more promises: "I will not begin by stating that absurd conclusion, as the proposition itself which I am going to encounter." And further: "I will not, in commenting on the gentleman's authorities, thank the gentleman with sarcastic politeness for introducing them..." Unlike his adversary, Wirt promised not to toss books around with "a theatrical air," nor play to the galleries for "laughs" at the expense of understanding, nor adopt a "partisan style of warfare," nor obfuscate the real issues by talking for hours on end.[92] He then proceeded to do all the things Wickham had done – in spades.

Wirt aimed to resuscitate the government's floundering cause, and not incidentally, to lower Wickham a peg or two. The first question he

[89] For MacRae's argument see, ibid. 27–56.
[90] Ibid., 56.
[91] Ibid, 59.
[92] Ibid., 59–60.

asked, one that intrigues historians in search of a distinctly American legal voice, was why, after excoriating the prosecution for resorting to English authorities to interpret the plain words of the Constitution, did Wickham spend most of two days resorting to English authorities himself? Why did he so quickly vanish "like a spirit from American ground" and end up magically "in the middle of the 16th century, complaining most dolefully of my lord Coke's bowels"?[93] And why, we might ask, after berating Wickham for dragging everyone through "a wilderness of investigation in England,"[94] did Wirt retrace Wickham's steps, challenging him case-by-case, point-by-point, authority-by-authority?

The clash of these two remarkable lawyers was the adversarial high point of the trial; who won is hard to say. What is clear is that both men, and indeed counsel on both sides, were stuck with English law and history. They were stuck because the commonly shared tradition of common-law learning provided them a way to think about law, a way to practice it, a way to argue about it. Because there was not yet a distinctive language of American constitutional law – and because the constitutional definition of treason, as both sides admitted, came directly from 25 Edward III – what English judges and legal authorities said about the meaning of those ancient words was grist for the mill.

Simply put, successful lawyers in Virginia in 1807, as elsewhere in America, were expected to make English law work for their American clients. Wirt, Martin, and Wickham belonged to the elite club who practiced Anglo-American law, as did St. George Tucker, Joseph Story, Jeremiah Mason, Daniel Webster, and countless others. And so did John Marshall; which brings us, as it brought Wirt, to the chief justice's spin on English law in *Bollman*.

The prosecution framed their indictment of Burr and mobilized their witnesses on the assumption that *Bollman* gave constitutional sanction to constructive treason. Like MacRae and Hay before him, Wirt undertook to justify their decision and in doing so he challenged Wickham to come clean. Why, he demanded to know, after denouncing the common law as a guide to interpretation and after insisting that common sense would suffice as a guide to constitutional meaning, did he waste time rummaging through English precedents? The reason was "the decision of the supreme court, in the case of Bollman and Swartwout. It was the judicial exposition of the constitution by the highest court in the

[93] Ibid., 61.
[94] Ibid., 73.

nation, upon the very point which the gentleman was considering…"[95]
According to Wirt, Wickham "knew that this decision closed against
him completely the very point which he was labouring," he kept it "sed-
ulously out of view." It was to hide the decision that Wickham "chose to
walk upon the waves of the Atlantic" in order to rear "a Gothic edifice
so huge and so dark as quite to overshadow and eclipse it."[96]

Confusion abounded. Wickham presumed to forestall debate by
declaring that the meaning of the Constitution was self-evident; Wirt
attempted to end debate by claiming that Marshall and the Supreme
Court had settled the matter in *Bollman*. The situation was rife
with irony. Here were the president's lawyers praising the wisdom of
Marshall and his Court at the very time Jefferson was trying to humble
both. Burr's lawyers on the other hand were compelled to marginalize
Marshall's opinion in *Bollman*. They also went on to argue that the doctrine of constructive treason, which might have crept inadvertently into
Marshall's opinion, was not supported by English legal authorities – this
while insisting that such authorities were not binding in constitutional
cases anyway.

Confusion begat talk; talk begat confusion. With professional egos
on the line, neither side would shut up. Since Marshall was reluctant to
stop the intellectual slugfest, he had to listen to arguments about what he
meant by what he had written in his own opinion. Along with the spectators, the jurors no doubt relished the intellectual fireworks, heavily
spiced as it was with sarcastic and mean-spirited personal exchanges.
Almost certainly, however, most of them did not understand the torrent
of black-letter learning coming from both sides.

In fact, the law arguments were now directed mainly to Marshall,
for the simple reason that Burr asked him to rule on the admissibility
of further evidence. Both sides and all authorities agreed that questions
of evidence were the exclusive domain of the court. And unavoidably
the question of evidence turned into a grand debate about the relationship between the jury and the judge in America. What Burr asked
for, in short, was for Marshall to keep the jury from hearing all further testimony not bearing directly on the overt act of levying war.
The prosecution insisted that the jury hear everything about Burr and
his plans (including what happened before and after the assemblage on
Blennerhassett's island that he so wisely absented himself from) and

95 Ibid., 61.
96 Ibid., 62.

then, with minimal intrusion by the court, decide whether or not he was guilty. Martin summed up the dispute late in the trial when he declared that the government "wants to lay all the evidence before the Jury, and we want to prevent it!"[97] Or to rephrase slightly, the defense trusted Marshall and the prosecution trusted the jury. To be sure Marshall got the point and to bolster his resolve, Martin supplied him with a long, impressive, and arrogant lecture on the distinct roles of judge and jury in American law.[98]

Jury-power was the all-purpose remedy for what ailed the prosecution's case, starting with the embarrassing fact that what they charged Burr with in the wording of their indictment did not correspond to the evidence they were prepared to present. In addition to being consistent with Jeffersonian faith in the common people, jury-power was also an antidote to the anti-republican implications of constructive treason on which their case rested.

Making the trial jury into the bulwark of American liberty, however, was not without its problems for the prosecution. To start with, there was no such creature as the *American* jury, since jury practice varied from state to state and from court to court. Indeed, at the very time the Virginia lawyers for the prosecution were celebrating the trial jury, St. George Tucker, Virginia's leading legal scholar, was bemoaning the sad condition of the jury process in his state.[99]

Also, as the recent convictions of Republican editors under the Alien and Sedition Acts proved, juries could not always be counted on to defend individual liberty. The trial of James Callender in the federal circuit court in Richmond in 1800 was particularly germane, because both Hay and Wirt were lawyers for the defense. What they learned that was relevant to the Burr trial was that domineering Federalist judges – Associate Justice Samuel Chase was the presiding judge – could bully jurors into submission. More to the point, what Chase did in the Callender trial closely resembled what Burr was asking Marshall to do, namely, to direct the jurors' deliberations by restricting the testimony they could hear.[100]

---

[97] Carpenter, *Trial of Burr*, 3: 414. Note: in my copy of Carpenter, vol. 3, due to an error in pagination, p. 414 appears immediately preceding p. 409. A second page 414 appears later. The text itself runs continuously.

[98] Ibid., 407–14.

[99] St. George Tucker, *Blackstone's Commentaries* (5 vols., Phil., 1803), 4: 64–74 (Note F. "Of the Trial By Jury in Virginia").

[100] For an illuminating analysis of this important case see Kathryn Preyer, "*United States v. Callender*, Judge and Jury in a Republican Society," in Maeva Marcus, ed., *Origins*

In order to pressure Marshall to permit the jury to hear all the evidence – and to pave the way for a guilty verdict even if he refused to do so – Wirt brought his gift of oratory to bear on the personality and character of Burr. What he labored to show was that Burr could be prosecuted for treason even though he was not present when war was supposed to have been levied. What called Wirt to the barricades was Burr's insistence that he could not be prosecuted for a crime, or treated as an accessory to it, until the crime had been established by trying and convicting those, like Blennerhassett, who were principals due to their presence when the crime was committed.

Wirt expressed his outrage at the apparent injustice of Burr's position in a series of rhetorical questions: "Will any man say that Blannerhassett was the principal, and Burr but an accessory? Who will believe that Burr, the author and projector of the plot, who raised the forces, who enlisted the men and who procured the funds for carrying it into execution, was made a cat's paw of? Will any man believe that Burr, who is a soldier bold, ardent, restless and aspiring, the great actor whose brain conceived and whose hand brought the plot into operation, that he should sink down into an accessory, and that Blannerhassett should be elevated into a principal?"[101]

And finally: "Who is Blannerhassett?" Supplying the answer to his own question was the master-stroke that permitted Wirt to do exactly what the defense objected to and what Marshall had forbidden: to address Burr's character rather than overt acts. If Wirt could persuade the jury that Burr was evil genius enough to betray his country, then it might not matter what Marshall instructed them about the law or what he ruled about evidence.

To demonize Burr, Wirt romanticized Blennerhassett and adorned his portrait with all those "flounces" and "furbelows" he found so offensive in Wickham's arguments and which he promised to forego. The truth is that Harman Blennerhassett came to America not only to escape the political turmoil of his native Ireland, along with the legal and social problems that came with his marriage to his niece, but also to make money. No doubt Burr sold him a bill of goods, but Blennerhassett's own ambition made him a compliant, if not an equal, partner in Burr's quest for wealth and glory – goals that Blennerhassett described in grandiose language.

of the Federal Judiciary: Essays on the Judiciary Act of 1789 (New York, 1992), 173–95.
[101] Robertson, *Reports,* 2: 95.

Harman Blennerhassett

In Wirt's portrayal, however, the young Irishman and his wife were Adam and Eve in the garden. A noble and innocent soul, "a man of letters," Blennerhassett sought only "quiet and solitude in the bosom of our western forests." He "carried with him taste and science and wealth; and lo, the desert smiled." Surrounded by music, beautiful gardens, a great library full of treasures, and blessed by a wife "lovely, even beyond her sex," he discovered paradise.[102]

"And such was the state of Eden when the serpent entered its bowers." Burr snaked himself "into the open and un-practiced heart of the unfortunate Blannerhassett" and infused "into it the poison of his own ambition," a "daring and desperate search for glory," and an "ardour panting for great enterprises." The noble young Irishman was transformed; his

[102] Ibid., 96.

"enchanted island" turned into "wilderness," and his loving wife left "shivering at midnight, on the winter banks of the Ohio..."[103] And so on.

And so what? What had Wirt accomplished, other than damning Burr in the eyes of generations of Americans and assuring himself a place in the annals of great American oratory? Wirt had accomplished several things that any hard-driving, result-oriented modern lawyer would appreciate, starting with the fact that he supplied a plausible justification for the prosecution's use of the doctrine of constructive treason. Deadly poison required a harsh antidote. In painting Burr the traitor in such harsh colors, Wirt may also have hoped to make it difficult, or at least embarrassing, for Marshall to rule in his favor, an outcome that Wirt and many others now feared was all but certain. All the more reason, then, for Wirt to address his remarks to the jurors. Like Rufus Choate, another great nineteenth century trial lawyer, Wirt understood that "Any thing may be said to a jury, if you see the Court seem approving, and the jurymen listen."[104]

Listen they did. And how could they resist, since Wirt enlisted the Genesis story and Milton's *Paradise Lost* to reach their hearts and minds?[105] In Wirt's dramatic monologue Burr was Satan, and Blennerhassett stood for the idealistic young nation tempted at the moment of its creation by Satan's false promise of wealth and glory.

On a less exalted level, Wirt's assassination of Burr's character was precisely what the government witnesses were prepared to attest to if Marshall would only give them the opportunity. And if Marshall did not give them that chance? Well, the jury got the message anyhow – thanks to the greatest theatrical performance of a very theatrical trial. Wirt summed up with a pep talk urging the jurors to do their republican duty by sending Burr to the gallows – whether as accessory or principal it mattered not.

Like Wickham and Randolph, though less subtly, Wirt also put Marshall on notice: "the court never says," declaimed Wirt, "that the evidence is or is not sufficient to prove what it is intended to establish. No court has such right." If by the court's ruling, he argued, it compels the jury to decide the question on the basis of partial evidence, would it

[103] Ibid., 97.
[104] Edward G. Parker, *Reminiscences of Rufus Choate: The Great American Advocate* (New York, 1860), 263.
[105] Robert A. Ferguson unpacks the symbolism in Wirt's speech in *The Trial in American Life*, 86–91.

not "thereby divest the jury of their peculiar functions?" The "province" of the jury "should not be invaded. The invasion is big with danger and terror."[106]

And finally, regarding Burr's motion to suppress: "Have you the power sir? I should like to know where the authority can be found to prove that you have it." And more ominously: "In the fluctuations of party, in the bitterness of rancor and political animosity, the judges may lead juries to one side or the other as they may think proper. They may dictate as to the existence of an overt act, and thus decide the fate of a prisoner. If a judge sitting on the bench shall decide on facts as well as law in a prosecution for treason, he may sacrifice or rescue whom he pleases. If he be a *political* partisan, he may save his friends from merited punishment or blast his foes unjustly." To do so would surely pave the way for "some ruffian Jefferies" to "mount the bench." You must not. "You will not bring your country to see an hour so fearful and perilous as that which shall witness the ruin of the trial by jury."[107]

Wirt concluded on August 25; Marshall handed down his crucial decision on evidence on August 31. During the intervening period both sides got in their final blows, and both warned Marshall that history stood ready to judge him. Perhaps the most instructive speech came from Benjamin Botts, who summed up the defense's case in a rambling, emotional, and powerful argument that denounced the pernicious influence of the partisan press, assailed jury competence, and denounced Jefferson for assuming powers that belonged exclusively to the judiciary. His conclusion that "the president's interference with the prosecution is improper, illegal and unconstitutional"[108] drives home one critical fact we need to know in evaluating the trial: that contemporaries were fully aware that Jefferson directed the prosecution from beginning to end.[109] Botts did not have to name names when he warned that even a virtuous, self-governing people could be "seduced by the arts of designing and influential men." And that, Botts concluded, is precisely what Marshall in the performance of his judicial duties had to prevent.[110]

Indeed, Marshall assumed he was preventing just such a seduction when on August 31 he ruled in favor of Burr's motion to suppress. It was a densely reasoned argument, the complex nuances of which will

---

[106] Robertson, *Reports*, 2: 98–99.
[107] Ibid, 121–2.
[108] Ibid., 169.
[109] Ibid., 151–92 for Botts's argument.
[110] Ibid., 164–73.

be considered in the following chapter. But the nub of the matter was, "No testimony relative to the conduct or declarations of the prisoner elsewhere and subsequent to the transaction on Blannerhassett's island can be admitted; because such testimony, being in its nature merely corroborative and incompetent to prove the overt act in itself, is irrelevant until there be proof of the overt act by two witnesses."[111] Except for the remote possibility of a rebellious jury, the verdict on Burr was all but settled. The verdict on Marshall himself, as we shall now see, was very much in dispute.

[111] Ibid., 445.

5

Judging the Judge

"The nation will judge both the offender and judges for themselves."
Jefferson to William B. Giles, April 20, 1807[1]

"...His Honor did not for two days understand either the questions or himself..."
Burr on Marshall, September 20, 1807[2]

"Our Treason Laws may be defective, but I believe Marshall's Conduct strictly and correctly legal as the Laws now stand."
John Adams to John Quincy Adams, February 12, 1808[3]

To judge Marshall's performance as trial judge – to see him as his enemies saw him – one needs to remember that the great chief justice was not yet great in 1807. To be sure, he was a popular figure in Richmond, where he and his family had resided since 1780. Thanks to his bold diplomacy in the XYZ affair in 1798, he was also a celebrated hero. Those in a position to know, friend and foe alike, agreed that he was a uniquely gifted lawyer. As evidence of promised greatness, there was his opinion in *Marbury v. Madison*, but that opinion had not yet achieved iconic status and neither had the man who wrote it. Whether Marshall would be a great chief justice – or indeed, whether he would be the first chief justice to be impeached – was all yet to be determined.

---

[1] Jefferson to Giles, April 20, 1807, Bergh, *Writings of Jefferson*, 11: 187–91, quote at 190.
[2] As quoted by Blennerhassett, Safford, *Blennerhassett Papers*, 412–13.
[3] John Adams to John Quincy Adams, Feb. 12, 1808, Adams Papers, MHS.

Virginia Republicans, numerous and well placed in 1807 and spurred on by a popular president, had decided feelings about that question. They remembered Marshall as Virginia's leading Federalist in the 1790s, a closet Hamiltonian named to head the Supreme Court by departing Federalist President John Adams to subvert President-elect Jefferson's democratic "revolution"; not for a moment did they believe that a judicial robe neutralized Marshall's partisan instincts. As for *Marbury*: Rather than a mark of genius, it was proof final of his aggrandizing agenda.

Two additional factors led Marshall's enemies to expect the worst in the impending trial. One was Marshall's barbed criticism of Jefferson and his party in the final volume of his biography of Washington, which appeared in April 1807. Even more to the point was his *Marbury*-like rebuke of the president's overreach in his Bollman opinion. Jefferson's decision to take charge of the prosecution in Richmond was almost certainly prompted by his conviction that Marshall would try to embarrass him again by siding with Burr.

Marshall knew that the lines of battle had been drawn and that he would be shown no mercy by the president, the ever-vigilant partisan press, perhaps even by the people themselves. The legal terrain was full of pitfalls and challenges, too. He had to keep nine talented and touchy lawyers on task and steer them away from personal attacks and partisan grandstanding. With no help from Judge Griffin, with no clear guidance from precedent, and with little time for study or reflection, he had to settle new and complicated matters of trial procedure.

Above all, there were important and perplexing legal issues to be decided: The constitutional definition of treason remained to be clarified; and the law of evidence pertaining to treason, touched on so briefly in Article III, Section 3, and in previous decisions by the justices on circuit, had to be settled. Marshall's own authority as a federal judge, especially as it related to the mythic power of the trial jury, was also on the line. Finally, embodied in the escalating rivalry between the president and himself was the profound issue regarding separation of powers that had been broached in *Marbury*: In 1807 as in 1803 the line between politics and law was the central issue.

Marshall understood all this: the "many real intrinsic difficulties" of the case, and how they were "infinitely multiplied by extrinsic circumstances," as he complained to his colleague Justice Cushing. Although he wished "earnestly" to consult with all his "brethren on the bench," he knew better: "Sincerely do I lament that this wish cannot be completely indulged." He could and did lean on the arguments of counsel, but

John Marshall

ultimately the decisions were his alone, to be rendered "according to the best lights I possess."[4]

For his effort he was depicted by his enemies as America's own "hanging-judge" George Jeffreys – never minding that it was not Marshall who wanted the hanging.

Feasting with the "Traitor"

The pending trial in Richmond had become the subject of political controversy long before it began; and Marshall found himself at the center of the storm well before he confronted Burr in the Eagle Tavern for arraignment on March 30, 1806. When Marshall committed Burr for a

[4] Marshall to Cushing, June 29,1807, Hobson, *Papers of Marshall*, 7: 60.

high misdemeanor instead of treason, as the government insisted, it was assumed by his enemies that he had taken sides with the traitor.

Several things gave instant traction to this notion, starting with Marshall's statement during Burr's commitment hearing on April 1. After quoting Blackstone, Marshall added that the great judge had not meant to say "that the hand of malignity may grasp any individual against whom its hate may be directed, or whom it may capriciously seize, charge him with some secret crime, and put him on proof of his innocence." Marshall hurried to point out that he was not referring to the conduct of the government – and his clarification appeared as a note in Robertson's *Reports* – but the damage was done.[5]

More damaging than Marshall's provocative reference to "the hand of malignity" was his appearance shortly thereafter at a party for Burr given by John Wickham. As reported in the April 7, 1807 issues of both the *Virginia Argus*[6] and the Philadelphia *Aurora*,[7] the story of Marshall's attendance at Wickham's party set off a firestorm. The author of the letter in the *Aurora* accused Marshall of polluting "the ermine of justice" by "coming into contact with an acknowledged criminal," one "who had been proclaimed a traitor by the executive of the union." The *Enquirer* of April 10 embellished the charge in an anonymous article entitled "A Stranger from the Country," which in fact was known at the time to have been written by Benjamin W. Leigh.[8] On April 22, the *National Argus* in Worcester, Massachusetts reprinted the article from the *Virginia Argus*. By the time the story was reprinted in the *Petersburgh Republican*, the dinner had morphed into the "Feast of Treason," which article then made its way into the *Democratic Press* of Philadelphia[9] and the *Republican Advocate* of Fredericktown, Maryland,[10] among many other Republican newspapers around the nation.

The "Feast of Treason" article accused Marshall of taking Burr "by the hand," of "joining in a Bacchanalian revelry, and drinking the toasts and sentiments of a traitor!" All this in plain sight. "Marshall, Burr,

[5] Robertson, *Reports*, 1: 11.
[6] Malone, *Jefferson*, 5: 302.
[7] "To the Editor of the Aurora," April 7, 1807 as reprinted in *The Sun*, May 2, 1807.
[8] William H. Cabell to Joseph C. Cabell, April 12, 1807, identified Leigh as the author. Joseph Carrington Cabell Papers, copies at Swem Library, College of William and Mary, from originals at UVM. Thanks to Charles Hobson for calling my attention to this letter.
[9] April 22, 1807.
[10] May 1, 1807.

and Wickham – a chief justice, a traitor, and a tory! Save us from such a *trio* of *honest* men."[11] Word spread as far north as Portsmouth, New Hampshire, where Fourth of July toasts to President Jefferson, "The Fair Daughters of Columbia," and General James Wilkinson (for his "patriotism, firmness and vigilance") also included a blast at the "Judiciary of the United States," hoping that its "honor" might be restored and that "its chief judge be no more found a companion to traitors."[12]

The partisan newspaper network of the early republic was obviously a force to be reckoned with.[13] Marshall was well aware of this fact from past experience, so why did he make himself vulnerable by attending Wickham's party? Could it be, as his critics claimed, that he was blatantly partial and simply did not care who knew it?

From the limited evidence available, it is difficult to answer these questions about Marshall's behavior. We know he attended Wickham's party, but we do not know for certain whether he knew, when he accepted the invitation, that Burr would be present; James Bradley Thayer reports that Marshall did not know. On the other hand once Marshall found out that Burr would attend, there was still time to decline. Indeed, Thayer heard from an unnamed relative of Marshall's that Marshall's wife Polly advised him not to attend, but that the chief justice thought it would be an insult to his old friend Wickham not to go. There is no evidence that Burr and Marshall conversed during the party; Thayer reports that the two men "sat at the opposite end of the table" and that Marshall left early.[14]

Still the fact remains that Marshall attended the party. When the guests toasted Burr's health, did Marshall lift his glass? We can only surmise that he did, since not to have done so would have been an egregious violation of established social convention. In fact convention, the gentlemanly tradition of the Richmond bar, and Marshall's long friendship with Wickham best explain his being there in the first place.

---

[11] From the *Petersburgh Republican* as reprinted in *The Democratic Press*, April 22, 1807.

[12] *New Hampshire Gazette*, July 21, 1807.

[13] On this point, see Jeffrey L. Pasley, *"The Tyranny of Printers": Newspaper Politics In the Early American Republic* (Charlottesville, 2001).

[14] Thayer's remarks were made in an address on the centenary celebration of Marshall's ascent to the Court. The printed version of Thayer's address contains no citations, however, and the relative who testified about Marshall's behavior regarding Wickham's party is not identified. See John F. Dillon, ed., *John Marshall: Life, Character and Judicial Services* (3 vols., Chicago, 1903), 1: 233–4.

Whatever the reasons for it, Marshall's presence was a costly lapse of judgment, one that, according to William H. Cabell, Marshall lamented "more than any act of his life."[15] Cabell believed that the act was unintentional, but what Marshall ought to have known and what ought to have warned him away was not that Burr might be at the party, but that Wickham was Burr's leading lawyer and Marshall's own friend. Marshall never tried to justify or explain his indiscretion publicly. Perhaps he remained silent simply because explaining might make things worse; at the same time, *not* explaining called forth the suspicions of the *Virginia Argus*.[16] The best Marshall could hope for was that his reputation for integrity would carry him through, and to some extent it did: Even Marshall's detractors at the *Enquirer* conceded that he did not "consciously" weigh in on Burr's side.

In the emergent age of popular politics, however, party allegiance counted as much as a gentlemanly sense of honor, and perception was just as important as truth, perhaps even more so, since truth was hard to come by and harder still to prove. Whether conscious or not, the indisputable consequence of the episode was to elevate the partisan tone of the proceedings and to give Marshall's political enemies another opportunity to assail his character. Later on in the trial, rumors circulated that Marshall and Wickham consulted privately about the course of the trial, this time over a game of chess.[17]

The Great Subpoena Debate: Law or Politics or Both?

The role which public perception played in the trial – a role measured by the sensationalist coverage of the trial in the press and the apparent gullibility of readers – is an indication that legal proceedings were no longer the exclusive domain of lawyers and judges and the elite portion of the public. It followed that editors interested in selling papers were not much interested in the un-dramatic aspects of Marshall's day-by-day conduct of the trial.

A fair reading of the entire trial transcript, however, shows that Marshall was evenhanded, modest and remarkably patient. If he failed to halt Martin's verbal assault on Jefferson, he also failed to stop

---

[15] William H. Cabell to Joseph C. Cabell, April 12, 1807, Joseph Carrington Cabell Papers (copy, Swem Library).
[16] As reprinted in the Pittsfield, MA *Sun*, May 2, 1807.
[17] Safford, *Blennerhassett Papers,* 355.

Wirt's tirade against Burr. Recall too that Marshall cut the prosecution considerable slack when they demanded the right to argue intent before they proved that treason had been committed. When he misspoke he apologized; when he was wrong he admitted it. When both sides were wrong, he let them both know. And when he did not know the answer he asked for time to study. When there was no "general rule" to be found, he said so and did not try to find one.[18] He also restrained himself when lawyers on both sides lectured him on his judicial duties, and warned him of the consequences of not fulfilling them.

In short, Marshall in *Burr* went out of his way to not be Justice Chase in *Callender,* which is to say he was neither highhanded nor domineering. This said, it is also true that Marshall's fairness has to be judged by his decisions on the great issues before him – the question of treason which he decided on August 31, and the question of whether he could subpoena a sitting president and order him to produce papers in his possession that the defense requested, and indeed appear in person if he failed to do so.

Marshall's decision to issue the subpoena *duces tecum* on June 13 was a dramatic highlight of the trial that lent itself perfectly to partisan spin. Coming on the heels of "The Feast of Treason" story, it appeared to many who were already predisposed to think so that Marshall had, in Wirt's words, made his court "a canal" through which Burr and his lawyers "may pour upon the world their undeserved invectives against the government."[19] Wirt was referring to Marshall's failure to stop Martin's unrestrained attack on Jefferson during the course of the argument over the subpoena, in which Martin lambasted the president for behaving like George III, if not God Almighty.

There is no doubt that Martin's verbal assault on Jefferson was a breach of adversarial etiquette that threatened the very goal of rational discourse Marshall professed to uphold. Nevertheless, before judging Marshall too harshly, it must be remembered that neither he nor anybody else could have known what Martin was going to say in the heat of battle. What he said, vitriol aside, was that Jefferson had launched a personal vendetta against Burr; other lawyers on Burr's team and Burr himself made the same point throughout the trial, albeit in less inflammatory language. As defense lawyers, to make such an assertion was part of their job, just as it was the duty of the prosecution to complain

[18] Robertson, *Reports*, 2: 536.
[19] Ibid., 1: 144.

about the defense's having done so; and the prosecution did complain with escalating vigor. The passions on both sides were no doubt genuine, but their complaints were also designed to put Marshall on the spot in the hope he might give them a break.

In fairness, however, ought Marshall to be blamed for the passionate political feelings that burst forth spontaneously during the long, grueling trial? The best he could do, and what he did in fact do, in response to Wirt's complaints at the conclusion of the rancorous day of argument on June 10, was to appeal to "the dignity" of the defense to stop "abusing" the government. Marshall was reluctant to interfere, but he wanted to make it clear that both sides "in the heat of debate" said things "of which the court did not approve," and that both "had acted improperly in the style and spirit of their remarks; that they had been to blame in endeavouring to excite the prejudices of the people; and had repeatedly accused each other of doing what they forget they have done themselves." He then urged both sides to "confine themselves on every occasion to the point really before the court; that their own good sense and regard for their characters required them to follow such a course; and it was hoped that they would not hereafter deviate from it."[20]

The offending parties paid but scant attention to Marshall's plea for moderation and restraint. And indeed it is hard to see how he could have made them behave differently except by exercising a heavy-handed authority that was against his nature, and which his enemies, and probably his friends, would have condemned him for using. As it turned out, there was condemnation aplenty when Marshall issued the subpoena to Jefferson on June 13. The personal nature of the confrontation between the two men was immediately apparent. Once again Marshall appeared to be siding with Burr the traitor; and once again he was condemned for using his court as a personal bully pulpit to chastise the president.

Whether Marshall secretly enjoyed once again lecturing Jefferson on his legal duties is impossible to know, but Marshall clearly went out of his way to rest his decision on solid legal and institutional ground. The court, he admitted, felt "peculiar motives" for manifesting a respect for "the chief magistrate of the Union." What those motives were, he did not say; but he did say that the court's respect had to be "compatible" with its "official duties," which in his opinion it was not.[21]

[20] Robertson, *Reports*, 1: 148.
[21] Ibid., 187.

On the subject of judicial duty, he spoke personally, explaining that he would "deplore most earnestly, the occasion which should compel me to look back on any part of my official conduct with so much self-reproach as I should feel, could I declare, on the information now possessed, that the accused is not entitled to the letter in question, if it should be really important to him."[22]

The letter in question was Wilkinson's letter to Jefferson dated October 21, 1806, which Jefferson had mentioned specifically in his proclamation of Burr's guilt on January 22, 1807. The subpoena as it was actually issued on June 13 requested not only the letter of October 21 but also "the document accompanying the same letter," which was Wilkinson's main narrative of the conspiracy, dated October 20, and which had been delivered to Jefferson along with the letter itself.[23] Thanks to Marshall's issuance of the subpoena and Jefferson's compliance, Burr and his lawyers would ultimately receive authenticated copies of both documents.

Since Burr's lawyers obviously required both documents to prepare his defense, it is difficult to see how Marshall could have ruled differently than he did. Even so, Marshall had no reason to think that the president would comply with the subpoena; indeed, given the bad faith between them, he had reason to think that Jefferson would not comply. Thus Marshall's resolute justification of his decision to issue the subpoena, which he grounded on an elemental principle of criminal procedure in capital felony cases: "So far back as any knowledge of our jurisprudence is possessed, the uniform practice of this country has been, to permit any individual, who was charged with any crime, to prepare for his defense, and to obtain the process of the court, for the purpose of enabling him so to do. This practice is as convenient, and is as consonant to justice, as it is to humanity."[24] He then rejected out of hand the prosecution's contention that the subpoena could issue only after the grand jury had brought an indictment. In Marshall's words: "Upon immemorial usage, then, and upon what is deemed a sound construction of the constitution and law of the land, the court is of the opinion, that any person, charged with a crime in the courts of the United States, has a right, before, as well

[22] Ibid., 188.
[23] *"Message from the President of the United States, transmitting a copy of the proceedings and of the evidence exhibited on the arraignment of Aaron Burr, and others, before the Circuit court of the United States, held in Virginia, in the year 1807* (City of Washington, 1807), Va. Hist. Soc., Rare Books, E334.J48, 1807.
[24] Robertson, *Reports*, 1: 177–8.

as after indictment, to the process of the court to compel the attendance of his witnesses."[25]

This basic right of criminal defendants to compulsory process, which Marshall located in the Sixth Amendment, was dispositive. The remaining and more dramatic question was whether, in order to secure that right, a subpoena *duces tecum* could issue to a sitting president. Connected to this issue was an even more explosive question: whether the court could compel the personal appearance of the recipient if the requested papers were not forthcoming. The subpoena addressed to Jefferson "commanded" him "to appear before the Judge of the Circuit Court…for the fifth Circuit," that is to say before John Marshall. Burr signed a formal waiver of personal attendance, however, noting that copies of the materials requested would be "admitted as sufficient observance of this process."[26]

Marshall's opinion was a forceful justification of the court's authority, including its power to compel performance. Concerning judicial authority: "The court perceive no legal objection to issuing a subpoena *duces tecum* to any person whatever, providing, the case be such as to justify the process." Concerning the obligation of the president to obey: while a king could not be summoned to appear in person, because it would be said to be "incompatible with his dignity," the president of the United States is no king – the same point Luther Martin had already made in much harsher language. "In this respect, the first magistrate of the Union may more properly be likened to the first magistrate of a state – at any rate under the former confederation." Then: "If in any court of the United States, it has been decided, that a subpoena cannot issue to the president, that decision is unknown to this court."[27] Marshall abruptly dismissed the argument that the duties of the president "demand his whole time for national objects," since "it is apparent that this demand is not unremitting."[28] Jefferson understandably took that remark as a

---

[25] Ibid., 180.

[26] For a photocopy of the original subpoena *duces tecum* see Aaron Burr Mss 2 B94a, Va. Hist. Soc.; also see the explanatory letter of R. Grayson Dashiell (ViHMss 2 B94 a1).

[27] Robertson, *Reports*, 1: 180–82, *Papers of Marshall*, 7: 41–43. In fact, Justice Chase on circuit refused to issue a subpoena *duces tecum* in the sedition trial of Cooper in 1798. Cooper, who served as counsel in his own defense, asked the court to issue a subpoena *duces tecum* to John Adams to attend the trial as a witness and bring relevant documents with him. Such was hardly a convincing precedent, however, since Justice Chase not only refused to issue the process but roundly berated Cooper for asking for it. Beveridge, *Marshall*, 3: 33–34.

[28] Robertson, *Reports*, 1: 181.

gratuitous personal slur. It was gratuitous because Marshall knew that Jefferson was not about to appear as a witness in his court and that there was no way to force him to do so.

The government's most compelling argument against the issuance of the subpoena, one that has resurfaced at critical times in American history, was that a president could not "for state reasons" be expected to comply with a subpoena ordering him to produce papers in his possession. On this point, Marshall spoke boldly, affirming that it was up to the court not the president to say what was relevant to the defense or inadmissible because of national security interests. Marshall granted that the letter requested by Burr raised "a delicate question," but added that there was "certainly nothing before the court which shows, that the letter in question contains any matter, the disclosure of which would endanger the public safety."[29] If such were the case, and if the matter in question were not "immediately and essentially applicable to the point," then such matter would be suppressed – but it was the court's call upon the return of the subpoena.

Marshall abruptly dismissed the prosecution's contention that a ruling in favor of Burr's subpoena motion would give "the countenance of the court to suspicions regarding the veracity of the witness" – that is, James Wilkinson.[30] That of course is precisely what the defense wanted to do, which is to say that their request for the subpoena was designed in large part to make the prosecution and the president look bad for building their case on Wilkinson's testimony.

The confrontation between the chief justice and the president over the subpoena – the tone of Marshall's argument, the complaints of the affront by Jefferson through his lawyers – was clearly not without its personal side. Their confrontation was also a textbook example (Madison's *Federalist* 51 being the text) of how the Constitution's separation of powers should operate: how the office holders in each branch, by zealously defending their institutional turf, would prevent a tyrannical concentration of power in any one branch. In the Burr trial, however, the danger came not from an overly powerful judiciary but rather from the executive branch backed by public opinion and a compliant Congress. Prompted by the president, Congress threatened to curb the Court's habeas corpus jurisdiction and even divest it entirely of its criminal jurisdiction. Jefferson also expected that Marshall's conduct of the

---

[29] Ibid., 186–7.
[30] Ibid., 186.

trial would lead to his impeachment which, had it occurred, would have been a devastating, if not fatal, blow to the independence of the federal judiciary.

Given the widespread hostility to the federal judiciary, and to him personally, Marshall's decision to subpoena the president was a risky move. Even so, his reasoned justification for issuing the subpoena – like his justification of judicial review in *Marbury v. Madison* – struck a timely blow for judicial independence in an age that had not fully accepted that principle.[31] The fact that Marshall escaped impeachment consolidated the victory – and he escaped in no small part because he conducted a fair trial while avoiding the judicial arrogance that had marred Chase's behavior in the Callender trial in 1800.

Marshall's example of independence along with his forceful defense of the court's subpoena powers would later bolster the Burger Court during the Watergate hearings in its victorious battle with President Nixon over executive privilege.[32] In 1807, however, the struggle between Marshall and Jefferson ended in a draw. While it is true that Jefferson complied with Burr's request for the letter of October 21 and the accompanying document of October 20, Jefferson (speaking through his lawyers in Richmond) never conceded that he was duty-bound to obey Marshall's subpoena.[33] The issue of the subpoena would resurface during the final stage of the trial, as will be noted shortly; and once again the contest between the president and the chief justice would end with both men defending their institutional turf.

The Decision that Freed Burr (Almost), Defined Treason, and Damned John Marshall in the Eyes of His Enemies

Marshall's decision of August 31 was the grand climax of the trial. The decision settled many things: the meaning of "levying war" first broached by the Supreme Court in *Bollman* was clarified. By implication

---

[31] On the long history of judicial independence, and especially on the struggle for judicial independence at the state level during the early republic, see Scott Douglas Gerber, *A Distinct Power: The Origins of an Independent Judiciary* (New York, 2011); on the development of the concept of judicial duty in England and America: Philip Hamburger, *Law and Judicial Duty* (Cambridge, 2008).

[32] As in Chief Justice Burger's opinion for the Court in *United States v. Nixon* 418 U.S. 683 (1974). On Marshall's relevance see Paul Freund, "Foreword: On Presidential Privilege, The Supreme Court, 1973 Term," 88 *Harvard Law Review* 13, 23–31 (1974).

[33] For Jefferson's position on the subpoena question and related matters see Malone, *Jefferson*, 5: ch. 18.

the contest between jury and judge was settled in favor of the latter (although the issue would surface again in the last phase of the trial). The matter of admissible evidence, the immediate point of dispute, was also settled. All of these things contributed to the jury's decision on September 1 to acquit Burr on the charge of treason.

What Marshall did to bring about the jury's verdict, although not to guarantee it, was to rule favorably on Burr's motion to suppress all further evidence that did not bear directly on the formal charge against him: that is, the charge that he had levied war against the United States on Blennerhassett's island on December 10. To rule on this question of evidence, however, Marshall also had to explain to the jury what the Constitution meant by "levying war" in Article III. And to do that he had to say what the Supreme Court had intended to say in *Bollman*. Beyond that conflicted decision were the circuit opinions of Chase, Paterson, and Iredell to be considered. And further back still, and most important of all, were the provisions regarding treason in the Constitution.

From the beginning to the end, the words in Article III loomed large, and this fact played to Marshall's strength. He was the "master spirit of the scene" in Richmond because he was a master interpreter of the written Constitution. Still, nothing he had done previously in this regard, *Marbury* included, rivaled his effort in the Burr trial. Although Marshall was still learning on the job in 1807, the trajectory of greatness was apparent.

A leading Marshall scholar referred to his Burr decision as "masterly," and so it was.[34] It was also the decision that drew the most fire from his enemies. In particular, what his critics found most objectionable was Marshall's ruling to withhold further evidence from the jurors, not only because it all but guaranteed Burr's acquittal, but also because, as with Chase in *Callender*, the ruling seemed to pit Marshall the conservative Federalist against the trial jury – the jury representing, according to republican theory, the sovereign people themselves.

However, what the critics did not do was to attend sufficiently to the entire opinion and to Marshall's minutely reasoned legal justification for his holding. According to Dumas Malone, even Jefferson probably did not read the opinion closely.[35] Hay found its excessive length and intricate reasoning off-putting, and like his boss, assumed that Marshall manipulated the law to serve partisan ends. Wirt too seems to have

---

[34] Hobson, *Papers of Marshall*, Editorial Note, 7: 7.
[35] Malone, *Jefferson*, 5: 339.

agreed, at least before the wounds of defeat had healed. With the possible exception of the essays of Lucius (aka William Thompson) published in the *Enquirer* and the Philadelphia *Aurora*,[36] most of the partisan press simply condemned the decision without analyzing it.

One person who took the opinion with utmost seriousness, however, was Marshall himself. One compelling reason for doing so, to which he alluded several times during the trial, was that a man's life was on the line. Also, Marshall was keenly aware of the importance of the constitutional question to be decided. Technically, as he observed, a single justice sitting on circuit could not settle the meaning of Article III, Section 3, especially since the Supreme Court en banc had already spoken. Marshall understood too that he could shape the law himself by clarifying what the Supreme Court meant by what he had written in *Bollman*. Nevertheless, all this is not to suggest that Marshall created treason law by himself, that he cut his doctrine out of whole cloth. Months of often learned discourse by the lawyers on both sides, the original words of the Framers, and the rich legacy of English law, were all indispensable elements in the final mix.

In addition, Marshall made an effort to solicit advice from his colleagues on the Supreme Court. Writing to his colleague Justice William Cushing early in the Richmond proceedings, he cut directly to the major issues, those that troubled the Court in *Bollman* and were certain to trouble Marshall in Richmond.[37] The most perplexing and weighty issue for which he wanted "the aid of all the judges" concerned the doctrine of constructive treasons. Specifically: "How far is this doctrine to be carried in the United States? If a body of men assemble for a treasonable purpose, does this implicate all those who are concerned in the conspiracy whether acquainted with the assemblage or not? Does it implicate those who advised, directed or approved of it? Or does it implicate those only who were present or within the district?"[38]

Whether Cushing consulted his colleagues on these legal points and whether he or they advised Marshall, as Marshall requested, is impossible to say for sure, but one thing is certain: these questions pressing on Marshall's mind in Richmond were legal in nature and not political. Legal also were the issues argued by counsel during the long trial; and they were argued in fact because they were *not* fully settled by the text of the Constitution, nor by the Court's decision in *Bollman*.

[36] Beveridge, *Marshall*, 3: 533–5 discusses the Thompson letters.
[37] Marshall to Cushing, June 29, 1807, Hobson, *Papers of Marshall*, 7: 60–62.
[38] Ibid., 60.

One thing that was settled by the Bollman decision is seen in Marshall's concession to Cushing that the Bollman Court "certainly adopts the doctrine of constructive treasons." And this is what the prosecution argued in Richmond and what Burr's lawyers vociferously denied. For Marshall, however, the question was not whether the doctrine of "constructive treasons" had been adopted in *Bollman*, but rather how far that decision carried the doctrine.[39]

In answering this question Marshall most likely got aid from his colleagues and certainly from the learned arguments of counsel in Richmond. In the final analysis, however, the call was his to make. And the authority of what he said depended on the quality of his own scholarly analysis and the persuasiveness of his own reasoning. Since the decision issued under his name alone, its reception as law would be inseparable from Marshall's reputation, which would in turn be linked with the record of his fairness as manifest in the trial itself.

Marshall understood both the opportunity and the pitfalls. To those waiting to denounce his effort and impugn his integrity as a judge, he had this to say: "That this court dares not usurp power is most true. That this court dares not shrink from its duty is not less true. No man is desirous of placing himself in a disagreeable situation. No man is desirous of becoming the peculiar subject of calumny. No man, might he let the bitter cup pass from him without self reproach, would drain it to the bottom. But if he have no choice in the case, if there be no alternative presented to him but a dereliction of duty or the opprobrium of those who are denominated the world, he merits the contempt as well as the indignation of his country who can hesitate which to embrace."[40]

◊ Rarely, if ever, among Marshall's many opinions, be they great or small, did the chief justice write so personally about the duties of judicial office. And nowhere in those opinions did he go to such lengths to ground his decision on logical analysis and discerning scholarship. Albert Beveridge concluded that Marshall's August 31 effort equaled, if it did not exceed, the best of his great constitutional opinions, being the only one "in which an extensive examination of sources is made."[41] Indeed, there is no better example of Marshall's mastery of the common-law methodology as applied to the new Constitution and the needs of the new nation. In this common-law interpretive universe, he was meshed

[39] Ibid., 60–62.
[40] Robertson, *Reports*, 2: 444–5.
[41] Beveridge, *Marshall*, 3: 504.

with the lawyers who argued the case so brilliantly; in fact he was the first among equals.

The adjudicative problems were complicated because the facts in the case were complex, because the issues were personally and ideologically fraught, and because the words in the treason clause of the Constitution were not as clear as they at first appeared to be, or as Burr's lawyers insisted they were. To be sure, the requirement that treason had to be proved "by two witnesses to the same overt act" (the Treasons Trial Act of 1696 required two witnesses but not to the same overt act) was itself straightforward. Its inclusion, moreover, was a sure sign that the Framers intended to prohibit the political uses of treason that had darkened English history.[42]

What muddied the waters was that the definition of treason as "levying war" against the government came pretty much verbatim from 25 Edward III, a fact that made several centuries of English case law, along with treatises and parliamentary acts regarding treason, an unavoidable part of the interpretive matrix. Rather than clarifying doctrine this long history opened up a confusing array of possible interpretations: Blackstone listed seven versions of treason, while Hay claimed he could detect at least fifteen. But whatever the number, it was clear that as a guide to a republican constitution, English legal history afforded ample room for both judicial discretion and judicial error.

So also did American legal history at the state and national levels in the post-Constitutional period. The debates of the Philadelphia Convention, conducted in secret, were not available; and even when they were published in 1840, they threw disappointingly little light on the meaning of Article III, Section 3. One thing that did illuminate the intent of the Framers, in addition to the two-witness provision, was the fact that the English Treason Act of 1351, as Sir William Blackstone explained, explicitly prohibited judicially constructed treasons. If the Framers of Article III had not read the old statute themselves, then assuredly they were familiar with Blackstone's account of Parliament's effort to keep judges from making treason law, as they had freely done before 1351.[43]

When Marshall read Blackstone on this point, and it is a sure thing he did, he certainly realized that the prosecution was asking him to do precisely what the great statute of 1351 prohibited. He was also aware,

---

[42] For Blackstone on the English rule and Tucker's observation on its American modification, see Tucker, *Blackstone's Commentaries*, 5: 357 and his footnote 21.
[43] Tucker, ed., *Blackstone's Commentaries*, 5: 84.

as were the lawyers in the trial, of Madison's warning in *Federalist* 43 against "new fangled and artificial treasons" that America's Constitution was designed to prevent.[44]

Blackstone and Madison provided clues as to the meaning of treason in the Constitution, but neither was binding. More directly apposite although still inconclusive were the positions on "levying war" taken by Justices Chase, Iredell, and Paterson in the 1790s. Their opinions were not controlling either, however, first, because they were circuit rulings; and second, as Marshall recognized, because the cases they decided involved acts taken in opposition to specific federal laws rather than efforts to overthrow the government. Obviously then, the most authoritative source available to Marshall in Richmond was his own opinion for the Supreme Court in *Bollman*. But as noted previously, it was also the most troublesome because his words in that opinion were not absolutely clear, and also because the prosecution could and did read into them a definition of treason sufficiently broad to embrace Burr's improbable western adventures.

With such wide latitude for judicial discretion, the particular questions to which the sources spoke ended up being mainly those framed by the prosecution's legal strategy, particularly by the initial decision to indict Burr specifically for levying war on Blennerhassett's island on December 10. Because those events were so unwarlike, the government needed to interpret "levying war" broadly; to legitimate this broad construction, they relied on their reading of Marshall's Bollman opinion. And to support their interpretation of that opinion, and perhaps to make it easier for Marshall to accept their argument, they turned to English sources and American decisional law from the 1790s.

Because the prosecution relied mainly on their own reading of his Bollman opinion, Marshall might have settled the matter peremptorily with a simple statement of what he meant in that opinion; and the main thrust of his ruling in Richmond was in fact a close textual and contextual analysis of his own words in the Bollman case. But the prosecution insisted, although not without contradicting Jefferson's bias against Blackstone and other Tory judges, that English treason law was a relevant guide to the intent of the Framers.[45] So reluctantly did the defense.

And so unavoidably, and uncharacteristically, Marshall turned legal historian. The definition of "levying war" he derived from English legal

---

[44] Benjamin F. Wright, ed., *The Federalist* (Cambridge, 1961), 310.
[45] Robertson, *Reports*, 2: 402–03.

history, however, was distinctly at odds with the sweeping definition
extracted by the prosecution. Marshall did concede their point that levying war did not always include actual hostilities, and he also agreed that
those who levied war did not in every instance have to be armed. His
main conclusion from English experience, however, was that "levying
war" required, if not actual hostilities, then a show of martial force,
"an assemblage with such appearance of force as would justify the opinion that they met for the purpose."[46] On its face, this definition did not
embrace the events of December 10 on Blennerhassett's island.

In short, Marshall viewed English law as moving away from the
broad definition of treason that the prosecution liked. His interpretation
of the opinions of Chase, Iredell, and Paterson fortified his conclusion:
"The Judges of the United States...seem to have required still more to
constitute the fact of levying war, than has been required by the English
books."[47] So too, as Marshall saw it, did the Framers of Article III, as
they set about to reshape the law of monarchical England to match the
republican spirit of the new nation.

By refuting the prosecution's interpretation of English law regarding
the meaning of "levying war," Marshall also undercut their reading of
his Bollman opinion. Still remaining, however, were portions of that
opinion that appeared to endorse constructive treason, or "constructive
presence," as Marshall called it. The specific question here was whether
Burr could be guilty of treason if he had not been present when war was
levied. To that question the prosecution answered "yes," and to prove
their point they confronted Marshall with his own words in *Bollman,*
which Marshall repeated and was about to clarify: "It is not the intention of the court to say that no individual can be guilty of this crime who
has not appeared in arms against his country. On the contrary, if war be
actually levied, that is, if a body of men be actually assembled in order
to effect by force a treasonable purpose, all those who perform any part,
however minute, etc., and who are actually leagued in the general conspiracy are traitors."[48]

Taken out of context, these words seemed capable of transporting
Burr to the gallows, especially since Marshall appeared to make the same
point at other places in his Bollman opinion. The defense was quick to

---

[46] Ibid., 416. Marshall explains *Bollman* on the meaning of "levying war," ibid.,
     407–23.
[47] Ibid., 414.
[48] *U.S. v. Burr,* 25 Fed. Cas. No.14,693 (C.C.D.Va.), 166.

challenge the logic of such an interpretation, but they were clearly worried that Marshall and his colleagues on the Supreme Court had conceded too much to their opponents. Both sides now pressed Marshall, sitting as a trial judge, for a definitive ruling on what he had said as Chief Justice and as the author of the majority opinion in *Bollman*.

Marshall responded in an opinion that laid the cornerstone of American treason law. For the prosecution lawyers who misread his Bollman opinion, he laid out the rules of interpretation that would have prevented their misreading. For the jury he explained the legal principles established in *Bollman* that should guide their deliberations. For one and all, he justified his decision to terminate all further testimony not directly related to the levying of war on Blennerhassett's island.

Marshall minced no words in setting forth the general principles of construction the prosecution violated in their interpretation of *Bollman*. Rule one: "Every opinion, to be correctly understood, ought to be considered with a view to the case in which it was delivered."[49] *Bollman*, that is to say, was a habeas corpus hearing regarding two men who were not involved in "executing the plan" that Burr had in mind, whatever that was. In short, the Bollman "opinion was not a treatise on treason, but a decision of a particular case…" Rule two: "General expressions ought not to be considered as overruling settled principles without a direct declaration to that effect."[50] That is to say, comments on treason in *Bollman* ought not to be construed out of context as overturning four centuries of English law, or a decade of reasoning by supreme court justices on circuit.

Rule three was especially telling since Marshall spoke as the author of the Bollman decision: "The opinion of a single judge certainly weighs as nothing if opposed to that of the supreme court; but if he were one of the judges who assisted in framing that opinion, if while the impression under which it was framed was yet fresh upon his mind, he delivered an opinion on the same testimony, not contradictory to that which had been given by all the judges together, but showing the sense in which he understood terms that might be differently expounded, it may fairly be said to be in some measure explanatory of the opinion itself."[51]

Rules one and two guided his exposition of *Bollman*; rule three explained candidly why his exposition deserved respect. Thus armed he

---

[49] Robertson, *Reports*, 2: 415.
[50] Ibid.
[51] Ibid., 421.

set out to say what the Court (and Chief Justice Marshall) meant to say about treason in *Bollman* – had that subject been properly before the justices. His exposition of the law boiled down to this definition of levying war: "It is said that war must be levied in fact, that the object must be one which is to be effected by force; that the assemblage must be such as to prove that this is its object, that it must not be an equivocal act, without a warlike appearance, that it must be an open assemblage for the purpose of force."[52]

To clarify further, Marshall quoted from his May 22 charge to the Richmond grand jury, when the meaning of his words in *Bollman* was fresh: "to constitute the fact of levying war, it is not necessary that hostilities shall have actually commenced by engaging in military force of the United States, or that measures of violence against the government shall have been carried into execution. But levying war is a fact, in the constitution of which force is an indispensable ingredient. Any combination to subvert by force the government of the United States, violently to dismember the union, to compel a change in the administration, to coerce the repeal or adoption of a general law, is a conspiracy to levy war, and if the conspiracy be carried into effect by the actual employment of force, by the embodying and assembling of men for the purpose of executing the treasonable design which was previously conceived, it amounts to levying war. It has been held that arms are not essential to levying war provided the force assembled be sufficient to attain, or perhaps to justify attempting the object without them."[53]

As to the guiding spirit of the Supreme Court's decision in *Bollman*, Marshall had one further observation to make and he quoted his own opinion in that case to make it, declaring, "it is more safe as well as more consonant to the principles of our constitution that the crime of treason should not be extended by construction to doubtful cases; and that crimes, not already within the constitutional definition, should receive such punishment as the legislature in its wisdom may provide."[54]

The constitutional meaning of "levying war" was now settled – at least for the purpose of ruling on Burr's motion to suppress further testimony. On that determinative procedural issue, Marshall made two points that settled the matter in Burr's favor. Point one: "That this indictment

[52] Ibid., 420.
[53] Ibid., 421–2. Marshall read his May 22 charge to the grand jury. Charles Hobson notes that no manuscript of that charge exists, noting further that Marshall "did not allow his grand jury charges to be published." *Papers of Marshall*, 7: 117, note 37.
[54] Robertson, *Reports*, 2: 420.

having charged the prisoner with levying war on Blannerhassett's island and containing no other overt act, cannot be supported by proof that war was levied at that place by other persons, in the absence of the prisoner, even admitting those persons to be connected with him in one common conspiracy." Point two: "That admitting such an indictment could be supported by such evidence, the previous conviction of some person, who committed the act which is said to amount to levying war, is indispensable to the conviction of a person who advised or procured that act."[55]

Marshall's argument here, which explained his ruling to suppress further testimony, was unanswerable. His first point meant that in presenting evidence and witnesses, the prosecution was confined to proving the precise charge levied in the indictment. Burr was charged with levying war on Blannerhassett's island and that was the charge he and his lawyers were prepared to refute. To proceed against him on charges not in the indictment would deprive him – or any criminal defendant – of the most elemental principle of due process. In Marshall's words: "The law does not expect a man to be prepared to defend every act of his life which may be suddenly and without notice alleged against him. In common justice the particular fact with which he is charged ought to be stated, and stated in such a manner as to afford a reasonable certainty of the nature of the accusation and the circumstances which will be adduced against him."[56]

Marshall's second point, which finessed the question of whether Burr could be guilty of levying war when he was not present at the time war was allegedly levied, was that before that question could be settled, it would have to first be proved that war had in fact been levied. Although Marshall noted that the question of "constructive presence" was not before the court, it would appear that he was prepared to endorse the principle that held that those who planned treason, and who rounded up recruits and procured supplies to implement it, could be tried for treason even if they were not actually present when their plan was set in motion. Marshall also went out of his way to emphasize that if the acts of planning, procurement and the like were considered treason, then those acts would have to be proved by two witnesses to the same overt act.[57] In any case, before an indictment for such acts would stand, the government would have to prove that war had actually been levied.

[55] Ibid., 423.
[56] Ibid., 424.
[57] In his letter to Cushing, Marshall acknowledged that the Bollman court had endorsed the doctrine of "constructive presence." Marshall to Cushing, June 29, 1807, Hobson,

Thus it all came back to what happened – or did *not* happen – on Blennerhassett's island on December 10. Marshall prudently refrained from stating his opinion as to whether the facts proved that war had been levied, since that question was for the jurors to determine on the basis of the evidence presented. But in ruling on Burr's motion to suppress, Marshall was emphasizing the relationship between the law and the facts they were to consider. As he explained, in a sentence that defies easy understanding: "It has been thought proper to discuss this question at large and to review the opinion of the supreme court, although this court would be more disposed to leave the question of fact, whether an overt act of levying war was committed on Blannerhassett's island to the jury under this explanation of the law, and to instruct them, that unless the assemblage on Blannerhassett's island was an assemblage in force, was a military assemblage in a condition to make war, it was not a levying of war, and that they could not construe it into an act of war, than to arrest the further testimony which might be offered to connect the prisoner with that assemblage, or to prove the intention of those who assembled together at that place."[58]

Marshall was careful to explain that the question of whether war had been levied "is not to be understood as decided."[59] But for practical purposes it had been, not because of anything Marshall said, but because the evidence already presented by the prosecution – the best they had to present – did not come close to proving that war had been levied. Before Marshall cut them short, Hay and his colleagues had presented fourteen witnesses, several of whom recounted in vivid language what they heard Burr say he intended to do, from which they surmised that he anticipated that thousands of westerners, who hated Spain and were doubtful about the government back East, would join Burr as he headed for New Orleans on his way to Mexico.

The problem for the prosecution was that no witness claimed to have seen this vast army on the move; and as Marshall observed, it would be impossible to hide such an army if it truly existed. What a couple of witnesses did see on the evening of December 10, instead of the assembling of a military force capable of taking Washington and Mexico by force, was the chaotic comings and goings of a bunch of young men

---

Papers of Marshall, 7: 60. Marshall explored the question of "constructive treasons" at Robertson, *Reports*, 2: 425–45. Regarding the two-witness rule as applicable to the crime of "advising or procuring treason," Marshall is emphatic (ibid., 436–7).

[58] Robertson, *Reports*, 2: 422.

[59] Ibid.

hurrying to escape the clutches of the Wood County militia. According to Marshall's definition of levying war, this motley band need not have committed violent acts or even have been armed. But they did have to exhibit "the appearance of force" competent to accomplish the crime they were accused of having committed. And this question was up to the jury.

Marshall's ruling on Burr's motion to suppress, the main target of Marshall's critics, has thus been misunderstood. Marshall did not in fact rule to withhold *relevant* testimony from the jury as charged. Nowhere is this distinction between relevant and irrelevant evidence more forcefully explained than by Luther Martin during the trial-after-the-trial.[60] What Martin argued and what Marshall ruled was that only those witnesses could be heard who were prepared to testify about the overt act of levying war on Blennerhassett's island. The government presented no further witnesses, one must assume, because they had none who could testify about that issue. What doomed the case – what freed Burr on the charge of treason, to put it another way – was not Marshall's ruling, but rather the fact that nothing happened on Blennerhassett's island, or anywhere else on the western frontier, that looked remotely like war levied against the United States.

Given the stubborn facts of the case, Marshall's ruling on evidence and the jury's deliberations led to Burr's acquittal. As a trial judge, Marshall rendered justice and defined the law to the best of his ability. He defined "levying war" in such terms as would permit the government to stop treasonable action before it turned into full-fledged warfare. He also agreed with the prosecution that Burr could have been convicted of treason without being present when war was actually levied – provided that it was established that war *had* been levied, and provided that there were two witnesses to Burr's activities that connected him materially to the act of levying war.

The principle Marshall enunciated here was compatible with one aspect of the English doctrine of "constructive treasons." What Marshall repudiated in English treason law – that which the prosecution tried to press on him during the trial – was the proposition that a conspiracy to commit treason was itself treason. For Marshall, a conspiracy to commit treason and treason were separate and distinct crimes.

---

[60] Carpenter, *Trial of Burr*, 3: 412. For Martin's discussion of the duties of the court in relation to those of the jury, see ibid., 407–14. Note: p. 407 appears immediately following p. 400.

By withholding irrelevant and inflammatory evidence, Marshall's decision encouraged the jurors to do what the law required: to give the accused the benefit of the doubt. At the same time, his decision also set forth a workable treason doctrine that enabled the government to defend itself against its own citizens who would use force to bring it down.

Needless to say, Marshall's enemies did not see matters this way. Impatient with nuanced and carefully drawn legal distinctions, they saw only the bottom line and assumed that Marshall had manipulated the law to free a traitor. None of Marshall's other opinions – not even *McCulloch v. Maryland* in 1819, not *Cohens v. Virginia* in 1821, not the Cherokee Indian opinions of the 1830s – elicited such a personally vicious response. The Baltimore mob that hanged Marshall in effigy, along with Burr, Blennerhassett and Martin, said it all. Even Marshall's favorable ruling on Hay's motion to re-try Burr for high misdemeanor, and possibly treason, in Ohio, where he rejoined the flotilla that departed Blennerhassett's island on December 10, did not quell the outrage. In fact with that decision, Burr himself joined the chorus of criticism against Marshall.[61]

Law and Politics in a Delicate Balance: The Chief Justice as "Examining Magistrate"

David Robertson stopped detailed reporting of the proceedings of the trial following Marshall's August 31 opinion and the jury's acquittal of Burr the next day. After recording Marshall's order presenting Burr to another grand jury in Ohio on September 9, he stopped reporting altogether and set about marketing the first two volumes of his reports. Robertson had good reasons to assume that the real trial was over and that the remaining business – the pending misdemeanor charge against Burr, the treason and misdemeanor charges against Blennerhassett, and the treason charges against Burr's subalterns – would be wrapped up expeditiously.

And by any count it should have been. It was apparent to all parties, for example, that Blennerhassett could not be convicted for treason when the main instigator had already been acquitted, and especially after Wirt's unforgettable portrait of Blennerhassett as an innocent victim of Burr's malicious charm. Treason charges against Jonathan Dayton,

---

[61] Beveridge, *Marshall*, 3: 528, quoting Hay to Jefferson, Oct. 21, 1807, Jeff. Mss, Lib. Cong.

Israel Smith and Comfort Tyler were almost certain to be dropped, too, since they had been indicted in the first place mainly to elicit testimony against Burr – thus the package of blank pardons.

Finally, pointing to a quick end to the trial was the fact that all the main participants desperately wanted the ordeal to end. The lawyers on both sides were exhausted and increasingly frustrated and testy. Burr was irritable and depressed and, according to Blennerhassett, was taking laudanum to ease his persistent stomach pain. After months in the hot seat Marshall needed a rest. Given the fact that further proceedings would necessarily be a reprise of much that went before, it would seem reasonable to assume that Marshall's previous definition of treason and his ruling on evidence in his August 31 opinion would settle outstanding questions.

Everyone was ready to pack it in – except President Jefferson. Writing to Hay six days after Burr's acquittal, Jefferson reaffirmed his position on the subpoena – that it was his call as to what should be divulged and not Marshall's – and then instructed Hay as to what course he should pursue: "I am happy in having the benefit of Mr. Madison's counsel on this occasion, he happening to be now with me. We are both strongly of opinion, that the prosecution against Burr for misdemeanor should proceed at Richmond. If defeated, it will heap coals of fire on the head of the Judge; if successful, it will give time to see whether a prosecution for treason against him can be instituted in any, and in what other court." As an afterthought Jefferson suggested that Blennerhassett and Israel Smith be prosecuted for treason in Kentucky.[62]

Thanks to Jefferson's instructions and Hay's compliance, the trial-after-the-trial lasted from September 3 until Marshall handed down his final commitment ruling on October 19 – proceedings that consumed all 418 pages of volume three of Carpenter's report of the trial. In important ways, the final phase of the trial was uniquely revealing. Exhausted lawyers on both sides returned to the fray, and if they behaved as they had done previously, they now did so with a fury that highlighted what had earlier been mostly suppressed; reputations were settled for better or worse; and longtime professional friendships were permanently severed. Also, in reprising previous arguments, points of evidence and points of law were clarified; so too were the respective positions of Marshall and Jefferson regarding the subpoena *duces tecum*. Even the secrets of the earlier grand jury proceedings were unpacked for all to see.

---

[62] Jefferson to Hay, Sept. 7, 1807, Bergh, *Writings of Jefferson*, 11: 365–66, quote on 366.

And most importantly, Marshall was put to a new test. This was especially true in the final phase of the proceedings during which he sat as a committing magistrate. In that role his responsibility was to determine whether there was sufficient evidence to commit Burr on charges emanating from events following the December 10 episode on Blennerhassett's island. In the principal treason trial Marshall evaluated arguments of counsel about the law in order to rule on what evidence the jury should consider; in the commitment hearings his duty was to evaluate both the facts and the law so as to determine whether there was reason to believe that a properly constituted grand jury would bring in an indictment.

The situation was fraught with painful choices and dangerous pitfalls that even John Marshall could not avoid. As frustrated counsel on both sides reminded him in no uncertain terms, his personal and professional reputation was on the line. Jefferson, who was anxiously watching events and calling the shots from Monticello, seemed destined to win no matter what Marshall did or did not do.

Burr's trial for misdemeanor as charged in the original grand jury indictment of June 26 lasted from September 3 through September 14, and consumed the first 110 pages of Carpenter's report. The proceedings opened on a hostile note when the question was debated as to whether Burr needed to be bailed again since he was already in the custody of the court. The investigation of the question once again took Marshall and the lawyers back to English common law, to the Judiciary Act of 1789, and to judicial decisions from the 1790s. Debate also ensued about the amount of bail, especially when Hay, following Jefferson's instructions, intimated that Burr might be charged with treason in the future, "either in Kentucky, Tennessee, or the Mississippi territory."[63] Marshall set bail at $5,000 according to the present charge, but not to a future one. After treason charges against Blennerhassett and Israel Smith were dropped, they were both bailed at $5,000 for the misdemeanor count. The charges against Jonathan Dayton were dropped and those against Robert Smith were declared by Hay to not be before the Court.

The spotlight was now on Burr who beat Hay to the punch by requesting full compliance to the previously issued subpoena *duces tecum* regarding the October 21 letter from Wilkinson to Jefferson. Burr finally settled for an authenticated copy of that letter. Burr's lawyers also insisted on seeing the entire November 12, 1806 letter from Wilkinson to Jefferson, arguing that selected portions of the letter had been used by Wilkinson

---

[63] Carpenter, *Trial of Burr*, 3: 14–15.

during the grand jury proceedings to save himself by incriminating Burr. While Wilkinson had written his letter to convince Jefferson that a military takeover in New Orleans was necessary to repel Burr's advancing army, in fact Wilkinson's real purpose in taking control of the city, which he did beginning November 25, was to silence those who knew of his former connection with Burr in the conspiracy.[64]

Sparks flew when Marshall issued a subpoena *duces tecum* to Hay ordering him to produce the letter. What the defense wanted to demonstrate – and this would be their major strategy for the remainder of the trial – was that Wilkinson and Jefferson were collaborating to convict Burr and that Jefferson was covering for Wilkinson, including his illegal actions in New Orleans. Hay was caught in a bind regarding the November 12 letter. Jefferson had given him explicit instructions to divulge only those portions of the letter that Jefferson had agreed to; Marshall ordered the full letter to be disclosed. Hay argued that "state secrets" were involved and refused to produce the letter, protesting that he was willing to go to prison before betraying "a sacred trust."[65]

Hay considered his obligation to cover up Jefferson's involvement a matter of personal honor; counsel for Burr looked on this obligation as a sign of weakness, if not corruption. Jefferson's ongoing involvement in the trial was by now apparent to all; also obvious was the fact that Hay was simply following the president's orders. Wickham drove home the point in his closing remarks on Saturday September 12, and in addition to calling Hay a puppet of Jefferson, also accused him of being "unacquainted with the facts, and ignorant of the law," and of having "repeatedly avowed the conviction of Burr's guilt," in violation of professional ethics.

A highly agitated Hay promised to answer the charge when the court met Monday, but could not help venting his feelings in a personal letter to Wickham written over the weekend. Hay repeated Wickham's offensive comments and then declared that those remarks constituted "a direct attack, upon my integrity, both as an individual and a public officer." After announcing that their long friendship was over, Hay concluded his letter by demanding a "public apology."[66]

---

[64] For a discussion of Wilkinson's plans concerning New Orleans and the November 12 letter see Abernathy, *The Burr Conspiracy*, 158–60.

[65] Ibid., 21–38 for the prolonged debate over the subpoena.

[66] George Hay to John Wickham, Sept. 16, 1807, John Wickham Papers, Part VI, Loose manuscripts, Division 14, Reel 3 of 3, Misc. Reels, Library of Virginia.

Wickham never apologized and the fact that no one believed Hay when he protested in open court "that he had never received any instructions or communications from him [Jefferson], nor could be governed by any 'orders on the subject from the executive,'" only made matters worse for the hapless prosecutor.[67] It was not easy being the president's man in Richmond.

Marshall's major opinion of September 14 contained several points, all of which doomed the prosecution's main argument. Point one concerned the indictment, which accused Burr of having launched the military expedition against Spain from Blennerhassett's island on December 10. The charge, said Marshall, was not for conspiring to launch an attack against Spain, but for actually doing so.[68] Moreover, the indictment contained no reference to conspiracy. Consequently all the evidence not directly related to the military expedition launched on the island was excluded – that is to say, all testimony of third parties, except as it applied to those events; all evidence of events regarding Burr's activities which took place elsewhere; and finally all acts of Burr's accomplices, except as they related to the events of December 10 on the island.

Hay realized that Marshall's ruling on evidence excluded almost all of the testimony he was prepared to present. One day after Marshall's decision, on September 15, Hay moved to discharge the jury. Marshall pointed out that the jury could not be discharged without the consent of both parties. Burr demanded a verdict and after twenty minutes of deliberation, the jury returned with an acquittal.[69] Blennerhassett called Marshall's opinion "an able, full, and luminous opinion as ever did honor to a judge, which has put an end to the present prosecution."[70] Jefferson considered the opinion one more reason for impeaching Marshall.

The second and final stage of the trial-after-the-trial began shortly after the jury's verdict, when Hay, following Jefferson's instructions, moved to commit Burr, along with Blennerhassett and Israel Smith, for levying war against the United States "at the mouth of the Cumberland river, in the state of Kentucky" and also "at Bayou Pierre, in the Mississippi Territory."[71]

[67] Ibid., 128.
[68] Carpenter, *Trial of Burr*, 3: 94.
[69] Robertson sums up the decision on the final two pages of his *Reports*, 2: 538–9; for Carpenter's fuller account see *Trial of Burr*, 3: 93–110.
[70] Safford, *Blennerhassett Papers*, 403.
[71] Carpenter, *Trial of Burr*, 3: 113.

Hay's motion put Marshall in a bind. On the most elemental level, the commitment hearing, if it should be granted, would mean that Marshall sitting alone would have to revisit and reassess much of the evidence previously heard – in the principal treason trial and in the misdemeanor trial which had just ended. To be sure, the issue would be probable cause only, but practically speaking it would be difficult not to let the previous jury verdict affect his decision of whether or not to commit Burr to yet another grand jury and possibly another trial. Aside from the question of his own capacity to render an impartial assessment of the evidence after all that had transpired, there was the question of whether he could hold up for yet another go-around.

Adding immeasurably to the physical and intellectual challenge now facing Marshall were the no-win political choices confronting him. While a ruling against commitment would obviously please Burr and his lawyers, several of whom were Marshall's personal friends, such a ruling would also strengthen Jefferson's case for impeachment. By contrast, sending Burr to Ohio for trial, if that were the outcome of the hearing, would appear to be bending to pressure from Jefferson and from public opinion. Either option would have been painful. In addition, a verdict of guilty in the new trial would, as Jefferson saw it, net not only Burr but also Marshall, for bending the law to free him in the earlier trial.

Marshall's first decision was to proceed with the commitment hearing; his second was to permit a wide range of testimony, some of which had been excluded by his August 31 decision and also by his September 14 decision. His rulings called forth a torrent of abuse, this time from Burr and his lawyers: "I found Burr, just after a consultation with his counsel," reported Blennerhassett in his journal entry of September 20, "secretly writhing under much irritation at the conduct of the Judge," claiming that "his Honor did not for two days understand either the questions or himself..." Burr instructed his counsel that Marshall should "be put right by strong language" or possibly even "abuse."[72]

Burr's lawyers now had their marching orders. Before setting Marshall right, however, they first had to turn up the heat on Wilkinson, who reappeared as the government's chief witness, and then to establish Wilkinson's collusion with Jefferson in their joint effort to convict Burr. If Burr had his conspiracy, then so did Jefferson and Wilkinson. Hay, whose demeaning association with the president had already been

---

[72] Safford, *Blennerhassett Papers*, 412–13, entry of Sept. 20.

shown, was also marked for public exposure. Burr's orders along with a sense of frustration shared by his lawyers made for some of the most dramatic courtroom action of the long, action-packed trial.

Eaton was called to the witness stand once again, and was once again humiliated, but Wilkinson as the chief witness for the government was the main target of the defense. As already noted, it was in order to establish the general's illegal action in New Orleans and Jefferson's compliance that Burr moved to subpoena Hay for the full text of the November 12 letter. More innovative still, at least for that time, was the request that the court call Littleton Tazewell, Joseph C. Cabell, and John Brockenbrough to testify about Wilkinson's testimony before the grand jury that had led to Burr's indictment back in May.

By probing the secret deliberations of the grand jury, Burr sought to demonstrate that Wilkinson had manipulated evidence in order to implicate Burr and disguise his own involvement in the conspiracy. This was a bold strategy, but also a risky one, since by showing Wilkinson's complicity in the conspiracy Burr might confirm his own involvement as well. Wickham's point was not that Wilkinson was guilty, however, but that both men were innocent. Wilkinson's crime was to perjure himself before the grand jury by tampering with evidence (the cipher letter and the letter of November 12), and by testifying falsely against Burr to save himself. If it could be shown that Wilkinson was acting at the behest of Jefferson, so much the better.

The testimony of Tazewell, Cabell, and Brockenbrough, though restrained, pretty much neutralized Wilkinson's testimony in the commitment hearings. The subpoena of the November 12 letter, since its contents were never fully disclosed, left open the possibility that Jefferson and Wilkinson were in close collaboration – the mere suggestion of which was all that Burr's lawyers needed to make their point.

Defense counsel's other major gambit, which kicked in as the time approached for Marshall's decision, was to lecture the judge about his legal authority and moral duty as an examining magistrate. Burr chose Luther Martin to deliver the message. Martin was not quite abusive, as Burr suggested he might be, but he was insultingly arrogant and brilliantly clever. Martin realized that a ruling by Marshall to commit Burr for a new trial would be to put Burr at the mercy of a new grand jury somewhere in the West, where it was all but certain that Jefferson's message of Burr's guilt had already taken root. To forestall such an eventuality, Martin demanded that Marshall use his legal power as committing magistrate – powers which Martin expounded with great authority – to end the trial. As Martin framed the issue it was judge versus jury: law against popular politics and public opinion.

Martin had reason to think that Marshall the conservative would get the point. And what if Marshall did not get it? Martin warned him of the consequences of bringing Burr to a new trial for the same crime in defiance of the constitutional protection against double jeopardy: "And there has been no judge dared to grant a new trial in such a case, to bring a person twice to answer for the same crime, and hazard his life ... If he does, his conduct might be approved, perhaps, at this moment, by a certain part of the community, whose minds have become highly inflamed against the prisoner; but I warn him, that, if he was so to play with life, he would find it the most unpopular of all the actions of his life; and, in a little time, he would find himself loaded with detestation."[73]

Those who had chastised Marshall for favoring the defense during the trial must surely have been surprised at Martin's dressing-down of the Chief Justice – and more surprised still when Marshall decided to commit Burr and Blennerhassett for trial in Ohio where they would answer to yet another grand jury. Marshall's ruling was straightforward and carefully reasoned; it was also politically calculated to make the best of a bad situation. Regarding the plea of *autrefois acquit* – that Burr had been tried once and acquitted – Marshall refused to rule, not because of his "fear to meet a great question," but because it was a constitutional question which ought to be settled by the full Supreme Court and not by a single judge sitting as an examining magistrate. After reviewing the evidence, Marshall concluded, "that the real and direct object of the expedition [Burr's flotilla] was Mexico."[74]

In short, Marshall did not buy the prosecution's argument that Burr's objective was to separate the Union and that he planned a direct attack on American territory in New Orleans as a first step; neither did he believe Burr's argument that his plan depended on a war with Spain, nor that a de facto war in fact existed at the moment Spanish troops crossed the Sabine River. Nor indeed was Marshall persuaded that Burr seriously intended to settle the Bastrop lands once it was clear that there would be no war. Instead, Marshall committed Burr and Blennerhassett "for preparing and providing the means for a military expedition against

---

[73] Carpenter, *Trial of Burr*, 3: 413. Note that due to an error in pagination, page number 413 (with different content each time) appears twice in Carpenter's report.

[74] For Marshall's commitment ruling see ibid., 409–18, quote at 409.

the territories of a foreign prince, with whom the United States were at peace." He also added significantly: "If those whose province and duty it is to prosecute offenders against the laws of the United States, shall be of opinion, that a crime of a deeper die has been committed, it is at their choice to act in conformity with that opinion."[75] The problem – and Burr's fate – was once again in Jefferson's hands.

One can readily understand why Burr and his lawyers were incensed and also why Blennerhassett reasoned that Marshall had succeeded in getting both Jefferson and Burr. A fairer assessment might be that the Chief Justice of the United States did not want to be hung out to dry by his old enemy, and that he was willing to offend Burr and his lawyers in order to avoid that fate – especially since it was Marshall's belief that Burr would never be brought to trial in Ohio anyway. Marshall did not emerge unscathed for the way he mixed law and politics – echoes of *Marbury v. Madison* – but he did escape the trap set for him by his old adversary.

The court records including Marshall's commitment ruling were forwarded to the federal district court in Chillicothe, where a grand jury indicted Burr and Blennerhassett for high misdemeanor.[76] As it turned out, neither man appeared for trial in Ohio, and as everyone including Marshall expected, the government abandoned further proceedings against both men. After seven months "the greatest criminal trial in American history" came to an end – not with a bang, nor a single conviction, but a whimper.[77]

Bashing Marshall

Even before the trial began, Jefferson had predicted that Marshall would be judged, and so he was. The president and his friends, including his lawyers in Richmond, had long since concluded that Marshall was a political judge. After the final commitment ruling, Blennerhassett reported that Marshall's professional friends had abandoned him for trying to "stroke" the "tiger of Democracy" rather than muzzling him.[78] Burr agreed that Marshall's friends as well as enemies believed that his

[75] Ibid., 418.
[76] See U.S. Circuit Court (7th Circuit). Ohio District. Records, 1805–1808, in the case of *U.S. v. Burr et al.* Section 4. Manuscripts, Mss1 Y854a 1–11, Va. Hist. Soc.
[77] Corwin, *Marshall and the Constitution*, 86.
[78] Blennerhassett to Mrs. Blennerhassett, Oct. 22, 1807, Safford, *Blennerhassett Papers*, 300; Blennerhassett to Mrs. Blennerhassett, Nov. 17, 1807, ibid., 516.

final opinion "was a sacrifice of principle to conciliate *Jack Cade*."[79] Blennerhassett himself, although he had admired Marshall for his integrity and fairness throughout the trial, concluded reluctantly that the Chief Justice "must be disposed to favor alike the ruin of Burr, Wilkinson and Jefferson."[80]

Richard Bates, another close observer of the trial, also proffered a political explanation for Marshall's behavior, one that had considerable traction at the time, as well as later on. According to Bates, "The judge in all probability wishes Burr to be acquitted for he is a Federalist, and the federalists are all friends to Burr, because Burr [is] a traitor who wished to sever the union, and because he is an enemy of Thomas Jefferson." It is worth noting that Bates himself withheld final judgment, declaring that he was "not ready to say that any opinion of his [Marshall's] delivered in this prosecution is an unconscientious one."[81] The Baltimore mob that hanged Marshall in effigy for "his *felonis* capers in open Court" was not so charitable.[82]

And neither were the leading administration newspapers. The most scathing and most widely circulated attack appeared in the *Enquirer* and the *Aurora* in the form of four letters. The author was William Thompson, who was also the author of previous attacks on Marshall in the *Enquirer*. Thompson sent the first lengthy draft of his diatribe to Jefferson who clamored for more. In "Letter the First," Thompson writing as "Lucius" proposed arraigning Marshall "at the bar of the public" in order to brand him "a disgrace to the bench of justice," and expose him as a leader of a Federalist conspiracy, who no less than Burr the traitor was out "to destroy the liberty and happiness of America." In subsequent letters Lucius detailed Marshall's partisan bias, which he claimed infused every aspect of the proceedings.[83]

For Lucius as for the president, *U.S. v. Burr* was vindictive politics pure and simple. As Lucius summed it up in the *Aurora*, Marshall had manipulated *"legal forms"* to reach a political objective and in the process destroyed both *"the spirit of justice, and the meaning of the law."*[84]

---

[79] Burr to Theodosia Burr, Oct. 23, 1807, Matthew L. Davis, *Memoirs of Aaron Burr* (2 vols., 1836), 2: 411–12.

[80] Ibid., entry of October 27, 466.

[81] Richard Bates to Frederick Bates, Sept. 20, 1807, Edward Bates Mss Collection, Va. Hist. Soc.

[82] Beveridge, *Marshall*, 3: 536.

[83] Beveridge discusses Thompson's attack at ibid., 533–5.

[84] From the *Aurora* as published in *The Democrat*, Nov. 28, 1807.

Or as Jefferson would explain to Hay later regarding the Burr trial, the law in Marshall's hands was "of a plastic nature."[85] In "Letter the Second," Lucius joined the president in inviting "the *people* of the U. States" to do some "justice" to the chief justice – by removing him from office.[86]

Thus the Burr trial reinvigorated the movement to impeach Marshall and reduce the power of the Supreme Court, which had been Jefferson's plan since Marshall's appointment in 1800.[87] Jefferson called on his friends in Congress to make it happen. Two months after the trial, Marshall was attacked viciously on the floor of the Senate – "with insidious warmth," recalled young Joseph Story, who witnessed the carnage – and indirectly threatened with impeachment.[88] Congressional Republicans also introduced a resolution for an amendment limiting the terms of all federal judges and permitting their removal by the president upon a two-thirds vote of each House.[89] When Senate Republicans moved to amend the treason provisions of the Constitution, Senator Giles and others got yet another opportunity to denounce the chief justice and the Supreme Court. Even John Quincy Adams, in his Report for the Senate Committee on the expulsion of Senator John Smith for his role in the Burr adventure, was harshly critical of Marshall's conduct of the trial.[90]

The campaign against Marshall, orchestrated by Jefferson and implemented by Thompson, Duane, Giles and others, treated the particulars of Marshall's conduct of the trial, but the all-embracing charge was that he was the leader of a vast Federalist conspiracy who played free and easy with the law in order to defeat the will of the people. Aside from the fact that the Federalists were no longer a force to reckon with in 1807, the evidence clearly indicates that it was Jefferson not Marshall who took the law into his own hands. It was Jefferson who initiated the case

---

[85] Jefferson to Hay, June 18, 1810, J. Jefferson Looney, ed., *Papers of Thomas Jefferson, Retirement Series*, 2: 473.

[86] *Aurora*, Nov. 25, 1807.

[87] Jefferson to Giles, April 20, 1807, Ford, *Works of Jefferson*, 10: 383–8, esp. 387.

[88] Story to Samuel Fay, June 18, 1807, W. W. Story, ed., *Life and Letters of Joseph Story*, (2 vols., 1851), 1: 157.

[89] Warren, *Supreme Court*, 1: 313.

[90] See the Report submitted by John Q. Adams for the Senate Committee on the expulsion of Senator John Smith for Smith's role in the Burr adventure in W. C. Ford, *Writings of John Quincy Adams* (New York, 1914), 3: 730–844 (10th Cong. 1st Sess., 56–63, Feb. 24, 1808).

precipitously on the basis of questionable evidence. Also by announcing Burr's guilt to the nation, Jefferson usurped the role of both the grand jury and the trial jury. Further, Jefferson violated established legal procedures when he encouraged and defended Wilkinson's law-defying actions in New Orleans; when he pressured his party in Congress to suspend the writ of habeas corpus; when he intervened personally in the trial of Bollman and Swartwout; when he took control of the prosecution in Richmond; when he attempted to manipulate witnesses by promising them pardons; and finally, when he authorized and encouraged a partisan newspaper war against Burr that made a fair trial difficult.

Jefferson's disregard of the law is easier to document than to explain, but it seems fair to say that his tendency to personalize history – and the office of the president – along with his dark view of judges and lawyers, played a significant role. Whatever the explanation for Jefferson's actions, it is worth noting that it was Marshall's decision – denounced as treachery by Jefferson's party-that in fact saved Jefferson, the champion of life and liberty, from having Burr's blood on his hands.

Equally ironic is the fact that Marshall's interpretation of treason, in contrast to the extreme version of English treason law relied on by Hay and company, comported closely with the republican principles of limited government and individual liberty that Jefferson and his party endorsed. The president's party had also championed the rights of the criminally accused in the sedition and treason trials of the 1790s, but it was Marshall, in both the Bollman and Burr trials, who defended and enlarged those rights.

Finally, regarding the independence of the jury, another cherished Jeffersonian principle that Marshall was damned for violating, the chief justice was as sound, if not more so, than the president himself. Jefferson did praise the republican jury, but he also inflamed public emotion against Burr, which he surely knew would influence the jurors. Marshall's August 31 decision, while it did limit jury discretion, also aimed to keep the popular prejudice against Burr from corrupting jury deliberations. Moreover, his authority to rule on matters of evidence, far from constituting judicial aggrandizement, was an authority almost universally held to be judicial in nature.[91]

---

[91] On the historical origins of judicial authority concerning rules of evidence see: James Bradley Thayer, *A Preliminary Treatise on Evidence at the Common Law* (1898; reprint Little, Brown, 1969), 180; and John Langbein, "The Criminal Trial before the Lawyers," *Un. Chicago Law Rev.*, 45: 263, 306 (1978).

In addition, Marshall's strenuous effort to explicate the law to the jury, while it revealed a conservative's skepticism about popular opinion, did not cross the line between informing and coercing. In any case, his ruling on evidence did not prevent the jury from going its own way if it chose to do so. What would have transpired had the jurors found Burr guilty on the basis of the evidence they heard is impossible to say. And in fact the jurors did have their say when they refused to find him straightforwardly "not guilty," but instead declared him "not proved guilty under this indictment under any evidence submitted to us." Their verdict freed Burr but invited the public to think he was really guilty.

Nevertheless, the jury also refused to convict Burr for what he might have intended to do, and might have done had thousands of angry citizens emerged magically from the forests of the West to follow him to New Orleans and Mexico City. We will never know for sure what Burr would have done had the opportunity to lead such a volunteer army presented itself. What we do know is that Marshall as a trial judge refused to speculate on the matter, which is to say he urged the jury to stick to the relevant facts as revealed in the evidence.

And so they did. Given the partisan passions of the day, this result was no small victory for the jury process and for John Marshall as trial judge. Concerning Marshall's attitude toward juries, it should also be recalled that his final order committing Burr and Blennerhassett to trial in Ohio put the matter in the hands of a grand jury, which was something the president ought to have done at the outset. Fuck Jefferson

Marshall's order to recommit Burr for trial in Ohio did not appease Jefferson, and given Marshall's dark assessment of the president, there is no reason to think that Marshall thought it would. In fact, neither Jefferson nor his supporters found a single thing to praise regarding Marshall's conduct of the trial. The newly emergent culture of democratic politics required villains to chastise, and Marshall fit the bill. In fact, long after the political accusations of the moment had been forgotten, the legacy of Jefferson's negative assessment of Marshall lingered on.

Marshall himself was not surprised at his critics. He expected the case to be hard and so it was: the most "unpleasant" one, as Marshall put it to Richard Peters, "ever brought before a judge in this or perhaps in any country which affected to be governed by laws." Marshall also noted somewhat wistfully that he could "have made it less serious" to himself "by obeying the public will instead of the public law & throwing a little more of the sombre upon others."[92]

92 Marshall to Peters, Nov. 23, 1807, Hobson, *Papers of Marshall*, 7: 165.

Clearly, Marshall understood the political pitfalls involved in the case; it is also clear that he did not succeed in avoiding all of them. But the fact that both sides ended up criticizing him strongly suggests that he favored neither, but rather was guided by a faith in due process of law and a deeply held sense of judicial duty. After rendering justice to the best of his ability, he shrugged off the insults heaped on him as best he could. When the ordeal finally ended, the chief justice "galloped to the mountains" to rest up for his fall circuit – and for the continued struggle with his old adversary that he knew was sure to continue.

The struggle between Marshall and Jefferson did continue – and indeed their ongoing personal animosity and ideological rivalry seems to encompass the central story of early national constitutional history.[93] When the contest between the two men resumed in the 1820s, as it did in the wake of Marshall's nationalist opinion in *McCulloch v. Maryland* in 1819, the specific constitutional issues had changed significantly from 1807. Populist states rights constitutionalism replaced opposition from the executive branch as the main threat to the Marshall Court. Talk of impeachment receded, too, as other measures to curb the Supreme Court surfaced in Congress – and as presidents like Andrew Jackson discovered that the surest way to change the Court's law was to change the Court's membership.

In this rapidly changing age, the constitutional relevance of the Burr trial also changed. Faced with the growing political power of states rights constitutionalism, and weakened by internal dissent on his court – both developments championed by Jefferson – Marshall toned down his nationalism. But he did so without surrendering the basic constitutional principles as set forth in the great decisions of the golden age. The one principle he did not compromise in this new age – the one above all others he affirmed in the Burr trial – was his commitment to judicial duty and judicial independence. Principled jurisprudence, as Marshall made clear when he defied President Jackson in the Cherokee Indian cases, remained the Supreme Court's first and last line of defense.[94]

[93] See R. Kent Newmyer, *John Marshall and the Heroic Age of the Supreme Court* (Baton Rouge, 2001), ch. 3: "Marshall, Jefferson, and the Rise of the Supreme Court," 146–209.

[94] Ibid., ch. 6: "Embattled Chief" and ch. 7: "Conservative Nationalist in the Age of Jackson," 386–458.

Epilogue

After the Dust Settled

"Our Parties will perpetually produce such Characters [as Burr] and such revolutions and as our Legislature and Executive will be always under the Influence of the Prevailing Party, I say We have no Security, but in the total and absolute Independence of the Judges."

John Adams, February 12, 1808[1]

"The courts of justice are the visible organs by which the legal profession is enabled to control the democracy."

Alexis de Tocqueville, *Democracy in America*[2]

Great trials of state like the one in Richmond are the stuff of history, but they cannot be expected to settle the historical narrative. Still, such trials are expected to settle certain things: the yes-or-no guilt of the accused; the facts on the ground that called forth the law that brought the accused to court in the first place; and finally the law itself. Ideally, the law should be stated with enough clarity and authority to be accepted by the public as fair and binding.

After months of learned discourse by some of the best lawyers in America arguing before one of its greatest judges, the Burr trial settled none of these – at least none fully and convincingly. Instead of bringing closure and catharsis, the trial as concluded by the enigmatic verdict of the jury perpetuated the debate – about Burr's innocence or guilt; about Jefferson's role; about Marshall's fairness; and indeed about the

---

[1] John Adams to John Quincy Adams, Feb. 12, 1808, Adams Papers, MHS.
[2] Tocqueville, *Democracy in America*, ed. Phillips Bradley (2 vols., New York, 1959), 1: 289.

180

reliability of the legal process itself. Instead of generating one convincing narrative, the trial generated several – which is why it affords such an intriguing glimpse of early national history. The miracle is that out of the partisan moralizing and character bashing came some legal principles consonant with the fundamental character of the young republic.

What the Trial Did Not Settle

Historians and biographers know a lot more about what Burr was up to than did Jefferson, Marshall, or the Richmond jury, but they too have struggled to understand the full truth about Burr's operations that landed him in Marshall's court.[3] Recent scholarly biographers agree that the object of Burr's expedition was not to separate the western states from the Union, nor to attack New Orleans, but rather to liberate Mexico from Spanish colonial rule. The unanswered question was whether Burr's plan was contingent on a war with Spain (in which case it would have been legal), or whether he continued his military activities after it became clear there would be no war (in which case he committed a high misdemeanor for violating the Neutrality Act of 1794).

On this question the historical record is inconclusive, the outcome of the trial even more so. It is true that Burr was acquitted of the misdemeanor charge by the jury, but it is also true that the government's case was flawed by an indictment, which by Marshall's ruling limited the evidence the jury could consider. What Marshall himself thought of the evidence, as noted previously, was that there was enough to try Burr for high misdemeanor for mounting a military expedition against the Spanish colonial regime in Mexico. The crucial question of what Burr planned to do after departing the mouth of the Cumberland was never answered by the courts, because the misdemeanor case against Burr in Ohio was never tried.[4]

Indeed, after looking at the contradictory accounts of what transpired during the years leading up to the Richmond trial, one is left to wonder if Burr himself really knew for sure what was he planned to do, since so

---

[3] Julius W. Pratt, "Aaron Burr and the Historians," *New York History* (1945), 26: 447–70, is a good place to start in charting the changing historical interpretations of Burr.

[4] Establishing the truth of Burr's claim at the trial that the object of his expedition was to settle the Bastrop lands has been difficult because most of Burr's extensive correspondence relative to his speculation in the Bastrop lands and other western land ventures was lost, due to the carelessness of Matthew Davis, with whom Burr left his papers. Lomask, *Burr*, 2: xiv.

much depended on unpredictable events – such as a war with Spain, or a conflagration on the Sabine River that looked like war or could be made to look like war, or even a spontaneous uprising of westerners, who hated Spain more than they loved the government on the Potomac. The problem was that Jefferson stopped Burr before he got to where he was going. What was ultimately missing at the trial and in the historical record as well was not just evidence but the facts on the ground that might have generated evidence.

Factual indeterminacy explains the difficulties and ultimate failure of the prosecution; it also accounts for the continuing debate about Burr's conspiracy and about Burr himself. The jury's verdict perpetuated the debate. Marshall entered "not guilty" on the record, to be sure, but the wording of the verdict – "not proved to be guilty under this indictment by any evidence submitted to us" remained as delivered.

One can only speculate as to why the jury hedged. Blennerhassett thought it was either "caprice" or "party spirit" but could not say which.[5] It was also possible that Richard E. Parker, "a very intimate friend" of Wirt and the one outspoken Jeffersonian on the jury, insisted on the equivocation as his price of going along.[6] Or perhaps the jurors were simply not sure of Burr's *real* innocence and wanted to somehow register their doubts.

In any case, the Scotch verdict invited critics to think that Burr had gotten away with treason, which left open the possibility that additional testimony from the untapped list of government witnesses would have proven him guilty, which in turn put the blame on Marshall for not permitting them to testify. Jefferson for one was certain of Marshall's culpability and hoped to prove it by instituting further proceedings against Burr for treason after Burr joined the flotilla that exited Blennerhassett's island on December 10. Jefferson's notion was that the evidence prohibited by Marshall's August 31 ruling in the principal trial would now be admissible and would prove Burr's guilt and expose Marshall's bias.

Marshall's enemies blamed him not only for withholding evidence from the jury but also for steamrolling the jurors, who presumably would have found Burr guilty on the evidence they had if left to their own deliberations. While it is true that Marshall took pains to clarify the law, which he no doubt assumed would guide the jurors, he did not attempt to direct a verdict – no doubt because he believed in 1807 what

---

[5] Safford, *Blennerhassett Papers*, 381.
[6] Wirt to Dabney Carr, Dec. 24, 1810, Kennedy, *Memoirs of Wirt*, 1: 292.

he stated in *U.S. v. Hutchings* in 1817: "that the jury in a capital case were judges, as well of the law as of the fact..."[7]

Whether Marshall would have set aside a jury verdict manifestly contrary to law as set forth in his decision of August 31 is impossible to say; it seems clear from Luther Martin's lecture on the duty of judges to rein in juries that the defense might well have expected him to do so if the jury had found Burr guilty.[8] Obviously, that possibility was never an issue; and in fact there is no credible evidence that Marshall faced an intractable or rebellious jury.[9] In fact the very opposite appears to be true. The jury in the trial-after-the-trial that acquitted Burr of high misdemeanor, for example, took only twenty minutes to deliberate. The jurors in the primary trial were nearly as quick in rendering their acquittal. Why the wording of their verdict deviated from standard practice remains a puzzle, but there is no reason to think they were motivated by hostility to Marshall or by a feeling that he had attempted to bulldoze them. It seems likely that the jurors were comfortable with the outcome simply because they were persuaded by Marshall's exposition of the law (which had a strong republican ring to it even if Jefferson did not see it that way) and by his ruling on evidence (which followed logically from this law). The fact that Marshall's friend and brother-in-law Edward Carrington was foreman of the jury guaranteed that Marshall's opinion was explicated during jury deliberations in the most compelling light.

In any case, those on the jury who were unwilling to defy Marshall's statement of the law but who still believed that Burr would have committed treason had Jefferson not stopped him could take some satisfaction knowing that the verdict that freed him did not really make him a free man. Jefferson may have lost the case in Richmond, but he ruined Burr in the process – or helped Burr ruin himself.

A Trial of Many Narratives

After the trial, life in Richmond returned to normal. Marshall headed for the "west country" as soon as his official duties ended; Jefferson

---

[7] 26 Fed. Cas., No. 15,429 (C.C.D. Va.) at 442. Special thanks to John Gordan III for the reference to the Hutchings decision; also see Gordan, "Juries as Judges of the Law: The American Experience," *The Law Quarterly Review*, 108: 272 (April 1992). Thanks also to Charles Hobson for noting that the Hutchings [sometimes Hitchins] case was originally reported in the Richmond *Enquirer*, Dec. 21, 1816.

[8] Carpenter, *Trial of Burr*, 3: 413. Note again the error in pagination.

[9] The nature and complexity of jury nullification is discussed in Norman J. Finkel, *Commonsense Justice: Jurors' Notions of the Law* (Cambridge and London, 1995), ch. 2.

hoped for some rest at Monticello, although he was soon forced to deal with deteriorating relations with England in the wake of the Chesapeake-Leopard Affair in July 1807. Burr began four years of self-imposed exile, traveling around Europe trying to sell his filibustering scheme to skeptical monarchs. Richmond's finest went back to their plantations, while ordinary folks, who had trampled one another to get a ringside seat, resumed their work-a-day lives. Those directly involved in the trial, and those who had witnessed it as well, all – whether rich or poor, famous or anonymous – took away their own recollections of the trial, shaped no doubt by their own unique angle of vision.

Fortunately, a few of those memories have survived to inform and enliven the historical record. Richard Bates was not writing history, but still left historians a useful clue as to what Virginians thought of Marshall's conduct of the trial. Then there was the young girl grown old who passed on her recollection of how Col. Burr brought her flowers and charmed the ladies of Richmond. Literary-minded observers like Washington Irving captured special moments such as Wilkinson's memorable confrontation with Burr. John Randolph left us some choice words about Wilkinson too, and about Jefferson as well. Young Winfield Scott praised Marshall's commanding courtroom presence, and judging from his own commanding role in the Mexican War in 1848, he also resonated to Burr's audacious plan to drive Spain from North America. And on it went: vignettes of history glimpsed randomly and preserved accidentally.

Unfortunately for historians, those most directly involved in the trial itself, with the exception of Harman Blennerhassett, felt little compulsion to write about it. One such was John Marshall, whose restraint was a mark of his character. The lawyers for the most part also said very little, no doubt because they considered winning and losing as merely part of their profession. This is not to say they did not have strong feelings about what happened. The sensitive and hot-headed George Hay in particular seems to have taken the defeat personally. Even during the trial he was hard on himself, and after the worst was over he even admitted to Jefferson that relying on Wilkinson as his chief witness was a mistake.[10] The trial also took a toll on Hay's long friendship with Wickham, and probably with some of the other defense lawyers who had ridiculed his performance. His letter of complaint to Wickham after one particularly bruising encounter was evidence that

---

[10] Hay to Jefferson, Oct. 15, 1807, Jeff. Mss, Adams, *History*, 927–8.

lawyering in Virginia, like so much else, was still a matter of personal honor.[11]

Personal feelings aside, Hay's life and career resumed without serious interruption. His marriage to James Monroe's daughter in 1808 gave him a seat at the table if he chose to take it. His professional career moved on at a steady pace as well. Two years later we find him arguing before Marshall in the Richmond circuit – and again defying party ideology by urging the court to indict under a federal common law of crimes. (Marshall dismissed the case without ruling on the federal criminal common-law question.)[12] In 1816 Hay defended the rights of Virginia in the great case of *Martin v. Hunter's Lessee* before the Supreme Court. He was appointed federal district judge for the eastern district of Virginia in 1826, which meant that he joined Marshall on the bench when the federal circuit court sat in Richmond; he served until his death in 1830.

Wirt appeared increasingly frustrated and irritable as the trial wore on, and according to Hay, gave up on Marshall's "integrity" after his issuance of the subpoena *duces tecum*.[13] His disaffection, however, if that is what it was, was temporary since he was soon praising the chief justice for his "power of analysis, the power of simplifying a complex subject, and shewing all its parts clearly and distinctly."[14] By 1827, Wirt announced to his friend Judge Carr that there was "not a better natured man in the world than the old Chief – and a more powerful mind was scarcely ever sent upon this earth."[15]

As for the trial itself, Wirt had reason to be personally gratified. Even before it was over, the Republican press made him a hero, celebrating equally his legal prowess and his spell-binding oratory.[16] Blennerhassett

---

[11] Wickham accused Hay of being unacquainted with the facts and ignorant of the law, and worse, of being influenced by "some person unseen and unknown, for whose discovery you professed great solicitude." Wickham's charge, said Hay, was not only "humiliating" but dishonored both his person and his professional reputation. According to Hay, Wickham's behavior ended their long friendship. Hay to Wickham, Sept. 16, 1807, John Wickham Papers, microfilm, Part VI, Loose manuscripts, Division 14, reel 3 of 3, Misc. Reel, Library of VA.

[12] Kathryn Preyer mentions the unreported case of *U.S. v. William Smith* in her "Jurisdiction to Punish: Federal Authority, Federalism and the Common Law of Crimes in the Early Republic," *Law and History Review* (Autumn 1986), 4: 245–6.

[13] Beveridge. *Marshall*, 3: 521.

[14] Wirt to Benjamin Edwards, Dec. 22, 1809, Kennedy, *Memoirs of Wirt*, 1: 272.

[15] Letter of Dec. 30, 1827, ibid., 2: 240.

[16] See *The Two Principal Arguments of William Wirt* (Richmond, 1808). This 221-page book was printed by Samuel Pleasants, editor of the pro-administration *Virginia Argus*.

also paid tribute to Wirt's "fervid and soul-thrilling eloquence" and his ability to sway "the minds of the jury with wonderful effect."[17] Jefferson expressed his gratitude by urging him to run for Congress, which offer Wirt politely declined. After several more years of highly successful practice in Virginia, President Madison appointed Wirt United States Attorney General in 1817. To Wirt's great credit he reformed that hitherto marginal office. His arguments for the government in the great constitutional cases before the Marshall Court, for example *McCulloch v. Maryland, Dartmouth College v. Woodward,* and *Gibbons v. Ogden,* soon won him national acclaim.

Wirt argued more cases before the Marshall Court than any other lawyer and the chief justice was among those who recognized him for the accomplished lawyer he was. Marshall no doubt also appreciated Wirt's powerful defense of the Supreme Court as an essential instrument of national government.[18] It is not hard to imagine what Wirt's states rights friends in Virginia thought of this argument, his defense of the 2d BUS's charter in *McCulloch v. Maryland,* and his decision never to appear *against* the Bank. Wirt also defied Virginia orthodoxy in *The Antelope* (1825) when as Attorney General he appeared on the side of the Africans who had been unlawfully enslaved.

Many counted Wirt's "serpent in the garden" speech his greatest triumph, but his defense of the Cherokee Indians against the land-greedy Georgians was much more to the point; and this time he had John Marshall on his side. The death of Wirt's beloved sixteen-year-old daughter Agnes in 1831 kept him from savoring the victory and may well have hastened his own death in 1834 at the age of sixty-two.[19] John Pendleton Kennedy dedicated Wirt's *Memoirs* "To the Young Men of the United States, Who Seek for Guidance to an Honorable Fame." They could scarcely have asked for a better model.

John Wickham, Wirt's great rival for distinction at the Virginia bar, has been undeservedly ignored by history – perhaps because he ignored it. Like Marshall, Wickham was so confident of his own gifts that he felt no need to advertise them. At any rate, he was too busy practicing law, looking after his numerous children, breeding racehorses, and tending

---

[17] Safford, *Blennerhassett Papers,* 297.

[18] For Wirt's defense of the Supreme Court, see his letter to President James Monroe, May 5, 1823. In this letter Wirt argued for the appointment of James Kent to fill the vacancy of Justice Livingston, who died in 1823. Kennedy, *Memoirs of Wirt,* 2: 152–6.

[19] See Wirt's heart-rending letter to Judge Carr, March 23, 1831, ibid., 343–4.

to his investments, his two plantations and many slaves. Not counting his lucrative practice, his extensive property holdings – enhanced greatly by two highly provident marriages – made him one of the richest men in the state. With the tragic death of his promising young colleague Benjamin Botts in the Richmond theater fire of 1811, followed by the deaths of Edmund Randolph in 1813 and Charles Lee in 1815, and by the departure of Wirt to his new office in 1817, Wickham reigned as the undisputed leader of the Virginia bar. Blennerhassett commended him not only for his "dignified and commanding" presence in court, but for his personal warmth and kindness.[20] John Randolph paid Wickham the highest compliment a southern gentleman could bestow, by bequeathing Wickham "his mare Flora" and "stallion Gascoigne," two of his prized thoroughbreds.[21]

Even Jefferson admired Wickham's talent – witness his attempt to retain Wickham in the highly controversial and intensely personal case of *Livingston v. Jefferson* (1810). Wickham declined and represented Edward Livingston instead, which brought him once again face-to-face with Wirt and Hay. The one man who did not think highly of Wickham was James Wilkinson, who challenged him to a duel for defaming his character during the trial. When Wickham suggested another court case rather than pistols, Wilkinson wisely dropped the matter.

Luther Martin was a dominant force during the trial, demonstrating time and again not only his talent for bombast but also his adversarial skill and his masterful knowledge of the law. Blennerhassett also described him as "one of the most benevolent men alive," a man whose "heart is overflowing with the milk of philanthropy…"[22] After the trial Martin was out of favor in the Old Dominion, and also briefly in his own state, indeed in his hometown of Baltimore, where he was hanged in effigy along with Burr, Marshall and Blennerhassett. He continued his successful practice, however, until poor health slowed him down: He suffered a paralyzing stroke in 1822, and until his death four years later remained in the care of his friend Burr in New York. Chief Justice Taney declared that that caretaking was the best thing that Burr had ever done; he also declared that Martin was one of the best trial lawyers he had ever seen.[23] In his freewheeling idiom, his contempt for authority, and his

---

[20] Safford, *Blennerhassett Papers*, 297.
[21] Bruce, *John Randolph*, 2: 625.
[22] Safford, *Blennerhassett Papers*, 510.
[23] Ashley M. Gould, "Luther Martin," in William Draper Lewis, ed., *Great American Lawyers* (Philadelphia, 1907), 2: 41, 43.

pragmatic use of English law, Martin was the most distinctly American lawyer at the Burr trial.

But Martin was not the only hard-hitting lawyer in the Burr trial. Whether the aggressive tactics of counsel on both sides signaled the demise of the republican community of lawyers in Virginia is a good question – one that would require another book.[24] Still, even a cursory glance suggests that the lawyers in the trial were torn between the traditional way of practicing law, where aristocratic social status, professional prominence, and courtroom decorum were closely connected; and the new age, when lawyers set aside social pedigree to make their living and their reputation by fighting it out in the courtroom. Luther Martin the iconoclast and street fighter was a full-time professional, but then so was Edmund Randolph. Family tradition rather than personal choice dictated the latter's legal career, however. Despite the high legal offices he held, and regardless of his numerous appearances before the Virginia Court of Appeals, he never relished the practice of law and did not really excel at it.[25] Randolph's authoritative demeanor during the Burr trial harkened to an earlier period when aristocrats spoke and plain folk listened. Wickham too displayed a touch of aristocratic hauteur during the trial, perhaps because he was one of the richest and most cultivated men in Virginia; he was also a lawyer's lawyer and a consummate professional with a killer instinct.

Most of all, it was Wirt who both sensed and embodied the tension in the profession between tradition and modernity. While he cherished the gentlemanly virtues of "the olden school" (virtues he did not find in his great rival William Pinkney), he was also a dedicated professional who lived by lawyering and loved nothing more than the give-and-take of adversarial combat with a worthy opponent. There is something old and something new in Wirt's remark regarding one friendly courtroom duel with Wickham, "I will give him a heat for the glory."[26] Remembering his own glory days in the Burr trial, he confessed, made him "feel young again."[27]

[24] An excellent place to start is A. G. Roeber, *Faithful Magistrates and Republican Lawyers: Creators of Virginia's Legal Culture, 1680–1810* (Chapel Hill, 1981) and Lee Shepard, "Lawyers Look At Themselves: Professional Consciousness and the Virginia Bar, 1770–1850," *American Journal of Legal History* (Jan. 1981), 1–23.

[25] See John Jay Reardon, *Edmund Randolph: A Biography* (New York and London, 1974), ch. 24 for a discussion of Randolph's legal practice.

[26] For Wirt on Pinkney, see Kennedy, *Memoirs of Wirt*, 1: 403–6; on battling Wickham, ibid, 2: 16.

[27] Wirt to Judge Carr, Feb. 17, 1817, ibid., 2: 16.

If Wirt relished the gentlemanly tradition of advocacy, he also noticed the subtle changes under way, as for example when he complimented Wickham for advancing the "noble science of defense." Wirt's intriguing comment has multiple possible meanings. As a reform-minded elite lawyer, he might well have been contrasting Wickham's professionalism with the backward state of Virginia's country practitioners. His compliment could also have been a riff on Edmund Burke's prophetic statement about American lawyers: how they were a feisty bunch, who were "acute, inquisitive, dexterous, prompt in attack, ready in defense, full of resources." More to the point, Wirt may have been comparing the sophisticated and aggressive tactics of Burr's defense team with the English defense bar as described by his friend St. George Tucker, where defendants in capital cases in the early eighteenth century were often not permitted counsel at all and where judges were expected to speak for the defendants.[28] In the second treason trial of John Fries in April 1800, Justice Samuel Chase would in fact attempt to implement the English rule, suggesting to Fries that he could do a better job than his defense counsel.[29] Wirt was not counsel in the Fries trial, but it can hardly be doubted that he knew of – and condemned – Chase's reliance on English trial practice.

If Wickham and company advanced the science of defense in America, as Wirt claimed, they also capitalized on the efforts of those who preceded them. The English Treason Trials Act of 1696 permitted defense counsel in treason cases, and American lawyers like James Wilson, in the spirit of that liberalizing act, were remarkably successful in winning acquittals in state treason trials during and after the Revolution.[30] And this is not to mention Andrew Hamilton's remarkable performance as defense lawyer for Peter Zenger in 1735, or John Adams's courageous

[28] According to Blackstone, "...it is a settled rule at common law, that no counsel shall be allowed to a prisoner, upon his trial upon the general issue, in any capital crime, unless some point of law shall arise proper to be debated." St. George Tucker, ed., *Blackstone's Commentaries* (Philadelphia, 1803) 5: 355. For St. George Tucker's criticism of English practice, see his footnote 17, ibid., 355–56. John Langbein traces the rise of the criminal defense bar in England beginning in the early eighteenth century. The shift that began in 1730, according to Langbein, could be traced to the Treason Trials Act of 1696, which the founding fathers consulted for the two-witness rule in Article III of the Constitution. See Langbein, *The Origins of the Adversarial Criminal Trial* (Oxford and New York, 2003), especially ch. 2.

[29] For a discussion of Chase's reliance on English trial practice see Stephen B. Presser, *The Original Misunderstanding: The English, the Americans and the Dialectic of Federalist Jurisprudence* (Durham, NC, 1991), 113.

[30] See Chapin, *The American Law of Treason*, 67–69.

efforts in defense of the British soldiers charged in the Boston Massacre of 1770. Still, the fact remains that never before the Burr trial had so many lawyers challenged the government – and the president of the United States personally – with such audacity and legal learning over so many months. And never before had there been such a concerted effort on the part of the government to mobilize public opinion with an eye to influencing the outcome of a criminal trial. Not surprisingly, a distinctly pragmatic motif could be detected in the proceedings, as counsel on both sides adjusted law in the books to popular politics, public opinion, and democratic juries.

Although one year after the trial Wirt complained that politics had triumphed over legal science in Richmond, judging by his own distinguished career, he retained a deep conviction that the all-out advocacy he witnessed in Richmond in 1807 was inseparable from the rule of law on which the Constitution and the federal Union rested.[31] It was this elevated view of the profession that prompted him to urge Republican President Monroe to defy partisan politics and appoint Federalist James Kent to the Supreme Court to fill the seat vacated by Henry Brockholst Livingston in 1823. A leading student of Wirt's career credited Wirt with both inventing and embodying the idea of the lawyer as advocate and guardian of the public good.[32]

Far more than the lawyers in Burr's trial, the plain folk associated with Burr – foot soldiers in his "army," friends and supporters who financed and encouraged him – have remained on the margins of history. This is certainly true of the young men who made their hasty exit from Blennerhassett's island and those who joined the flotilla later. Burr seems to have never fully apprised them of what he was up to, leaving them instead with the impression that they would settle the Bastrop lands or maybe fight Spain if there was a war. Before fleeing to escape Wilkinson's posse, Burr thanked them, wished them well, and left them to fend for themselves. A few went back East with nothing to show for their efforts, except the tales they could tell to their children and anyone who would listen. According to local historians, a good many of them stayed on in the Southwest to become farmers, merchants, teachers, and lawyers. Whether they settled on the Bastrop grant is unclear, but

---

[31] For Wirt's gloomy assessment of the Burr trial and the future of the Union, see Wirt to Benjamin Edwards, Dec. 22, 1809, Kennedy, *Memoirs of Wirt*, 1: 273.

[32] H. Jefferson Powell, "William Wirt and the Invention of the Public Lawyer," *Green Bag* (Vol. 4, No. 3, Spring 2001). Powell cites Wirt's letter to Monroe, May 5, 1823.

probably they did not, since the title to the grant was in serious doubt. For Burr, settling the great Southwest was a default plan and, when the need arose, a legal defense of his conspiracy.[33] Regarding the latter point, John Marshall was not persuaded, as his final decision to commit Burr for trial in Ohio indicates.[34]

Subalterns in Burr's army – Comfort Tyler, Israel Smith, David Floyd – were never brought to trial; neither were Blennerhassett, Senator Jonathan Dayton of New Jersey, and former Senator John Smith of Ohio. Nevertheless, all of them in one way or another paid a price for Burr's ambition. William Eaton also paid heavily for his brief encounter with Burr. Rather than help convict Burr, Eaton disgraced himself. Admittedly, Eaton made his own trouble but he was also used badly by Burr who tried to recruit him, and by those in the administration who attempted to purchase his testimony. Writing to Wilkinson in February 1808, Eaton demanded to know how it was that he had "talked of *Dukedoms* and Principalities." Wilkinson could give no credible explanation because there was none to give. In a later speech, Eaton declared what had become common knowledge by the end of the trial: that the government's chief witness had been connected for "more than two years" with the Burr conspiracy and had turned states evidence to save his own hide.[35]

During cross-examination in the latter phase of the trial, Eaton begged the court and the jury to "look through all the pages of my life" for proof of his honesty and sense of duty.[36] Jefferson, who still continued to praise Wilkinson as a great American patriot, paid no heed; neither did the government's lawyers in Richmond who had counted on Eaton's testimony. When the common folk of the city remembered Eaton, they did so for his exotic dress and wild behavior during the trial rather than

---

[33] See the entry of August 23, 1807, in Safford, *Blennerhassett Papers*, 353. Malone concluded, "The validity of Burr's title, in the eyes of American authorities, was questionable to say the least." Malone, *Jefferson*, 5: 256. For the litigation surrounding the Bastrop land see Mary K. Tauchau, *Federal Courts in the Early Republic: Kentucky 1789–1816* (Princeton, 1978), 139, footnote 66. For a detailed history of the Bastrop grant, see Jennie O'Kelly Mitchell and Robert Dabney Calhoun, "The Marquis de Maison Rouge, The Baron de Bastrop, and Colonel Abraham Morehouse," *The Louisiana Hist. Quart.* (April 1937), 20: 289–462.

[34] Carpenter, *Trial of Burr*, 3: 410–11.

[35] Eaton to Wilkinson, Feb. 6, 1808, [Charles Prentiss,] *The Life of the late General William Eaton* (Brookfield, MA, 1813), 403–04, cited in Abernathy, *The Burr Conspiracy*, 270–71.

[36] Carpenter, *Trial of Burr*, 3: 236.

his heroic role in the Tripolitan War. The "Lion of Berne" died in 1811 at the age of forty-seven.[37]

Unlike Eaton, Doctor Bollman emerged as something of a hero for his unwillingness to compromise the truth – even when the President of the United States made him an offer. He did not write an account of the trial for posterity, but his emphatic refusal to accept the pardon offered by Hay and Jefferson for a crime he did not commit remains a monument to his integrity. Bollman's account of Burr's expedition given trustingly and naïvely to Jefferson and Madison, and later to the Court, makes a strong case that Burr's intention was not to sever the Union, but rather to free Mexico from Spanish rule. After the trial Bollman wrote a few pamphlets on banking, but played no further part in American history.

Samuel Swartwout, who spoke persuasively to the grand jury of Burr's peaceful intentions, remained his steadfast friend during the painful period immediately after the trial and after Burr's return to New York from Europe in 1812. Swartwout also ingratiated himself with Andrew Jackson by challenging Wilkinson to a duel, a duel that never came off. With Burr's encouragement, Swartwout supported Andrew Jackson's campaign for the presidency and became Collector of the Port of New York for his efforts. Upon leaving that office, Swartwout was charged with misappropriating over one million dollars. Like Burr, Swartwout also spent his final years under a cloud.

James Wilkinson's reputation for double-dealing was fairly well-established before the trial, but his performance in Richmond confirmed the worst. Why this final judgment was so unrelievedly harsh, however, is not so clear as it first appears to be. Wilkinson's service to Spain as "Agent 13" was obviously a blemish on his character, although extorting money from Spain was not something most Americans of the time, certainly not most westerners, would hold against him. In his favor, when forced to choose his loyalties in 1806, he chose his own country and in so doing, helped avoid war with Spain, which he might have easily precipitated. It is worth noting too that there was no solid evidence indicating that Wilkinson seriously contemplated a separation of the Union.

In any case, Wilkinson's whole career of adventurism came into focus in the Burr trial and most damningly in his effort to save himself by accusing Burr of treason. Rather than applaud Wilkinson for exposing

---

[37] For a favorable view of Eaton and his role in the Burr trial see the article by Louis B. Julia H. Wright and Julia H. MacLeod, "William Eaton's Relations with Aaron Burr," *Miss. Valley Hist. Rev.* (March 1945), 31: 523–36, cited in Malone, *Jefferson*, 5: 240.

Burr, many, including John Randolph, rightly accused him of distorting the truth in a cowardly maneuver to save his own hide. Wilkinson's law-less behavior as the military dictator of New Orleans and his self-serving mistreatment of Bollman and Swartwout doomed his reputation. If not for such actions, Wilkinson might have gone down in history as one of those buccaneers who roamed the borderlands of the unfinished nation in search of gold and glory.

Following the trial, the general found himself under constant offi-cial scrutiny. In 1808, at John Randolph's urging, the House conducted an inquest into whether he had been in the hire of Spanish officials. Daniel Clark, Wilkinson's former friend and business associate in New Orleans, supplied chapter and verse in his book, which appeared in 1809.[38] In 1810, the House launched two further inquiries. One focused on Wilkinson's activities in the Southwest and his involvement in the Burr conspiracy; the second investigated charges that he had neglected troops under his command when they were quartered in New Orleans in 1809–1810. Trial by court-martial in 1811 acquitted him on all counts. Another trial in 1815, this time regarding his military command on the Canadian border during the War of 1812, also ended in an acquittal – mainly, it would appear, because the regular army officers on the court liked Wilkinson more than they did the government in Washington.[39]

Wilkinson attempted to redeem his reputation with the publica-tion of his three-volume *Memoirs of My Own Times* (1817), but the detailed evidence of venality and duplicity that surfaced during the trial left an indelible impression. During his time of troubles, Wilkinson got no help from Jefferson, who refused to answer his general's correspon-dence, nor any from Madison, who to Wilkinson's distress, supported the court-martial proceedings against him.[40] Why a man of the world and a discerning judge of character such as Burr put so much trust in such a well-known intriguer may seem hard to explain, except that both men were inordinately self-centered and ambitious, and both perceived the American Southwest as a source of fame, glory and wealth for the taking.

In many ways Harman Blennerhassett was the most pathetic charac-ter in the story. There were other losers to be sure, but the Irishman had more at stake than anyone except possibly Burr himself. Wirt was correct

---

[38] *Proofs of the Corruption of General James Wilkinson*, 1809.
[39] Linklater, *Artist in Treason*, ch. 29.
[40] Ibid., especially ch. 28: "Madison's Accusations."

to depict him as a romantic – witness Blennerhassett's pretentiously naïve "Querist" essays in the Marietta *Ohio Gazette*, September 1806, fantasizing about Burr's kingdom-to-be in Mexico and intimating that it would be a good thing all around if the western states separated from the Union. True, these essays were speculative ruminations, not plans for action, but taken out of context they could be readily used against Burr, which may explain why Burr's lawyers strongly discouraged Blennerhassett from appearing in his own defense, which he was prepared to do.[41]

Blennerhassett may have been a loose cannon, but he was also a close and often insightful observer of the Richmond proceedings. He acknowledged Marshall's ability but also criticized his conduct during the second phase of the trial: for granting unjustified leeway to the prosecution; for ignoring his own previous decisions; and generally for bending to popular opinion, presumably to atone for his decision that led to Burr's acquittal in the first treason trial.[42]

Blennerhassett's private journal also documented his own growing realization that Burr's main concern all along was Burr. No doubt Burr deserved to be faulted, but like all narcissists he may well have deceived himself as much as he deceived others. At the same time, Blennerhassett was not a babe in the woods and neither was his devoted and tough-minded wife, who enthusiastically supported the enterprise and stuck by her husband when it failed. Both bought into Burr's grand scheme because they wanted more than their "garden of Eden" could offer.

Blennerhassett played for high stakes and lost everything. Gone was the prospect of a happy future with his wife midst his books, his scientific equipment, and his gardens. Gone was his reputation and gone as well was the money he loaned Burr, which, in addition to the $30,000 he spent building his island paradise, was pretty much all of the fortune he had brought with him to America. Blennerhassett's attempt to retrieve some of his investment by threatening to expose Burr and Alston in

---

[41] See, for example, the entry for August 13 in Safford, *Blennerhassett Papers*, 323, where he mentions that his brief had "entered on the thirteenth folio." Blennerhassett was in close contact with Randolph, Wickham, and Botts, all of whom agreed to defend him pro bono if his case went to trial.

[42] Safford, *Blennerhassett Papers*, 412–13, entry of September 20, where Blennerhassett recalls that Burr was "secretly writhing under much irritation at the conduct of the Judge," and urging that he should in the future "be put right by strong language," presumably his own.

print failed miserably. Alston, who had already lost $50,000 of his own money on Burr's project, was not about to lose more, and Burr, who was barely one step ahead of his creditors, was in no position to repay Blennerhassett even if he wanted to.

If Wilkinson was the perfect scoundrel, then Blennerhassett was the perfect victim. After a failed effort to grow cotton in Mississippi, Blennerhassett and his wife hit the road, calling on old friends for help. Blennerhassett's main legacy to history was a bundle of letters and a journal, published by William H. Safford in 1864. In his writings we see Blennerhassett grappling painfully with his failed dream, with the suffering he inflicted on his family – and with the deceitful behavior of Burr. Blennerhassett honorably refused to testify against Burr when pressured by the administration, although doing so would have eased his own situation.[43] He did conclude, however, that "the little emperor" was "a heartless swindler" who was as bad as Wilkinson, since he pretended to be a friend.[44] Blennerhassett, who was offended to hear Burr brag about his success with the ladies, would not have been surprised to hear that Burr had conned his new wife, Madame Eliza Jumel, out of several thousand dollars before she saw the ruse and divorced him.[45]

Jefferson on Burr for the Record

More than any of his contemporaries, Jefferson influenced the historical narrative about the trial and about Burr. Despite Burr's acquittal – indeed his two acquittals – it was the president's public proclamations of guilt that stuck. Jefferson continued the attack even after the jury's September 1 verdict to acquit – this despite his celebration of the jury as the bulwark of liberty. As noted previously, Jefferson ordered Hay to press forward with the misdemeanor charge against Burr in Richmond, and if that failed, to bring him to trial in Ohio.[46]

Hay's second effort to convict Burr failed, but several weeks of additional testimony (as recorded in 418 pages of Thomas Carpenter's report) provided a rich source of material that was mined selectively for evidence of Burr's guilt. Even after the trial was officially over, Jefferson continued

---

[43] Blennerhassett mentions the offer made by Jefferson's emissary William Duane to turn states evidence (and possibly perjure himself) in Safford, *Blennerhassett Papers*, 356–8.

[44] Ibid., 461, 506 and passim.

[45] Lomask recounts the sordid tale, *Burr*, 2: 395–403.

[46] Jefferson to Hay, Sept. 7, 1807, Bergh, *Writings of Jefferson*, 11: 366.

his campaign of vilification. Addressing the General Assembly of North Carolina on January 10, 1808, for example, he denounced Burr, without naming him specifically, as a "parricide" who endeavored to "bring into danger the union of these States, and to subvert, for the purposes of inordinate ambition, a government founded in the will of its citizens, and directed to no object but their happiness."[47]

The president also called on his supporters in Congress to join his crusade against Burr.[48] One who answered Jefferson's call to action was young John Quincy Adams, who apparently was contemplating defection to Jefferson's party. Adams's Report for the Senate Committee on the possible expulsion of Senator Smith of Ohio for his association with Burr not only recommended Smith's expulsion but condemned Burr and Marshall as well. Indeed, according to John Randolph, Adams was more interested in getting Marshall impeached than he was in getting Smith expelled from the Senate.[49] Like Jefferson, Adams treated Marshall's attention to the common-law rules of due process – "the narrow forms prescribed by law" – with ill-disguised contempt. Despite Adams's efforts, however, the Senate fell one vote short of endorsing the committee's recommendation.

Adams's performance was roundly denounced as political pandering by the Federalists, but his Report put a stamp of approval on the president's actions and invited others to join the ranks of Burr-haters and Marshall-doubters. While Adams would later join the chorus of those who praised Marshall for putting the Constitution on a solid foundation, his dark view of Burr and his critique of Marshall's role in the trial appear to have found traction in his grandson Henry's brilliant and influential history of the early republic.[50] John Adams, it should be noted, was sharply critical of his son's Report – for its "Levity of Expression" and for its failure to appreciate the importance of due process as set forth by Marshall.[51]

Jefferson also went after Burr with his remarkable pen. No man of his generation wrote more brilliantly – or so purposefully. Jefferson wrote about everything under the sun, but many of his letters from the 1790s

[47] Saul K. Padover, *The Complete Jefferson*, 528.
[48] Richardson, *Messages and Papers of the Presidents*, 1: 429.
[49] See Randolph's remarks in the debate in the House of Representatives, Feb. 1, 1808, 20th Cong., 1st Sess.; also Warren, *The Supreme Court in United States History*, 1: 314, footnote 3 from previous page.
[50] Adams's Report is found in Ford, *The Writings of John Quincy Adams*, 3: 175–84. See esp. 176.
[51] John Adams to John Q. Adams, Feb. 12, 1808, Adams Papers, MHS.

onward, all of which he meticulously saved, aimed to explain and justify himself to posterity and to set the record straight about his enemies. Although these letters were addressed to private individuals, they were rarely entirely private. Some, like the infamous letter to Philip Mazzei criticizing Washington, appeared accidentally in the public domain, to be sure. Many, however, were clearly written to shape opinion, inspire action, and influence the writing of history. As Jefferson confessed to Martin Van Buren at the end of a long letter concerning political events of the 1790s, "I have written you a very long letter, or rather a history."[52]

Such was the case with the letters discussing Burr, Marshall, and the Richmond trial that appeared in Volume Four of his *Memoirs*, the first "collected edition" of Jefferson's writings. Edited by his grandson Thomas Jefferson Randolph, the four-volume work was published posthumously in 1829 and was immediately billed as "the text-book of republicanism."[53] In writing about the Burr conspiracy, Jefferson portrayed himself as a man of iron resolve who never faltered or erred. In a letter to Lafayette, for example, he denounced Burr's conspiracy as "one of the most flagitious of which history will ever furnish an example" – a scheme to separate the Union and subvert American "freedom." Writing to George Hay, the president referred to Burr as a "criminal" who was "the rallying point of all the disaffected and worthless of the United States," the "pivot" of foreign intrigues designed to weaken America.[54] If Jefferson overrode due process of law to stop Burr, he did so by his own reckoning to save the nation – even though he conceded early on that the nation was never really in danger.

When it came to Aaron Burr (and to John Marshall as well), Jefferson was not inclined to ponder the gradations of human nature between good and evil. According to Jefferson's dichotomus moral calculus, Burr was simply a corrosive evil that had to be destroyed. At no time during the trial or in the years following did Jefferson question the correctness of his assessment. Neither did he consider the possibility that the means he chose to bring Burr down – that is, a frontal assault on due process by a sitting president – might constitute a dangerous precedent for the young nation.

[52] Jefferson to Van Buren, June 29, 1824, Ford, *Works of Jefferson*, 12: 357–72, quote at 371.

[53] Merrill D. Peterson, *The Jefferson Image in the American Mind* (Charlottesville, 1998), 29.

[54] Jefferson to the Marquis de Lafayette, July 14, 1807, Thomas Jefferson Randolph, ed., *Memoir, Correspondence, and Miscellanies from the Papers of Thomas Jefferson* (4 vols., Boston, 1830) 4: 96–98; Jefferson to Hay, Sept. 4, 1807, ibid., 10.

Burr as Icon and Anti-Hero

Burr made only a half-hearted attempt to counter Jefferson's assault on his reputation. With characteristic nonchalance he simply left his papers in the care of his New York friend Matthew Davis, with instructions to publish posthumously whatever he thought appropriate. Davis's two-volume edition of the *Memoirs of Aaron Burr* (1836–1837) was not well reviewed. By acknowledging that he had omitted correspondence from Burr's paramours – several were married women from prominent families – Davis inadvertently provided ammunition to Burr's detractors who could now claim that he was a sinner as well as a traitor.[55]

Whatever their shortcomings, however, the *Memoirs* did challenge Jefferson's assessment of Burr. It is hard to read Burr's youthful letters, his wartime correspondence, and his tender parental letters to Theodosia, for example, without sensing the unfairness of Jefferson's blanket condemnation. Davis also took the fight directly to Jefferson – by documenting his effort to destroy Burr after the disputed election of 1800; and by mobilizing evidence indicating that Burr's "conspiracy" intended only to free Mexico from Spanish colonial rule and this only in case of a war with Spain. On this point, history came to Burr's aid. Burr did not live to witness the Mexican War in 1848 when President Polk and General Winfield Scott did precisely what Burr himself had set out to do in 1807. He did, however, live to see Texas revolt against Spanish rule, which according to one of his early biographers, prompted him to declare, "I was only thirty years too soon! What was treason in me thirty years ago is patriotism now."[56]

By the time of the Mexican War, American expansionism had generated an elaborate rationale of cultural superiority called Manifest Destiny. By contrast, Burr proclaimed no grand theory regarding civilization's westward march to justify his western scheme; neither did he claim that God commanded him to liberate Mexico from Spanish oppression. Rather than rationalizing his actions, Burr let them speak for themselves. And long before his "conspiracy" took shape, he had begun to calculate the profits to be made in the West. While still

---

55 Davis, *Memoirs of Burr*, 1: v–vi. For Burr's extensive treatment in American literature see: Samuel H. Wandell, *Aaron Burr in Literature* (Port Washington, NY, and London, 1936), and Charles F. Nolan Jr., *Aaron Burr and the American Literary Imagination* (Westport, CT, 1980).

56 Parton, *Burr*, 670.

vice-president, he concluded that Mexico could be taken by force of arms and bold leadership.[57] If Jefferson's government refused to act, Colonel Burr would take up the slack. He never doubted his ability to lead the charge – indeed, to take charge of history. Burr liked Andrew Jackson because he was a military man of action. No doubt he would also have agreed with Theodore Roosevelt's martial approach to foreign policy, and with Roosevelt's opinion that Thomas Jefferson was "the most incapable executive who ever filled the presidential chair."[58]

Whatever may have been Burr's faults, false modesty and hypocrisy were not among them. In short, Burr put his own spin on Jefferson's famous phrase regarding the pursuit of happiness in the Declaration of Independence. As Gordon Wood has observed, it was precisely Burr's perceived disdain for the idealism of the Revolution that constituted "the real treason of Aaron Burr" in the eyes of Jefferson and many other statesmen of the new republic.[59] Even so, a case could be made that Burr's self-tailored "pursuit of happiness" was as representative of the American ethos as was Jefferson's lofty idealism. Burr's notion that political campaigning could be "a great deal of fun" and yield some "honor & profit" to boot was American to the core – and light years in advance of the likes of Washington, Adams, and Jefferson.[60]

If Jefferson believed that Burr was a traitor to the values of the Revolution, he also believed that Burr was an actual traitor who deserved to hang. John Adams did not go quite so far, but after the trial he warned his countrymen not to confide in men like Burr "for their political guides" lest "calamities, devastations, bloodshed and carnage" might follow.[61] Adams was apparently referring to the dangers of secession and civil war, and when both occurred contemporaries were tempted to revisit Burr's conspiracy. One who did so with lasting effect

[57] Consult Isenberg, *Fallen Founder*, 282–92 for a discussion of Burr's western schemes.

[58] Theodore Roosevelt, *The Naval War of 1812* (1882), as quoted in *American Heritage Dictionary of American Quotations* (New York, 1997), 255:5.

[59] Gordon Wood, "The Real Treason of Aaron Burr," *Proceedings of the American Philosophical Society,* vol. 143, no. 2 (June 1999), 280–95.

[60] Burr to Aaron Ward, January 14, 1832, Kline, *Political Correspondence of Burr* 2:1210–11. Kline makes the point in "Aaron Burr as a Symbol of Corruption in the New Republic," in *Before Watergate: Problems of Corruption in American Society,* ed. Abraham Eisenstadt et al. (New York, 1978), 74.

[61] Adams to Richard Rush, Oct. 25, 1809, quoted in John A. Schutz and Douglass Adair, eds., The *Spur of Fame: Dialogues of John Adams and Benjamin Rush* (San Marino, CA, 1966), 172.

on the popular mind was Edward Everett Hale, whose didactic story written in 1863, called "The Man Without a Country," was clearly modeled after Burr.[62]

Before linking Burr to the Civil War, however, it should be recalled that it was Jefferson's states rights ideology rather than Burr's conspiracy that was used to justify southern secession in 1860. If Burr's conspiracy stood for anything other than his own ambition, it was the militant expansionism that found fruition in the Mexican War and came to characterize American foreign policy during the remainder of the century and beyond. In 1807 Burr preferred to fight first and then talk, while Jefferson favored diplomacy over war – even if it meant using James Wilkinson as his emissary. Ironically, Burr's militant nationalism closely resembled that of his great rival, Alexander Hamilton.[63]

Burr's image as a gung-ho expansionist was not his only legacy; neither has he been remembered solely as Wirt's serpent in the garden. In the years following his death, Burr became a model anti-hero, a loner who faced cultural ostracism with dignity and courage. And certainly there was much to task both. Despite his acquittal, most Americans considered him a traitor – and what was worse, a traitor who escaped his just deserts. Also under indictment for murder in New York, he could not return home or resume his law practice. After a hasty farewell to friends he headed for Europe, where he spent four degrading years peddling his debased western project and sponging off old friends to keep bread on the table.[64]

What followed his exile was even more devastating. He returned surreptitiously to New York City in 1812, but before he could get settled, news arrived in late June that Theodosia's eleven-year-old son, and Burr's only grandchild, had died unexpectedly. Not long after came the crushing news that Theodosia herself had been lost at sea off Cape Hatteras, while on her way to visit him. The two people he loved the most and whose existence had sustained him during his trial and exile were gone.

Ironically the tragic trajectory of his life appeared to meliorate his character. Before the Richmond trial, he had behaved as though fame

---

[62] See Ferguson, *The Trial in American Life*, 100–106.

[63] For Hamilton's position consult Gordon Wood, "Alexander Hamilton and the Making of a Fiscal-Military State," in his *Revolutionary Characters: What Made the Founders Different* (New York, 2006), ch. 4.

[64] [Burr] *The Private Journal of Aaron Burr* (2 vols., New York, 1903), written for his daughter Theodosia, recounts in graphic detail his trials and tribulations during his years of exile, as well as his determination to survive.

and glory were his birthright; after the trial he bore the pain of failure and ostracism with manly defiance. He resumed his law practice with considerable success, attempted to repay some of his debts, and looked after his stepchildren and his ailing companion Luther Martin. Burr's capacity for friendship never deserted him and neither did the small band of old friends who stuck with him to the end.

While Burr's life fell painfully short of its early promise, he never complained (except for an occasional outburst about the Virginia Dynasty, the fecklessness of the Madison administration, and the mediocrity of James Monroe). Without apology or self-adornment, he was what he was – which is precisely why he appealed to twentieth-century iconoclasts who were wary of fancy talkers and weary of hypocrisy and moralizing. Blennerhassett had a point when he referred to Burr as "Lord Chesterfield," but in the New Yorker's open defiance of polite conventions of any sort, Burr was also America's very own Lord Byron. For the poet William Carlos Williams, as for other modern critics of bourgeois irresolution and smugness, Burr stands out as a man of action "in the American grain."[65]

Jefferson and Marshall on Law and Republican Liberty

The ordeal in Richmond was a watershed in Burr's life and a stain on his historical reputation. In comparison, the president and the chief justice suffered very little; both resumed their official duties and their personal lives without serious interruption. While the historical reputations of the two men suffered a bit as historians picked up the argument started by contemporaries, few critics would question their greatness: Jefferson for reasons too numerous to mention retained his place in the pantheon of great Americans, just as Marshall emerged unchallenged as "the great chief justice" and the representative figure of American law.

Greatness, however, only history can bestow, and in 1807 the jury was still out. Jefferson and Marshall no doubt understood that their confrontation in the Burr trial might figure in the final reckoning. If Jefferson appeared paranoid, it may well have been because he felt surrounded by Marshall and his relatives and friends: in Kentucky, Joseph Daveiss and Humphrey Marshall; in Richmond, Marshall's brother William, clerk of the circuit court, and his brother-in-law Edward

---

[65] William Carlos Williams, *In the American Grain* (New York, 1925). The essay on Burr is called "The Virtue of History," 188–207.

Carrington, foreman of the trial jury. In addition, there was John Randolph, whom Marshall chose as foreman of the grand jury, along with his friend Wickham, with whom Marshall was accused of conspiring to settle the case.[66] Even Blennerhassett, who admired Marshall, speculated that "the well-known spirit of clanship and co-operation with which the Marshalls and all their connections are so uniformly animated" predisposed the chief justice to "ruin" Jefferson and perhaps Wilkinson and Burr as well.[67]

Jefferson in turn was determined to ruin Marshall and saw the trial as an opportunity to do so. Judicial corruption was the immediate charge; judicial power was the motivating fear. The president wanted the world to know that "from the beginning of the trial," the chief justice was determined to "clear Burr" by keeping the public from seeing the damning evidence of Burr's guilt and his own malfeasance. Jefferson assumed that the new proceedings he ordered against Burr in Ohio would in fact generate such evidence. By charging Burr for events that transpired at the mouth of the Cumberland River the witnesses who had been excluded by Marshall's ruling of August 31 (on the grounds they were not prepared to testify as to the levying of war on Blennerhassett's island) would now be permitted to testify. When they did, the whole world would discover that Burr had been guilty all along and that Marshall had covered for him. As the president explained to Hay, "These whole proceedings will be laid before Congress, that they may decide, whether the defect has been in the evidence of guilt, or in the law, or in the application of the law..." For good measure Jefferson instructed Hay to have an authenticated copy of Marshall's opinions sent along.[68]

Clearly, the trial was not only about Burr, nor about the definition of treason, nor even about the personal antipathy between the president and the chief justice. Also at issue, as both men fully appreciated, was the role of the federal judiciary in the governance of the new nation. This question had divided the parties since the 1790s and had taken on new urgency with Justice Chase's impeachment in 1805 and Marshall's opinions in *Marbury* and *Bollman*. Jefferson believed that the will of the sovereign people was best represented by the elective branches of government, especially as they operated at the state level. Marshall believed

---

[66] Blennerhassett reports the rumor in the Aug. 23, 1807, entry in his private journal, Safford, *Blennerhassett Papers*, 354–5.
[67] Entry for Oct. 27, 1807, ibid., especially 465–6.
[68] Jefferson to Hay, Sept. 4, 1807, Bergh, *Writings of Jefferson*, 11: 360–61.

that the Constitution placed the federal judiciary on a par with the elective branches and armed it with the authority to uphold the law even in defiance of a popular president. In Richmond, the standoff between the two men and the two branches of government they represented was dramatized by the contest over the subpoena *duces tecum,* but the tension between law and politics permeated the entire trial.

At the basis of the law-politics dispute symbolized by Marshall and Jefferson lay their profound disagreement as to the nature and the source of law itself. Marshall was not a legal philosopher and most assuredly not a legal theorist; for him the common law took the place of both philosophy and theory. Training and experience taught him that common-law decisions embodied the wisdom of past generations as it was distilled incrementally by lawyers and judges grappling with the real problems of real people. Recovering these time-tested rules and adjusting them to changing circumstances was what lawyers and judges were trained to do. This is not to say that past decisions always controlled in Marshall's common-law universe; but even when they did not, such decisions still constituted the starting point of adversarial discourse – witness the proceedings in Richmond. Long before Tocqueville famously made the point, Marshall operated on the conviction that the bench and the bar, armed with the conservative methodology of the common law, stood between the people and their rulers as a restraint on the sudden impulses of both.

If Marshall's approach to law privileged the wisdom of the past, Jefferson's looked to the potential of the present and the future. As a champion and political beneficiary of the sovereign people, newly mobilized by his own party, the president favored legislation over judge-made law. He also rejected Marshall's notion (and that of most lawyers of the age) that adherence to common-law precedents eliminated personal and ideological bias in judging. According to Jefferson, judges did not discover law, as they claimed, they made it. Even more dangerous in his opinion, judges like Marshall claimed the right to review and even override laws made by the people's elected representatives. In 1776, Jefferson insisted that the judge ought to "be a mere machine."[69] He never changed his mind, at least when it came to Marshall, whose use of common-law rules of evidence to free Burr exemplified the "plastic nature of the law" he feared would lead to judicial tyranny.[70] For Marshall's part, he saw

[69] Jefferson to Edmund Pendleton, Aug. 26, 1776, Julian Boyd, ed., *The Papers of Thomas Jefferson* (Princeton, 1950), 1: 505.
[70] Jefferson to Hay, June 18, 1810, Looney, *The Papers of Thomas Jefferson: Retirement Series,* 2: 473.

Jefferson's determination to convict Burr in defiance of the established rules of procedural due process as proof positive that common-law judges and lawyers were indispensable in a republican polity that was fast becoming a popular democracy in which the voters were subject to manipulation by partisan demagogues.

For Jefferson the duty of his office was clear. Writing to Doctor James Brown a year after the Burr trial, he analogized Wilkinson's flagrant disregard of legal process in New Orleans – and by implication his own treatment of Bollman, Swartwout, and Burr – to the bold leaders of the American Revolution: "There are extreme cases where the laws become inadequate even to their own preservation, and where the universal resource is a dictator, or martial law."[71] More to the point was the president's letter of February 3, 1807 to W.C.C. Claiborne, Governor of the Territory of Orleans, justifying his own and his general's illegal measures used against Burr and his followers: "On great occasions every good officer must be ready to risk himself in going beyond the strict line of law, when public preservation requires it; his motives will be a justification as far as there is any discretion in his ultra-legal proceedings, and no indulgence of private feelings." By Jefferson's reckoning, such decisive but "ultra-legal" action not only strengthened public confidence in the administration, but also provided "a wholesome lesson too to our citizens, of the necessary obedience to their government."[72]

Jefferson did not temper his radical views with the wisdom of hindsight. Writing to John B. Colvin, September 20, 1810, he defended his law-defying treatment of Burr and his fellow conspirators at great length, while denouncing the "weakness of the law, apathy of the judges, active patronage of the whole tribe of lawyers, [and the] unknown disposition of the juries…"[73] Raising his actions to the level of general theory – he even tossed in a hypothetical reference to his constitutionally questionable acquisition of Louisiana to make the point – he appeared to be saying that popularly elected presidents following their own version of "the law of necessity" and national "self-preservation" were answerable only to the opinion of the American electorate. Judging from the *Virginia Argus,* many of them praised "the great and good Mr. Jefferson, as the political savior of his country; as the man who alone could bring us back to the pure standard of republicanism from which we had gradually

---

[71] Jefferson to Brown, Oct. 27, 1808, Ford, *Works of Jefferson*, 11: 53.
[72] Bergh, *Writings of Jefferson*, 11: 150–51.
[73] Ibid., 11: 146–50, quote at 148.

been diverging...".[74] Jefferson took the risk and no doubt accepted the accolades.

So here was the standoff in Richmond: On one side stood Jefferson, elected by the people to be the champion of republican virtue. On the other side stood Marshall, whose common-law approach Jefferson saw as a retreat from the great moral questions of "right or wrong," an approach based on "small objections" and legal niceties.[75] Jefferson believed that the arcane matters of legal evidence and due process should yield to the unhindered judgment of a citizen-jury spurred on by an elected president armed with the sword of republican justice. For Marshall, rules of evidence were the heart of due process just as due process was the essence of the rule of law – the principle above all others his oath of office required him to uphold.

From Courtroom Chaos Some Sound Law for the New Nation

In Richmond, Marshall ended up doing precisely and emphatically what Jefferson insisted that judges had no authority to do: he made law. He did so not by infringing on legislative authority, as the caustic editorial in the *Virginia Argus* claimed, but rather by seeing to it that Burr got a fair trial – which is to say he clarified the constitutional meaning of treason in order to decide what was proper evidence for the jury to see.[76] Marshall arrived at this constitutional position by weighing precedents and authorities from the past, by reference to the circumstances at hand as debated by counsel during the adversarial process. So common-law judges had reasoned for centuries.

Marshall's opinion, delivered in the afternoon of August 31 to a packed house, was followed the next morning by the jury's acquittal. The words were barely out of the jury foreman's mouth before the fusillade began. Nothing in Marshall's long career on the Court – not *Marbury,* not *McCulloch,* not the Cherokee decisions – matched the personal virulence of the attack that took place in Congress and in newspapers across the nation. The partisan press (spearheaded as usual by the Richmond *Enquirer* and Duane's Philadelphia *Aurora*) not only denounced Marshall

---

[74] *Virginia Argus,* Oct. 7, 1807.
[75] Jefferson to Hay, June 20, 1807, Bergh, *Writings of Jefferson,* 11: 239–42; also see Jefferson to Hay, Sept. 4, 1807, ibid., 360–61.
[76] The editorial claimed that Marshall "felt himself to be *legislating* on the subject of treason," this while consciously ignoring precedent to do so. *Virginia Argus,* Dec. 4, 1807.

as a partisan judge but also accused him of being a traitor. William Thompson's *A Compendious View of the Trial of Aaron Burr,* published in Petersburg, Virginia less than one year after the trial ended, weighed in with 138 pages of unrelenting abuse.[77] And this was just the beginning. According to Henry Adams efforts to impeach Marshall would almost certainly have succeeded except for the distraction created by the Chesapeake-Leopard Affair in July 1807.

What is revealing about these attacks is that they denounced Marshall's political bias and his character but rarely grappled with the legal reasoning in his actual opinion.[78] This failure to grapple is not surprising since Marshall obviously made no effort to placate the ordinary reader. Beveridge called Marshall's opinion a "state paper" and so it was, but it was a lawyer's document, not a literary production. Even as law, it did not soar like *McCulloch* or *Cohens v.Virginia,* or go straight to the point like his dissent in *Ogden v. Saunders.* In contrast, the Burr opinion (because of the complex issues involved and the multiple authorities evaluated) was long, technical, and sometimes difficult to follow. Had critics made the effort, however, they would have discovered that Marshall's common-law laden analysis put American treason law on a republican foundation – one that was consistent with the intent of the Framers, the ratifiers, and thoughtful statesmen in both parties, including the party of Jefferson.[79]

It may seem strange that a conservative such as Marshall should have put a liberal stamp on treason doctrine – that is to say, that a champion of strong national government and executive authority should have announced a doctrine that limited the discretionary power of both. The paradox disappears, however, when it is recalled that Marshall's opinion followed that of the conservatives at the Philadelphia Convention, who took the wording of Article III directly from the English Treason Act of 1351. In defining treason only as levying war and giving aid and comfort,

---

[77] William was the brother of John Thompson whose critical letter to Marshall played a part in the congressional race of 1798; apparently, hating John Marshall ran in the family.

[78] On the distinction between "legal and nonlegal narratives" see Ferguson, *Trial in American Life,* especially 24–28.

[79] The most sophisticated evaluation of Marshall's decision, one that refutes Edward Corwin's claim that Marshall was guided by his hatred of Jefferson, is found in Robert K. Faulkner, *The Jurisprudence of John Marshall* (Princeton, 1968), "Appendix II. Marshall and the Burr Trial." Willard Hurst, *The Law of Treason in the United States: Collected Essays* (Westport, CT, 1971) reasons that Marshall's decision followed the intent of the Framers.

the Framers deliberately chose to depoliticize treason by *not* drawing on the other treasonable activities listed in that famous statute, the most sweeping of which was "compassing," that is, imagining the death of the king. The inclusion of the two-witness provision in Article III, borrowed from the Treason Trials Act of 1696, speaks to the same point.[80]

Among the Framers, James Wilson of Pennsylvania was the acknowledged authority on English legal history. He was one of the leading defense attorneys in the Pennsylvania treason cases during the 1770s, and as the dominant figure on the Committee of Detail in Philadelphia, he was also chiefly responsible for the restrictive wording and stiff evidentiary provisions in Article III.[81] As a member of the Pennsylvania ratifying convention, he praised the restrictive nature of the treason provisions of the Constitution, a point he also emphasized in his law lectures in 1790–1791 at the College of Philadelphia.[82] The other key figure on the Committee with Wilson was Marshall's friend Edmund Randolph, who shared Wilson's restrictive view of treason and who undoubtedly carried that view to Richmond in 1807.

Marshall made some law then, but he did so by drawing on English treason law, the Framers of the Constitution, and the lawyers who parsed both for his use. And this is not to mention Burr and Jefferson, whose clash defined the factual environment of the case. In the final analysis, however, it was Marshall's call. His opinion was neither a freewheeling improvisation, nor simply an echo of previous authorities. By building on the liberal elements in the English legal legacy, he put flesh on the skeletal phraseology in the Constitution: by narrowly defining "levying war"; by distinguishing between treason and the conspiracy to commit treason; by clarifying and reaffirming the two-witness provision; and by insisting that the prosecution be held strictly to the wording of the formal indictment.

The extent to which Marshall's decision accounts for the relative paucity of treason prosecutions over the years is impossible to measure with any precision. Justice Jackson was no doubt correct, however, when in *Cramer v. U.S.* he observed, "We have managed to do without treason prosecutions to a degree that probably would have been impossible except while a people was singularly confident of external security and

---

[80] Willard Hurst discusses the English background of the treason clause in his *The Law of Treason in the United States: Collected Essays* (Westport, CT, 1971), ch. 1 and 2.

[81] For Wilson's role at the Philadelphia Convention see ibid., ch. 4.

[82] See Hurst, *Law of Treason*, 136–7. For Wilson's law lectures consult Robert G. McCloskey, ed., *The Works of James Wilson* (2 vols., Cambridge, 1967), 2: 663–9.

internal stability."[83] Marshall's decision, moreover, did little to restrict the power of Congress to punish activities other than treason deemed to be a threat to national security, as for example in the Espionage Act of 1917 and the Sedition Act of 1918. This was precisely the point made by Rufus King during the debates over the treason clause during the Philadelphia Convention, and the one reaffirmed by Justice Jackson in *Cramer v. U.S.* in 1945.[84] In fact, by distinguishing conspiracy to commit treason from actual treason, Marshall himself identified conspiracy, with its less strict standard of proof, as a likely area for congressional legislation.[85]

Two decisions, even when rendered by America's great chief justice, did not settle the course of American law. Still, the fact remains that Marshall's restrictive definition of "levying war" in Article III worked to discourage prosecutions under that clause. Hardly less influential was Marshall's warning in *Bollman* regarding the danger of treason prosecutions by elected officials in times of popular hysteria. Thus could Justice Jackson quote Marshall in *Ex parte Bollman* to support the Court's decision to reverse a treason conviction driven by post-WWII anti-German hysteria. Jackson quoted Marshall on the duty of the Court to maintain "a deliberate and temperate inquiry" when dealing with a crime that is certain to "excite and agitate the passions of men," and to remember that it is "more safe, as well as more consonant to the principles of our constitution, that the crime of treason should not be extended by construction to doubtful cases…"[86]

Marshall's rulings during the Burr trials on due process and the procedural rights of criminal defendants have also retained their relevance after two centuries. Marshall's insistence on the court's duty to hold the prosecution and the jury to relevant evidence is a case in point; other oft-cited principles concern the right of criminal defendants to compulsory process, their right to confront witnesses against them, and their

---

[83] Opinion in *Cramer v. U.S.*, 325 U.S. 26, 45–46 (1945).

[84] For King's statement, see Max Farrand, *The Records of the Federal Convention of 1787* (3 vols., 1911), 2: 347; for Jackson's statement, see 325 U.S. at 45.

[85] Circuit Judge Fitzhugh also recognized the hiatus in federal criminal code when he observed, regarding the charge of treason brought against Bollman and Swartwout, that while Congress had made misprision of treason a crime, it had not yet chosen to punish other more serious crimes short of treason itself [as for example, conspiracy to commit treason]; since "there is no intermediate class of offences of a treasonable nature between misprision and treason, it must be treason." *U.S. v. Bollman*, 24 Fed. Cas. No. 14,622, at 1196.

[86] 325 U.S. 47; *Bollman* at 4 Cranch 75, 125, 127.

right to be tried only on the formal charge in the indictment.[87] Of all the procedural rights championed by Marshall in the Burr trials (*Bollman* as well as *U.S. v. Burr*), none was more important than the right of the accused to the writ of habeas corpus. Not surprisingly it was Marshall's opinion in *Bollman* that Chief Justice Taney quoted when, in the case of *Ex parte Merryman,* he challenged Lincoln's temporary suspension of the writ during the Civil War.[88]

What Marshall did in *Bollman*, and what made his opinion relevant to justices like Taney and Jackson, was in William Cranch's words to "poise the scales of justice, unmoved by the arm of power, undisturbed by the clamor of the multitude."[89] Balancing the scales of justice was the defining duty of judges and the special obligation of an independent judiciary.

Creating and maintaining an independent judiciary – defining the authority of the federal courts and protecting them from their political enemies – was Marshall's constant concern during the Burr trials and his most lasting legacy. Due process of law, especially as it concerned the procedural rights of criminal defendants, was the high ground on which Marshall chose to battle the president and his party. Marshall's ruling on the admissibility of evidence that finally settled Burr's fate then was not an arcane legal nicety nor a usurpation of authority, as Jefferson claimed; rather, it was a universally accepted power belonging to the court, one that went to the heart of the Court's constitutional function.

If *Marbury v. Madison* was Marshall's first effort to define that function in the new scheme of government, then *U.S. v. Burr* (including *Ex parte Bollman*) was the second. And nowhere during the trial did he set forth the court's uniquely legal role in the constitutional scheme of government more forcefully than when he issued the subpoena *duces tecum* to Jefferson. Marshall's point was that the right to a fair trial according to due process of law was a foundational principle of constitutional government in America. If due process went to the heart of constitutional government and the federal courts were the chief guardians of due process, it followed that the federal judiciary and the federal Constitution were inseparably connected.

---

[87] For a thoughtful discussion of the continuing impact of Marshall's decisions in the Burr trials, see Peter Charles Hoffer, *The Treason Trials of Aaron Burr* (Lawrence, KS, 2008), 184–8.

[88] *Ex parte Merryman*, 17 Fed. Cas. No. 9,487 (C.C.D.My., April term 1861), 152. Taney cites and quotes Marshall, "my great predecessor," at 152.

[89] Dissent, *U.S. v. Bollman*, 24 Fed. Cas. No. 14,622, at 1192.

As he well knew and as the standoff over the subpoena makes clear, Marshall had no way to compel the president to recognize the constitutional authority of the judiciary. What Marshall had that the president did not have, however, were the words of his opinion as embodied in the written records of the court, which could be consulted by future courts. Marshall had the last word, then, and words were Marshall's forte. Thus it was Marshall's impassioned defense of due process and judicial independence in the subpoena debate, rather than Jefferson's private opinion on these matters, that echoed down the corridors of American history.

Never were Marshall's principles more apposite, or his example of judicial independence more relevant, than in the epic struggle between the federal courts and President Richard Nixon during the Watergate hearings resulting in *United States v. Nixon* (1974). There were of course substantial differences between Nixon in Watergate and Jefferson in the Burr trial, the main one being that Nixon himself was on trial. Nevertheless, the similarities are striking, especially in regard to Nixon's claim that the president was above the law. In his interview with David Frost, Nixon was asked whether a president "could do something illegal" if he thought it was in the "best interests of the nation." Nixon replied, "when the President does it, that means that it is not illegal."[90] Nixon appeared to be saying that the president can in certain circumstances make his own law, whereas Jefferson declared that if necessary he could knowingly violate the law. Which option is worse is hard to say, but both violate the guiding axiom of the Constitution: that ours is "a government of laws, and not of men."

In addressing Nixon's unconstitutional actions in *U.S. v. Nixon* then, it was altogether appropriate that Chief Justice Warren Burger's opinion for a unanimous court rested squarely on Marshall's ruling on the Court's power to issue the subpoena *duces tecum* to Jefferson in *U.S. v. Burr*. In his analysis of the case, Professor Paul Freund identified the four basic rules in Marshall's argument that the Burger Court employed, but Chief Justice Burger himself went straight to the point when he declared,

---

[90] In this regard, see the opinions of Republican judges Duckett and Fitzhugh and the argument of federal attorney Walter Jones in *U.S. v. Bollman*, 24 Fed. Cas. No. 14,622, (C.C.D.Columbia, 1807), 1189. Jefferson's defense of illegal executive action, as expressed in his letter to Dr. James Brown and to the governor of Louisiana, were discussed earlier. The transcript of the Nixon-Frost interview is reported in the *New York Times*, May 20, 1977, Sec. A, p. 16. The Nixon-Frost exchange is quoted in Sanford Levinson, "Slavery in the Canon of Constitutional Law," in Paul Finkelman, ed., *Slavery & the Law* (Madison, 1977), 105.

"The generalized interest in confidentiality," even when claimed by the President of the United States, "cannot prevail over the fundamental demands of due process of law in the fair administration of criminal justice."[91]

Certainly there can be no guarantee that the Supreme Court or other federal courts will always, like the Burger Court, follow Marshall's example of resisting executive overreach. It was one thing to say no to Thomas Jefferson when the fate of the nation, even by Jefferson's own admission, was never at risk from Aaron Burr. It is quite another to assume that the federal courts will challenge a president who has assumed vast new powers in an age of perpetual war, when there are no longer three thousand miles of Atlantic to shield the nation from harm. The irony is that judicial independence in an age of perpetual war, either hot or cold, is hard to come by precisely when it is needed most. At any rate, as John Adams wisely observed, Marshall's example of restraining an overzealous president remains to instruct and inspire.

The role of Marshall and the lawyers in the Burr trial also contains lessons for historians seeking to understand the dynamics of early-nineteenth-century legal culture in the United States. What we see in the Burr trial – what helps account for the fireworks and the chaos, as well as the constructive outcome of the trial – was the collision of English legal doctrine nurtured over centuries of monarchical government against the living needs of the new nation. For all the talk about republican law, English common-law institutions, principles, and terminology permeated every aspect of the proceedings. At times it appeared as if the common-law tradition itself – with due process and rule of law at its core – was on the line.

At the same time, however – and no less important than the English legal legacy in the Burr trial – was the freewheeling, pragmatic, non-ideological willingness of counsel on both sides to pick at will from English precedents and to modify what they chose as it suited their needs. Marshall may have put his own imprimatur on American treason law, but nine lawyers arguing strenuously and at times brilliantly for seven months showed him the way. Their joint effort provided a civics lesson for the thousands who followed the trial, even those who complained of the outcome.

---

[91] 418 U.S. at 707–708. See Haskins and Johnson, *The Foundations of Power*, 2: 271–2, footnote 182. Paul Freund is quoted to the effect that *U.S. v. Nixon* drew heavily on and confirmed the principles asserted by Marshall in the Burr trial. See Freund, *Harvard Law Review* (1974), 88: 13, 31.

In short, the Burr trial affords historians a unique glimpse of judicial lawmaking in the young republic – at a time when legal institutions and legal doctrine were nearly as unsettled as the American Southwest that activated Burr's restless mind. The legal arguments and techniques of adjudication in Marshall's courtroom were also in flux, at once deeply rooted in English soil but also pointing to the time when American law and lawmakers would stand on native ground. In a sense Marshall himself exemplifies the transitional nature of the moment. Only five years into his job, the chief justice still had one foot in the eighteenth century – which is to say that his judging was a work in progress.[92] His main opinion in the Burr trial in fact seems closer to *Marbury* – where he spent several pages expounding on the ancient writ of mandamus and ended up borrowing Blackstone's tenth rule of statutory construction to rationalize judicial review – than to his bold exposition of American constitutional law in *McCulloch* or *Gibbons*.[93]

As a full-time professional who made a living from the law and made law his life's work, Marshall looked to the future; but he was also an eighteenth-century common lawyer before he became the great expounder of the Constitution. He was also a natural-born member of Virginia's ruling elite who approached his work on the bench as a matter of public service. During the trial this sense of *noblesse oblige* translated readily into his deeply held and frequently stated belief in judicial duty – the same that led him to stand firm against the pressure of public opinion and the threats of impeachment emanating from the White House.[94]

President Jefferson was likewise governed by a sense of public duty, one also traceable to his membership in Virginia's ruling class. The irony is that these two elite sons of the Old Dominion should have stood for such divergent views of republican government, indeed such radically different views of the American Revolution. Marshall opted for liberty under law and looked to the taught tradition of the common law for guidance; Jefferson viewed liberty through Enlightenment spectacles and trusted its care to the newly proclaimed sovereign people speaking through their elected representatives. Aaron Burr had little use for philosophies of any sort; add him to the mix and the trial became a

[92] See William E. Nelson, "The Eighteenth-Century Background of John Marshall's Constitutional Jurisprudence," *Michigan Law Review*, (1977–1978), 76: 893–904.
[93] Robert Clinton comments on Marshall's reliance on Blackstone in his Marbury v. Madison *and Judicial Review* (Lawrence, KS, 1989), 18–20.
[94] The concept of judicial duty and its development over time is treated insightfully in Philip Hamburger, *Law and Judicial Duty* (Cambridge, MA, 2008).

republican morality play in which law, politics, ideology and character were inseparably intertwined. Little wonder then that the citizens of the new nation were so "jostled" by the trial, or that historians continue to ponder the way lawyers, judges, presidents and larger-than-life characters like Aaron Burr went about fashioning law for the new nation.

Index

Made in the USA
Middletown, DE
22 January 2019